A GUIDE TO CONTEMPORARY

FRENCH LITERATURE

FROM VALÉRY TO SARTRE

by WALLACE FOWLIE

Meridian Books
THE WORLD PUBLISHING COMPANY
Cleveland and New York

AN ORIGINAL MERIDIAN BOOK

Published by The World Publishing Company
2231 West 110th Street, Cleveland 2, Ohio
First printing July 1957
Seventh Printing, September, 1967
Library of Congress Catalog Card Number: 57-10834
Printed in the United States of America   7 BP 967

ACKNOWLEDGMENTS

Some of the pages in this book have been rewritten from essays that have appeared in the following periodicals and books:

Accent
Poetry
Sewanee Review
The Culture of France in Our Time
Spiritual Problems in Contemporary Literature
Mid-Century French Poets

For the preparation of this volume, I am grateful for the fellowships extended to me by

The Guggenheim Foundation
The Yaddo Foundation
The Huber Foundation
The Newberry Library

29~12

A Guide to

Contemporary French Literature

CONTENTS

INTRODUCTION: *The French Literary Mind*

In the literary tradition of France, eloquence, both oral and written, is a ceremony. It is true that in every literary tradition, eloquence, by its very nature, must become to some degree the stylization of language, but in France the instinct to make of language a highly formalized expression is deeper and more permanent than in other traditions. Each of the great masterpieces in French literature seems extraordinarily aware of the public to which it is addressing itself, of the presence of a public, of a public mind which must be subjugated and enchanted according to well-established rules of subjugation and enchantment.

And that is why the first trait of the French literary mind always seems to be its sociability or even what we might call its worldliness. The French writer is always addressing some one, even when he is speaking on that subject which has become a favorite since the days of the Renaissance when Montaigne wrote his *Essays:* the subject of solitude. Because of this attitude of the French writer, which is more an instinct than an attitude, born of a need to communicate and to establish a relationship between his thought and the minds of other men, his works are characterized by a tone of bareness, of separateness. They often give the effect of arias sung in the midst of great silence, sung at some distance from the world, even if they are directed toward the world. This is sometimes described as the classical spirit in French art, and works composed in this spirit have the inflections of a pleader and a lawyer whose skill is used to combat and convince and seduce.

Such works, and they have occurred in all periods of French history, illustrate the solitude of literary speech. But such speech-solitude, because of its ceremonial aspect, is floodlighted. Its contrived effect, so carefully planned to provoke, hold, subjugate and enchant, may often appear a pure theatricality. The writer in the French tradition resembles a performing artist. In French schools the primary literary exercise is that of textual explication, by which a single page of a writer is made to serve as a revelation of his particular art and thought, and even the art and thought of his period. Only a very highly self-conscious and even histrionic art permits such examination and such treatment, whereby a novelist is studied not in his novel, but in a single paragraph from his novel, and a poet is studied in a single sonnet. This habit of study has helped to convert French literature into a series of celebrated set-pieces. Renan is known for his prayer on the Acropolis and Proust for the passage on the madeleine cake dipped in a cup of linden tea.

A single page can be separated from its book and exist autonomously in its own brilliance, in much the same way as a speech in a French conversation may be taken out of its context and seen to be a distinct and singular creation. At French dinner parties the general effect may be that of conversation, or at times of hubbub, but when listened to more attentively, the conversation of each dinner guest will be seen to be a monologue, recited both simultaneously and independently. French eloquence, whether written or spoken under the stimulus of a physically present public, is expression ritualistically conceived.

The reason for this solitariness of the French literary voice, what we might name the primary secret of the French literary mind, is the fervent identification it establishes with the past. If the finished product of French writing often gives us the impression of an aria sung in the center of a vast space, of a form stripped of nonessentials and bare in an almost heroic vulnerability, we know that its strength comes from its alliance with an allegiance to the tradition of its past. The dependence of a French writer on other writers who preceded him is acknowledged and emphasized. French art is knowingly the renewal of tradition and not the discovery of the new. The writer in France learns his particular role and vocation in terms of those past writers with whom he is in sympathy as well as those with whom he is in disagreement. Many French masterpieces have been born from a quarrel. The loneliness of the French writer, which now might be termed his uniqueness, comes from this will to determine himself by his affiliations and disagreements. The French writer knows that originality is an unimportant and even an illusory goal in art. The seeming new really draws upon the old.

I have taken courses in French literature both in America and Paris where the professor actually never got to the author announced as the subject of the course, where all the time was spent·in discussing the forerunners of the author. We learned all about the writers whom the author had read during his lifetime and to what degree he had been influenced by them, but by then we had reached the final lecture, and although we had learned much of what lay behind the literary work in question, we had no time to consider the work itself.

Such an approach, which treats literature as a renovation of the past, as a prolongation, rather than as an original creation, explains to some degree the attitude of the French people toward their writers. The pride which the French feel in their writers and their awareness of them even if they do not always read them, are singularly French traits. The recent death in Paris of Paul Valéry, in July 1945, became an event of national significance. I refer to the example of Valéry in this connection because he is as far removed as it is possible to be from the type of popular writer. As a poet, he is one of the most difficult France has ever produced, and one who will rank among the greatest; and as a prose writer, he is even more difficult. The stylistic and philosophical difficulty of Valéry's art would seem to relegate him to a very small circle of initiates, but it is a fact that, even long before his death, he was a universal figure in Paris, a symbol and justification of French pride in literary tradition.

In the homage which France paid to Paul Valéry, the dignity of the literary mind was extolled once again. The case of Valéry signifies that once more in France acknowledgment was made to the belief that the literary artist, no matter how esoteric or difficult, represents a significant fusion between the present and the past. Valéry had not always been kind or approving in his treatment of the past. He has derided, for example, and in a tone of considerable malice, some of the most hallowed sentences of Pascal, sentences which have been explicated for generations in the lycées and universities, and precisely those belonging to passages which we have been calling arias. But the French, as well as possessing a sense of tradition, have an iconoclastic sense which rather enjoys a scene of destruction when it is carried out with deftness and critical sharpness. Valéry's very attack on the sentences of Pascal has thrown them into greater relief than ever, and one day there will be books written for and against Valéry's attack on Pascal.

If Valéry is anti-Pascal and anti-philosophers in general, he is on the other hand a disciple of Mallarmé, who directed him closely in his vocation as poet. The discipleship has helped to define Valéry's particular position in French poetry and to redefine the art of his master. Valéry's debt to Mallarmé is so significant that professors in future courses on Valéry will perhaps not feel compelled to go beyond a discussion of Mallarmé's poetry.

The French, more insistently than other national groups, use the names of their writers as symbols which stand for much more than the actual literary work. They represent attitudes of mind and vary-

ingly successful efforts to study the mystery of man.
The French use the names of Racine, Descartes, Villon, as others say Orpheus, Socrates, Venus. And
French writers also use these names almost as talismans or as epithets of saints and sinners invoked during self-examinations. The literary past in France is
constantly testifying and representing. Thus Valéry
orientates his own thought by declaring himself a
critic of Pascal and a disciple of Mallarmé.

The art of speech in France is almost identical with
the art of persuasion. One of the surest means to per-
suade is to speak intimately and personally, to take
the reader into confidence, to speak confidences.
When the French writer employs this device, he
speaks, not about his mother or wife or child, as the
writer of another tradition might do, but about the
author whom he reads passionately and with whom
he has formed a spiritual liaison. Baudelaire is most
personal when he writes of Edgar Allan Poe; Claudel
when he tells the effect of Rimbaud on his life;
Valéry when he describes his conversations with Mallarmé.

At moments of national crisis, the French turn to
their writers, because the writer is by definition in
France the man who writes about the world of his
heart but who also looks at the world itself and seeks
to integrate in his writing some considerations concerning the affairs of the world. On the one hand,
Valéry can compose such a pure poem as *Narcisse,*
which contains the description of a forest scene and
the exploration of a psychological dilemma. And on
the other hand, he can write such an article as *La
Crise de l'Esprit* which, although it was written soon
after the end of the first World War, stands today as

one of the most penetrating statements on the political and sociological dilemmas of modern man. The first sentence of the essay has become a celebrated exordium in France: *Nous autres, civilisations, nous savons maintenant que nous sommes mortelles.* It is this kind of sentence we have been trying to describe as the beginning of an aria. It is both resonant and arresting: "We civilizations know now that we are mortal." It has the solitariness of a single voice speaking to a vast public which in this case is both France and the modern world. It is the voice of a pleader who is going to speak, through deep sensitivity to the past, to his own world on the subject of the abyss of history.

So the literary mind of France, nourished as it is on the past, may analyze whatever subject persists in tormenting man: politics, morals, theology, philosophy. Literature, the most complex of the arts, involves all these subjects and many others, and in France, more than in other countries, the people turn to the particular form given to these problems by the literary artist. The ideas of the sixteenth century are perhaps best expounded in the *Essays* of Montaigne; the moral and religious problems of the seventeenth century may be studied in the sermons of Bossuet; modern man's psychological barriers are for the French more significantly analyzed by a Baudelaire or by a Proust than by a Freud. When we read such a passage as that of Valéry which begins with the words, *Nous autres, civilisations, nous savons maintenant que nous sommes mortelles,* we realize that the writer in France has replaced the prophet. The writer has learned, through the exercise of his form, which is the practice of lucidity, of stripping and condensing, how to see everything in its absolute meaning. Valéry in his passage on the mortality of civilization, and Péguy, another writer-prophet of France, when he speaks of the modern tendency of changing a mystical state into a political state, both attain in their writing to the absolute meaning of an event.

But this role of tradition in the make-up of the French literary mind is only one aspect. It gives to the writer a feeling of solidarity with the past and an urgency to continue a movement rather than to found a new one. This dependence of the French writer on earlier writers, which grows in many cases to something akin to religious fervor, is not however an enslavement of mind, but, paradoxically, a liberation. Montaigne is better able to formulate his thoughts when he reads Seneca and Sextus Empiricus. Pascal, in denouncing Montaigne, found his own voice in the seventeenth century; and Gide, in our day, in his approval of Montaigne, received confirmation in many of his own attitudes as writer.

The French genius, however, cannot be defined solely by this habit of integration with the past. French genius is not just one thing. It is characterized by infinite variety and richness, by the most opposing traits. After establishing a relationship with the past, it then establishes another kind of relationship with the present. The second secret of the French literary mind is the dialogue it creates with another mind of its time. No major view on man, and no particular kind of sensitivity is allowed to exist alone in France for very long. The French genius asserts itself by creating some miracle of equilibrium. It discovers in its own age an opposing voice, usually of power equal to its own, and therefore is able to grow more vibrantly according to its own distinctive qualities. French art seems to develop in the form of a dialogue. But this dialogue is conciliation, or rather balance and counterpoint. Each of the two voices remains independent and clear, but much of its clarity and independence is derived from the existence of the other voice.

The provinces of France, each one so different from all the others, prefigure and control to some degree the multiple varieties or variations of French art. Long before the classical opposition of Corneille and Racine, so minutely studied in the lycées, there existed at the very beginning of France in the twelfth century, one of the most dramatic dialogues between French minds. Throughout the history of France, Brittany has produced literary minds which seem to be characterized by agility and suppleness on the one hand, and by a tendency toward mysticism and poetry on the other. Pierre Abélard, the twelfth-century philosopher, who was also poet and lover at one time in his life, had this kind of mind: both critical and mystical, both lyric and independent. He is usually considered one of the forerunners of the French analytical and rationalist spirit, adept in argumentation and subtlety. But Abélard's philosophy and theology were attacked by a contemporary, a man equally powerful but in a different way. Saint Bernard was Abélard's adversary. He was a Burgundian, of a race vastly unlike the Breton. The genius of the Burgundians is that of organizing, constructing, synthesizing. The Roman legionnaires had settled in Burgundy and had perhaps bequeathed some of their respect for authority and their sense of order and even their physical prowess. It is still believed that the best soldiers in France come from Burgundy.

A clash was inevitable between these two men. Abélard's spirit was critical, analytical and even destructive; whereas Bernard's spirit was bent upon protecting authority and tradition, eager to preserve and synthesize, and determined to use his full power in accomplishing those ends. So Bernard, the man of action, opposed Abélard, the reflective thinker. The passion of order and synthesis opposed the passion of thought and analysis. The same warning which Saint Bernard gave to Abélard in the twelfth century has been spoken in our day by Valéry in the essay already quoted, *La Crise de l'Esprit*. Man's investigation and knowledge may grow to such an extent that they become dangerous for himself and for the world. That was why Saint Bernard intervened in the career of Abélard, and that is the reason today for Valéry's question about knowledge. We can easily realize the threat which such knowledge represents for civilization. It is not an exaggeration to say that today a civilization appears as fragile as a human life.

The twelfth-century dialogue of Abélard and Bernard, which was a pattern of counterpoint established between a spirit of analysis and a spirit of synthesis, continues in varying ways in each great period of French history. In the Renaissance, the humanism of a Rabelais who believed in the natural goodness of man, was offset by the humanism of a Calvin who preached the corruption of human nature. In the seventeenth century, one of the most significant dialogues for the subsequent development of French writing, was that between Descartes and Pascal. Descartes furthered his so-called method of doubt so that human reason might attain to truth. It would not be fantastic to consider Descartes' philosophical treatise, *Discours sur la méthode,* as the first of the psychological novels in French literature wherein reason in its purest state is the protagonist. But Pascal, in the same years, and in no uncertain terms, was asking mankind to humble itself: *Raison, humiliez-vous;* and telling mankind that "the heart has its reasons which reason does not understand." Thus the intellectual enterprise or adventure of Descartes cannot be separated from the more deeply tormented and spiritual adventure of Pascal. One was necessary for the other in this persistent pattern of French thought where each age seeks to conciliate opposite tendencies, where analysis is opposed to synthesis, realism to idealism, action to contemplation, thought to sentiment.

More than other countries, France favors and supports and values the existence of opposing minds at any given moment of its history. In that country which has developed to such a high degree the art of argument and discussion and conversation, no single voice is ever allowed to be heard for any length of time. I suppose that no teacher ever had such abundant and even hysterical success as Abélard, and yet his revolutionary spirit, brilliant as it was, negative and demolishing according to that form which holds and stimulates young students, was not unchallenged and was finally subjugated by the sterner, more dogmatic, although far less subtle and scintillating, spirit of Saint Bernard.

There exists throughout the history of French literature, from the earliest writings in the French language, the courtly romances, for example, of Chrétien de Troyes in the twelfth century, up to the plays and novels of the Existentialists in Paris today, a profound and persistent unity of inspiration. What unites all the major works of French literature is the psychological inquest of man, an inquest to which each one seems dedicated.

The effort to study man, to explore the secrets of his mind and his desires, to define his position with respect to life and death, to the cosmos and to truth, is the motivation and the activity of the French literary mind. Many answers have been given to these questions in the various periods of French history, but all the individual questions might be summarized by the one large question: what is man? And this question provides the stimulation and subject matter of French writing, whether it be the *ballades* of the gangster-poet Villon in the fifteenth century or the involved psychological novel of Proust in the twentieth. The French writer turns instinctively not to the collective problems of mankind, but to the personal, more secretive and individual problems of a man. He believes that only through the laborious exploration of self can he attain to any aspect of universal truth.

In the so-called central period of French culture, in the classical age of the seventeenth century, there occurred an exceptional harmonization between this permanent interest of the French writer in psychological study and the philosophically Christian view of man which lies at the basis of everything we call French. The study of man became at that

time, more uniquely than it had previously, the study
of man's corruption. Classicism and Christianity were
united by the doctrine that man is not born good.
The mystery which man brings to the world is not
his innocence, but his knowledge of evil, his corrupti-
bility. The experience of evil is the subject matter of
the tragedies of Racine, the maxims of La Rochefoucauld, the fables of La Fontaine and of every other
literary work of the classical age.

Descartes' very method itself, which was expounded in France as well as in Holland and elsewhere
in Europe just prior to the reign of Louis XIV, consists in a descent into one's own mind and a removal
from one's mind of all those notions falsely acquired
which cannot be arrived at by rational intuition.
We have already mentioned Descartes' *Discours sur la
méthode* as a kind of introduction to the impressive list of psychological novels, the type of writing
which, since the tragedies of Racine, has dominated French literature. Descartes' celebrated
Cogito, ergo sum is the axiom on which he built his
metaphysical system. It is the point of departure in a
revolution not so much of ideas as of a method which
has had a long history and which is not yet terminated.

Pascal, contemporary with Descartes, initiated a
further revolution, which has had an equally fertile
history. Descartes' analysis of the basic simple truths
which man discovers in himself by means of his rational intuition is paralleled in time by Pascal's revolution of the human heart and of sentiment. The
logic of Descartes, which is always however that of a
single hero, is offset by the turbulent dark poetry of
Pascal's torment. The "abyss" which he bears within

himself is Pascal's symbol of the barrier which separates him from truth and helps to objectify the personal anguish generated by his self-inquisition.

The psychological inquiry which has been carried on
uninterruptedly by the French literary mind since
Descartes and Pascal, continues in varying proportions the influence or the example of these two men.
On the one hand, the spirit of a method may be primary. This becomes equivalent almost to a cult of
ordering and organization, of evidence, analysis and
synthesis where structure and compositional form are
uppermost in the mind of the creative artist. Flaubert is a leading example of this type of writer. And,
on the other hand, a spirit of disquietude and even of
anguish, manifesting itself in the lineage of Pascal,
where the study of man is carried on in an austere
trembling and fearfulness, where the complexities of
the heart overbalance the logical reasonableness of
the mind. Some of the greatest artists belong to this:
Racine, Baudelaire, Rimbaud, Mauriac, Malraux. To
them I would attach the contemporary group of
French writers known as the Existentialists.

Existentialism illustrates all the permanent traits
of the French literary mind, but especially the close,
fervent exploration of psychological man. In Sartre's
play *Huis Clos* he forces each of the three characters
to turn inwardly upon himself and to reveal to the
other two his most personal secrets and motives. The
first part of the play is a reduction to zero of the
pretense and deceit and even imagination of the three
characters. It is an effort to begin all over again from
the most basic and simple truths concerning three
case histories. This is in a way an application of what
is usually called the Cartesian method, which is the

most lucidly rational approach to any given problem. But this is only the beginning of the play. The three characters find themselves in hell, which appears to them in the form of a Second Empire living room, and here we come upon the Pascalian aspect of the play. The room is hell for the three characters because they are not free to escape from it. It is what Pascal calls the "abyss" or the obstacle in one's nature which prevents happiness.

This play of Sartre contains therefore two subjects which we associate especially with French literature. First, the logic of an analysis or an inquisition which may be called the Cartesian influence; and secondly, the problem of man's happiness or salvation, which may be called the Pascalian influence. Cartesian and Pascalian are two adjectives which designate method and problem, and their commingling in the writings of Descartes and Pascal themselves, as well as in subsequent writers like Baudelaire, Rimbaud and Sartre, is the specifically French quality and paradox in literary art.

We use the word "paradox," or we might have used "irony," because of the extreme logicality and sense of order with which the French artist approaches the problems of the most dizzying illogicality. The towering disproportion between man's desire (idealism or thirst or aspiration) and man's capacity (realism or limitation or existence) is the subject matter of literature, and the French consider it with a disarming clarity of vision and a mathematical preciseness, whether the work be the seventeenth-century *Méditations* of Descartes or the twentieth-century treatise on *L'Etre et le Néant* of Sartre.

Existentialism, as the newest expression of the

French paradox, takes its point of departure from a fundamental axiom, "Existence precedes essence," as fundamental as Descartes' *Cogito, ergo sum.* Sartre has often repeated that man exists first and then defines himself later. Man is only what he makes himself into. He projects himself into his future. With such statements, Sartre immediately defines doctrines on human liberty and responsibility which are strongly reminiscent of Pascal's. If the key words used by the Existentialists in describing man's state: despair, abandonment, anguish, nausea, have their counterpart in Pascal's vocabulary, Descartes' sentence about man conquering himself rather than the world (*se vaincre plutôt soi-même que le monde*) is likewise applicable to Sartre's belief that man is the ensemble of his actions and that every human project has a universal value.

Existentialism has its roots in the past. Its writers have established a debate or a dialogue with other contemporary writers. And it has revised all the basic metaphysical and psychological problems of man: action, liberty, responsibility.

The outstanding trait of the French genius, that on which all other traits depend, is its spirituality. I believe that the equilibrium which the French writer establishes between himself and the historical past, between himself and his contemporary world, and between himself and the problem of man, is due to an exceptional power of spiritual discernment. It is a willingness to avow and unmask the spiritual turmoil and aspiration of man. More than a willingness, it is a habit, centuries old, of considering virtue common sense, of considering intuition that faculty by which one attains truth. Literature in France has had an incomparable tradition in its awareness of a spiritual mission. No matter what the subject matter may be, and no matter what philosophical stand the individual writer takes, the most apparent word in his vocabulary and, I dare say, the most frequently used word in French literature, is *esprit* and its derivatives, *spirituel* and *spiritualité*. No matter what kind of writer is speaking on human destiny, a Villon or a Pascal or an Existentialist, the mystery of the subject is best articulated by the word "spirituality."

Everything that can be designated as essentially French seems to come from their understanding of the individual, of their prized concept, *la personne*. For the French, to comprehend the destiny of their country is to comprehend the destiny of man. France is the vocation and the study of the individual.

Throughout their history, the French have never ceased believing in what we might call the "absolute of man." I mean the absolute which exists in each man and which can be attained only through perpetual analysis of himself and struggle with himself. This belief in the absolute of man is what might be designated as French pride, vastly different from the humanistic pride of the Renaissance, when man was sensuously glorified by painters and poets, and vastly different from the racial pride of a culture myth. French pride has its roots in a profoundly pessimistic view of man: he has lost through greed and perversity a great heritage of peace which has to be won back by relentless struggle and purification.

This is the key to French writing in every century: in the poetry of Villon, in the story of Rabelais' giants, in the thoughts of Pascal, in the novels of

André Malraux. French pride comes from this extraordinary awareness of man's imperfection and a courageous measuring of his dilemma. André Gide has summarized this in one of his sentences: *Je n'aime pas l'homme, j'aime ce qui le dévore.* ("I don't like man, I like what devours him.") But to this very special form of pessimism is added a particular kind of optimism: a belief in the dignity of this struggle, in the ultimate capacity for reform in man and society. Behind every limpid portrait of man which French civilization has produced, behind every Gothic representation of Judas, behind every character of Balzac, behind every clown of Rouault rises the archetype of human greatness. France has given to the meaning of freedom the will to bind oneself to the ideal through a fierce embracing of what is actual and real and even debased in man.

I suppose that no nation in the world is so diverse as France, so divided, so made up of contradictory individuals. France to the outside world often resembles a multiplicity of political parties, of social classes, of beliefs and ideas. But especially, at those very moments in its history when France appears to us the most divided, it appears to each Frenchman as one and unified. At the moments of greatest fever when France seems split asunder, it is then that she is magically composing past and future, fusing them, unifying, uniting and resolving. Its literary mind never allows France to lose its conscience.

Literature is the deepest memory of the world. In France, in particular, literature is the most powerful reassembling force of conscience. It is true that dogmas, philosophies and ideals will appear contradictory in France, and in any other country, for that matter.

But if these contradictions, which are the product of the mind, become also the product of the literary mind and are cast into a formalized product, the artistic work, they have the chance of becoming a stabilizing factor in periods of turmoil and crisis. Literature is a vast register of everything: myths, psychology, philosophy, theology; but it is a reality, because of its form, which helps us to bear and understand that nightmare, infinitely more chaotic and contradictory, which is life.

France recently passed through a military crisis and is now engaged in an economic crisis. But there is a third kind, which implacably follows the other two, and which is the most subtle and significant of all: the intellectual or spiritual crisis. Here, on the third crisis, the focus and strength of literature are felt. I have already referred to the example of Paul Valéry and his lecture, *La Crise de l'Esprit,* written at the close of the first World War. At that moment of depletion, France was able to turn to one of her literary minds in order to see more clearly into the problems facing her. Valéry belongs to no recognizable group of writers, such as Communists or Catholics or Existentialists. He is, therefore, as Gide is, a more purely literary figure, disinterested and supremely independent.

His death coincided with the end of the war, and again, as in 1919, France turned toward him as a clarifier of contradictions. The long creative effort of Valéry's life was directed toward a study of the activity of man's spirit or of man's mind. The word *esprit* in French means both spirit and mind, and it is one of the most frequently used words in Valéry's texts. In one of his earliest writings, published before the end of the nineteenth century, Valéry asked the question, "What are the powers of a man?" (*Que peut un homme?*) and he was still asking the same question in the pages he was writing at the time of his death in 1945.

He never deviated from the most central problem of man, from a consideration of the deepest part of man's being, of what he called *le moi pur* ("the pure self"). Valéry's enterprise of fifty years, twenty of which were spent in total literary silence—an admirable lesson of rigor and severity toward oneself—was an enterprise of denuding the intellect, of stripping off false notions and precepts and prejudices from the mind. The activity of the mind consists for Valéry of two parts: transformation and conservation. By these two activities the present and the past are harmonized.

This enterprise of a literary mind, which is spiritual in its deepest sense, stimulates the demon of knowledge who always represents a grave danger for spiritual man, but Valéry pursued his adventure with an admirable French balance of wit and seriousness, of science and maliciousness, of incredulity and naïveté. There was always in him the trace of the young student's mind: brilliant and supple, affectionate and destructive. He liked to demolish traditions and then walk about joyfully in the debris. He used to call the devil "a very attractive literary character." But levity was always offset by seriousness. Valéry composed out of the problem of knowledge a work in prose and a work in poetry where light is juxtaposed with nocturnal shadows. The experience of being human for Valéry is, in its spiritual sense, equivalent to feeling that "there is something from all men in each

of us and something from each one of us in all men."
(*Il y a de tous dans chacun et de chacun dans tous.*)

The most constant theme in the writings of Valéry he learned from the example and methods of Leonardo. It is a theme which, more than other literary themes, defines and limits the work of the artist and emphasizes the primacy of the spirit in the activity of the artist. An artistic work, according to this doctrine, is never terminated. It is abandoned. A poem or a painting, therefore, represents a fragment of some greater exercise or adventure carried on, not within the realm of matter, but within the realm of the spirit.

PART 1

ONE

VALÉRY: *The Intellectual Quest*

His passing confirmed Paul Valéry as the national poet of France. As "national" as a poet can be in France, where ordinary citizens are as persistently individualistic as artists, and where each citizen and artist expresses his love of country by his unremitting criticism of other Frenchmen. A few years ago, at the death of Henri Bergson, which occurred just after the Germans occupied Paris, Valéry read at a session of the Académie Française a brief eulogy on the philosopher whom he called "the last thinker of our period" (*le dernier homme pensant de notre époque*). This we are tempted today to apply to Valéry himself. But France has always been fertile in geniuses. Valéry is not the last poet or the last thinker of France, or even of his own period. However, he belongs to a very small group of French poets: Villon, Racine, Baudelaire, Mallarmé, Rimbaud —whose work is incomparable. Valéry joins them in that today his work is total as theirs is, and consecrated to the resurrection in verse of what is deepest in man.

Paul Valéry was born on the 30th of October, 1871, of a Corsican father and an Italian mother, in the city of Sète on the Mediterranean. There he lived until thirteen, attending without too much eagerness the Collège de Sète. To the learning of books, he preferred perhaps the vision of the sea and the fishing boats loaded with glistening tuna fish. In 1884 his family moved to Montpellier. This was an abrupt change from a city on the sea to a city of gardens. He continued to study, now at the Lycée de Montpellier, in the same desultory fashion. Vacations, until his fifteenth year, were spent in Genoa, with his mother's family.

At eighteen he began a year of military service at Montpellier, and it was during this year that the first decisive event of his life occurred. In May 1890, on a terrace café he entered into conversation with a young Parisian dandy. They discovered mutual interests in Baudelaire, Verlaine and Wagner. Later, the Parisian dandy, whose name was Pierre Louÿs, sent to Valéry in Montpellier his closest friend from Paris, a young Calvinist bourgeois who was writing his first book. This second friend, André Gide, succeeded in luring the provincial to Paris, where at the end of 1891, Louÿs led him to the rue de Rome, number 89. There, on the fourth floor, the door was opened by the master himself, Stéphane Mallarmé, who received Valéry into his close circle of disciples and artists.

Between Mallarmé and Valéry grew both spiritual affinities and artistic divergences. It would be impossible to exaggerate the importance of Mallarmé's example on the younger poet. He found in the salon on the rue de Rome a luminous example of poetic purity and poetic pride, a religious sentiment for the art of conciseness. He learned that France, so universally called the country of reason and clarity, possesses a long tradition of lyric obscurity, and that the dream of Maurice Scève in the sixteenth century was similar to Mallarmé's, the dream of singing of the pure self.

While incorporating Mallarmé's lesson on the prestige of the word and the symbol, Valéry moved gradually toward another hero of art, toward another lesson, not so much on art as on the creative process in art. Mallarmé's example was never replaced for Valéry, but to it was added Leonardo's. Valéry turned away from contemplation of the work of art itself in order to study the manner in which it was executed. He turned from aesthetics toward mathematics, architecture, psychology.

After the early poems and two brief prose works, Valéry entered a long period of literary silence. Between his twenty-fifth and forty-fifth years he occupied minor positions in the War Ministry and the Agence Havas, but published nothing and did little or no writing. Mallarmé too had felt the seduction of silence. During this protracted retreat from literature, Valéry matured inwardly and intellectually. Baudelaire somewhere mentions *ce perfectionnement de mon esprit,* and it was this development and perfecting of self, preferred by mystics and philosophers to the more facile fame and union with the world, which Valéry underwent during his twenty years silence.

Not until the first World War did Valéry again occupy a place in French letters. At the beginning of the war, André Gide requested permission to publish a volume of Valéry's early poetry. After first refusing, he consented and set about writing for the book a new poem which he planned to make fifty lines in length. He worked on it from 1914 to 1917, and when completed, *La Jeune Parque* counted five hundred lines.

In 1925, three years after the publication of *La Jeune Parque*, Valéry was elected to the Académie Française. The new poem and the publication of his early poetry had made him one of the most discussed poets of the day. He occupied the thirty-eighth chair in the Académie, the one previously held by Anatole France. In his acceptance speech, Valéry did not once mention by name his predecessor. This was a species of literary vengeance, because Anatole France had once been reckless enough to underestimate the importance of Mallarmé. Later, in 1931, Valéry himself had to deliver the speech of welcome to the new member of the Academy of that year: le maréchal Pétain. In 1938, the chair of poetry at the Collège de France was created for him. The social success of his public lectures recalled the success Bergson had known previous to 1914.

Valéry's voice was weak, but by arriving early and securing a seat near the desk, one could listen to an animated conversational tone, sentences admirably formed and varied, but dealing with concepts and ideas which were difficult to follow. There were few helpful transitional passages. He elaborated only the summits of his thought. One had the impression of being given great lights on many subjects, particularly on the subject of Valéry's own mind, and deliberately not being given the substance or the groundwork of the assumptions and the illuminations. But

Valéry was a sage and not a teacher. His prose sentences are not incomprehensible, but they do contain much more than their surface meaning. They are imbedded in the occult and come from the deepest and most concealed part of his mind. It is we who have to change ourselves in order to comprehend them. The poet's death has made his oracular statements absolute. We who are still changing have to take all the steps toward their comprehension.

One of the most attractive traits in Valéry's character was his conviction that the genius has no particular claim on the world, no particular privilege to seek out. During the course of his first lecture, given in the salon of Adrienne Monnier in Paris, he happened to be speaking of Poe, and made the statement that the American poet had not received the recognition his genius entitled him to. But as soon as he heard his own words, he corrected himself by saying to his auditors: "What I have just said is ridiculous. The man of genius has no claims." (*Ce que je viens de dire est absurde; le génie n'a aucun droit.*)

Like most men of ideas, he looked very little at nature. The spectacle of his heart interested him much more than the spectacle of a landscape. Once on a hilltop in Hungary someone pointed out the valley of the Danube to him. He glanced rapidly at it, and then turning back to his traveling companion, Georges Duhamel, said: "No matter where I travel, I am always shown the same view." (*J'ai beau voyager, on me montre partout le même paysage.*)

His life was consecrated to exploring the resources of the mind. He opposed all fixed systems of philosophy and showed little approbation for philosophers.

He took pride in his own position of integral agnostic which left him no regrets for any firmer beliefs. Lightness and wit characterized his own convictions which were constantly undergoing modifications.

Valéry placed little importance on the personal habits, manners and affections of great men. In time the world will probably learn more about the manner in which Valéry worked, but that may well be the only personal aspect of his life which will be revealed. After his period of silence, during the active part of his career when so many demands were made upon him, he rose at five in the morning, prepared his own breakfast and worked until nine. They were the only hours of quiet and reflection which Valéry reserved for himself, the only hours when his thought could be distilled into words and prepared for that strange communication we call a book.

Philosophy and art were not professions for Valéry. They were a kind of climate in which the philosopher and the artist might live and discover themselves. Creativeness is not the goal because, as Mallarmé had so consistently taught in his poems and in his conversation, the perfect poem is the one which is never projected outside the intellect. So, a philosophical system and a published poem are betrayals of the mind and imperfect replicas of man's creative power. The so-called completed masterpieces of art and the torment of Pascal astonished Valéry and even irritated him.

In the botanical garden of Montpellier where Valéry used to walk as a boy and where as a young man he walked with his friends from Paris, Louÿs and Gide, he discovered the tomb of Narcissus in one of the many fountains. It was there doubtless that he first meditated on the mythological figure of Narcissus who was destined to become the angel of his symbolism. The leaves were dry and brittle. The lines of the fountain seemed clear and ancient. The sun filtered through the branches and struck the surface of the water which was mirror to the sky and trees and to the face of the young poet who bent over it.

Valéry has three poems on the theme of Narcissus. The second of these, and the most profound, *Fragments du Narcisse,* does not deal with the myth as a simple story of metamorphosis, but as a complex drama, central to the thought of Valéry and to the psychological inquiry of the contemporary artist.

Inaccessible to himself, this Narcissus created by Valéry is a kind of philosopher in his search for self-knowledge. He is also the hero of sterility, bearing spiritual affinities with Hamlet, with Gide's André Walter and with the contemporary hero of inaction and self-analysis. Valéry's twenty years' silence is reduced in *Narcisse* to an afternoon, but the briefer silence is also pregnant with thought and meditation. The cool body of Narcissus is his sole defense against the dead who await him. He can therefore love only himself, and pray the gods to arrest the daylight as it diminishes. The poem ends in the disorder of evening shadows. The inaccessible love of Narcissus disappears as his lips touch the darkening waters and scatter the image he loved.

If *Narcisse* is the poem of Montpellier: of gardens and shadows, of self-love and youth—*Le Cimetière Marin* is the poem of Sète, of Valéry's return to his native city on the sea, to his ancestors in their marine graveyard. Immobility in this poem is not that of a single individual, as it was in *Fragments du Narcisse,* it is the immobility of nature, of the sea and of the sun poised on the zenith. Always throughout the work of Valéry persists the mirage of power, the possible omnipotence of the human mind. The problem explored is that of the soul, of whether it is one of the myths of mankind, or the great reality of man. The contemplation of the sea, ever stable and enduring, gives to the poet the experience of an ecstasy in which the "pure" self and the "pure" cosmos meet, or derive their existence one from the other.

These two poems of the fountain and the sea illustrate the two states of being in which Valéry studies his favorite subject: the principle of his own functioning, the autonomy and the potency of his own mind. First, as Narcissus, he studies the multiple selves of a single man, the constant changes in nature which surrounds him, and the duration of time with its endless vicissitudes and intermittences. Secondly, as the poet walking over the tombs of his ancestors and contemplating the constancy of the sea, he studies the image of stability and the nontemporal. On the one hand, he analyzes the principle itself of living, of all that is personal and transitory in an individual. And on the other hand, he abstracts himself from life, in his search for the universal and the permanent.

French art is especially the art of dialogue. One voice is seldom heard alone in France. The classical opposition between Corneille and Racine is in reality a dialogue. The two voices of Descartes and Pascal are not discordant. To the voice of Montesquieu one should add Rousseau's. To Mallarmé's voice one will have to add henceforth Valéry's. French harmony is not simple. It is markedly contrapuntal. The dialogue between Valéry and Mallarmé is one of the most recent in French poetry. It will be listened to as attentively as two other impassioned dialogues of our period, the one Péguy held with Corneille, and the one Claudel held with Rimbaud.

Mallarmé taught the modern world how to read poetry. Valéry will teach the future world how to consider behind the poem the spiritual depths from which it rises. It is the new dialogue between rigor and profundity. Between rigor taught by Mallarmé, rigor of form, of architecture, of symbol—and profundity taught by Valéry, profundity of source, of mystery, of knowledge.

Valéry never disavowed his debt to Huysmans' novel *A rebours*, where he first saw the name of Mallarmé, and to Mallarmé himself who was the greatest influence in his life. Mallarmé has been the most subtle proposer of enigmas in French literature, and Valéry was to continue and prolong this role of his master. Whereas Mallarmé's favorite topic was the art of poetry, Valéry's became the act of poetry, the mystery of the poetic mechanism. The world was made to end in a book, according to Mallarmé, but Valéry formulated a new goal for himself: knowledge concerning the secret laws of poetry. Beauty implies a method. Valéry was concerned with discovering this method and ridding poetry of all "mystery," a word he strongly disliked. He never held a salon like Mallarmé's, and never became the master or head of a group. There was nothing of the patriarch or the pedagogue about Valéry. And yet he was always kindly and animated in café groups of

younger poets. He treated them as friends and intimates rather than disciples, and willingly discussed
any subject: Descartes, Degas, Josephine Baker.

His confidant and devoted secretary, Monod, assures us that the early Valéry was a prolific poet. In
Genoa, in the summer of 1892, he lived through what
is now referred to as his "night," comparable to similar experiences of Descartes and Pascal and Mallarmé
himself. It was an experience of liberation, a sudden
awareness of his vocation which had been preceded by
a period of anguish and distress. Valéry always manifested a marked disdain for literature in the ordinary
sense. The novel especially was distasteful to him.
Once Gide lent him a copy of *Martin Chuzzlewit*
which he returned the following day saying that he
had sampled the book enough to see how it began and
how it ended. He had looked at it enough to see
de quoi il retournait, and his curiosity was satisfied.
More subtly than Voltaire in the eighteenth century, Valéry has been in our age the emancipator and
the iconoclast. His lesson is perilous for the believer.
Unless his work fortifies the reader's spirit, it may
well turn out to be a destructive force. His own spirit,
so liberated and attentive, gives one often the impression of moving about in a vast intellectual desert.
"In the beginning was the Joke, and the Joke was
God," he once said to Edmond Jaloux. (*Au com-
mencement était la Blague, et la Blague était Dieu.*)

A great deal has been written during the last one
hundred years about the poet and the subject of poetry. At its center, the controversy over "pure poetry" raised the issue to its most acute state, at which
time Paul Valéry, as principal spokesman, devised certain formulas which have gone very far in calming the

controversy and offering to both sides formal defini-
tions on which the criticism of poetry will probably
rest for some time to come.

The subject of a poem, Valéry tells us, is about as
important to a poem as the name of a man is to the
man. It has to be there, but it tells us as much about
the poem as a man's name tells us about the man. The
thought of a poem exists, to be sure, but it is concealed in the substance of the poem. In order to explain this, Valéry uses an image of a very telling nature. He compares the thought of a poem to the
nutritive element in a piece of fruit. We eat the fruit
and experience a delight without always being aware
that we are being nourished at the same time. Nutri-
tion is in the fruit as thought is in the poem, but we
cannot separate it from the pleasure we enjoy in the
acts of eating or reading.

A poem will represent in words what the poet
might have wept over, what he might have exclaimed
about. Tears, caresses and sighs are all behind lyric
poems, but because poems are representations, art-
fully conceived, they are close to being games. When
Valéry uses such a word as "game" (*jeu*), he is careful
to add that this game is solemn and significant. He
is unwilling to accept any rigid definition of purity
in poetry. It is impossible to conceive a poem, he says,
that would have only poetry in it.

From a phrase in a preface written by Valéry, Abbé
Bremond devised the subject matter of a book on
pure poetry, in which he called it the lyric trance
preceding literary creation. This he described as the
moment of inspiration or ecstasy where human reason is suspended, and which the poet afterwards will
try to explain or communicate. Valéry, in opposing

this doctrine, seems to deny the power of inspiration, or to stress the importance of deliberate labor on a text. Ronsard and the Romantics had based much of their poetic theory on Plato's doctrine in the *Ion*, concerning poetic madness or delirium. But Valéry revives the cult of reason and assures his readers that there is nothing exceptional or mysterious in the poet's make-up. To the work itself he always preferred the study of the problems of making a poem.

And yet Valéry does leave an opening for the more traditional view of the poet and his subject. He says there are two kinds of verse: that *given* to the poet and that *calculated* by him. The given line is the one which seems to originate without any effort on the part of the poet and is therefore a purely gratuitous gift of the gods. Valéry has acknowledged that he himself has known some of those imperious verbal illuminations which come in a fixed combination of words and which seem to demand that a poem be written around them. The line, *Pâle, profondément mordue*, came to him once in this way. It is not a line especially meaningful by itself, but by adding other lines to it he composed a stanza, and then by gradually adding other stanzas he created the poem *La Pythie*. In another instance, the cadence of a line came first to Valéry and obsessed him to such a degree that an overwhelming desire grew in him to find words to suit the cadence. It was the ten syllable line, with the caesura after the fourth syllable, which demanded a reality and which ended by growing into his most celebrated poem, *Le Cimetière Marin*. He claims to have begun its composition without any knowledge of its subject matter.

The given line, for Valéry, is the one endowed with

the most magic. It originates in a seemingly magical way, and then it persists in the work as the line we repeat the most often, the line we return to, finding it always impossible to modify. Valéry quotes an opening line from a Baudelaire poem as an example of this type of verse, as one that must have "come" to Baudelaire:

La servante au grand coeur dont vous étiez jalouse

In terms of meaning, "The warmhearted servant of whom you were jealous," Valéry judges the line equivalent to the condensation of a Balzac novel, and then he goes on to claim its power as pure poetry. The proof of this power is in the rhyme it calls forth in the following line:

Et qui dort son sommeil sous une humble pelouse

The rhyme word, *pelouse*, "lawn," under which the old servant sleeps, is quite inaccurate for a French cemetery, but no accusation of impropriety has ever been leveled against Baudelaire. The beauty of the line is strong enough to cover up any defect of vocabulary.

These anecdotes are lessons in the power of words as used by poets. The meaning that is given to them is something else. "My lines," Valéry once said, "have the meaning that you give them." We owe to Valéry also a conversation he recorded between Mallarmé and Degas over this problem. In addition to his painting, Degas was interested in writing sonnets. One evening, at the home of Berthe Morisot, he complained of the difficulty he had in writing, and said, "I wasted my day on a sonnet which doesn't come off. And yet I don't lack ideas. I am full of them. I have too many." Mallarmé answered him, saying, "You don't make sonnets with ideas, Degas, you make them with words." One of the principal tenets of Mallarmé's doctrine states that the poet should learn how to yield the initiative, in the creation of a poem, to the words themselves. He taught that the verse re-created a total word, new and foreign to ordinary language, a word characterized by its incantatory power.

Mallarmé and Valéry continued and deepened one of the aspects of modern poetry founded in France by Poe and Baudelaire. It is concerned with the practice and the mastery of the means of poetry, with the belief that the subject of a poem is important only as a means of expression which should exist within the poem as an integral part of its texture.

In his celebrated definition of symbolism, Valéry states that the new poetry is simply trying to recapture from music what belongs to it. But in the practice of so-called symbolist poetry, he revived and adhered to all the classical rules of prosody. The act of writing poetry is a bending of the will to all kinds of constraints. If the music of language is to be rediscovered and recreated, a long process of "research" is necessary in the sound of syllables and the meaning of words and the phrases of words and their combinations. Music may well be the art in which intention and form are the most perfectly fused, and poetry, if it is to imitate or equate music, must contain symbols which will permit endless interpretations. The symbol in poetry establishes a relationship between things and ourselves. It is a kind of bond uniting man with the universe. Valéry appropriates some of the oldest symbols (or myths) of the world,

Narcissus and the Fates, which are the titles of two of his greatest poems. Most of the poems in *Charmes* take their titles from the leading symbols: *L'Abeille, Palme, Les Pas, Au Platane, La Ceinture*.

Valéry is a singer of knowledge, of subterranean knowledge, where thought may be studied at its birth, in the intermediary stage between the subconscious and the conscious. His poems are seen to be more and more the condensed dramas of knowledge. They are metaphysical debates, as in the poems on Narcissus, where a veritable self-inquisition takes place. At the beginning of *La Jeune Parque,* we learn that some kind of metaphysical catastrophe has taken place, and the poem develops the consequences of this catastrophe. Albert Thibaudet called *La Jeune Parque* the most difficult poem in the French language. It is hardly that, once its central problem is seen clearly. The youngest of the Fates wonders whether she should transcend life or accept it. At the end of the poem she does affirm the power of life in a gesture of gratitude which is an answer to the suicide of Narcissus, and which is also confirmed at the end of *Le Cimetière Marin,* a further exhortation to life.

It will be difficult, more difficult than with most writers, to find out who Valéry was and what his thoughts were. He reveals himself to some degree when he talks of the men he admired. Of Leonardo da Vinci, for example, who was always dreaming of the universe and the rigors imposed on man. Of Descartes, also, who for Valéry was the incomparable artist working on the hardest of materials. Of Voltaire, whom he read at the time of his death and whom he saw as the most supple of men, the quickest and the most attentive. Behind the seemingly cold perfection of Valéry's poems and behind the hard intellectuality of their subject matter, readers today are beginning to sense a hidden deep tenderness and compassion. He himself once wrote that at the extreme point of each thought there is a sigh. (*A l'extrême de toute pensée il y a un soupir.*) What he reacted against was the obvious sentimentality of poets which he equated with pornography. Valéry moves his readers without saddening them.

His work still appears startlingly new and difficult. During these few years since his death, those who knew him the best have written more about the man himself and his relationship to his work than about the work. He gave slight heed to his fame and his greatness. His deftness and brilliance in conversation are still remembered, but his attitude and manner are more described than the subjects he spoke of. Playing with his cigarette or his monocle, he rarely chose a subject of conversation but infused into whatever topic was discussed formulas and witticisms which made any further commentary useless. In his spontaneous and scintillating speech, this Frenchman, who was half Corsican and half Genoese, seemed to be relaxing from the rigors of the early hours. It was always difficult for those who saw him and heard him to think of him as a great poet, a great prose writer and a thinker who will probably be more invoked in the years to come than any of his contemporaries.

No one denounced more vigorously than Valéry the sentimentality and lamentations with which poetry too often allows itself to be compromised or satisfied. In a letter he once pointed out the eight lines which he considered the most perfect he had written. It is the brief passage describing a sunset in *Fragments du Narcisse: O douceur de survivre à la force du jour.* Then, with his customary self-disparagement, added to his note that these same lines of his are totally devoid of any ideas. In his personality were traits of asceticism, of haughtiness, of belligerency, but above all an exceptional simplicity which seems to be the mark of most men of genius. During a half century, from Narcissus to Faust, Valéry practiced on himself a spiritual discipline which covered up the personal dramas the world may never learn about him.

He seemed always absent from the world and present in it at the same time. Once, on his way to a meeting of the French Academy, he paused before a window display to look at a beautifully printed page of poetry. He had been working that morning on a poem of his own and was still obsessed with rhythms and choices of words. He thought he was still working on his own page as he looked through the window, and began trying to make substitutions of words. But the printed words resisted him. They could not be modified. It was only then that he realized he was looking at a page of *Phèdre*.

TWO

GIDE: *The Sensual Quest*

The continuing interest in André Gide, since his death in February 1951, is a denial of the belief that a great writer is neglected for at least a time after his death. The many recent publications about him are for the most part personal testimonials to the man, written by close friends who call upon their memories of meetings with Gide, of conversations and events. No contemporary personality is more complex than Gide's, and no writer did more than Gide to stimulate controversy and contradiction about himself. During at least half of his literary career, if not all of it, he was obsessed with how the future would judge him and his work. He never ceased following the changes which took place in his mind and attitudes and judgments, changes which many critics have called contradictions and inconsistencies, but which testify rather to Gide's relentless self-inquisition.

One of his final words, spoken on the day of his death to the eminent physician Jean Delay, almost in-

Itiated a literary quarrel. Delay was alone with Gide and asked him whether he was in pain. Gide answered: "It is still the struggle between what is reasonable and what is not." Immediately two Catholic writers, François Mauriac and André Rousseaux, interpreted this statement as a tragic hesitation between Faith and Reason. The formula is enigmatical and resembles the final words of some of Gide's books, *Les Nourritures Terrestres*, for example, and *Thésée*. But so close a friend as Roger Martin du Gard refuses to see in it anything sibylline or mystical. At the end, Gide had two attitudes he exposed to his friends. One was in his words, *C'est bien. C'est très bien,* which they interpreted as meaning, "This is the way I hoped to die, lucid up until the end. I am submitting reasonably to the inevitable." The other attitude was more sorrowful when tears would come to his eyes in saying farewell. This final oscillation was for Martin du Gard one between his acceptance of the natural law and his sorrow at leaving his friends. And this oscillation is expressed in the phrase: *Toujours la lutte entre ce qui est raisonnable et ce qui ne l'est pas.*

At the time of his death, Gide had received the official sign of consecration, the recognition of his century that he was one of its major writers. The Nobel prize, awarded to him in 1948, indicated that his work had attained a degree of accepted universality, and the continuing attacks of the younger avant-garde writers was proof enough that his work was still being read by all ages and still sufficiently vital to initiate violent opposition. The miracle was that Gide had become a "classical" writer by the time of his death, while remaining a "dangerous" writer. In keeping with a great European tradition, he uttered at the moment of dying a statement so mysterious that already it has been exploited in varying and contradictory ways.

This man who, more than any other artist, invented for his age the term "restlessness" (*inquiétude*), ended his life in a seeming calm and resignation. Gide, in every book, including his final posthumous message, *Et nunc manet in te,* is both hero and poet irreconcilably. He is the poet who sent his wife the admirable letters which she destroyed in a moment of deep despair, and he is also the man whose life destroyed the remarkable harmony which once existed between Madeleine Gide and himself. From all the touching testimonials concerning Gide during his last year and at the moment of his death, it would seem that after a long lifetime of vacillating, contradictory search, he ended by choosing himself. A tone of affirmation, a marked denial of God, a belief in the void of death, provide a different portrait of Gide, a final one, which will have to be added to the long series his books have already fashioned.

Beyond the enigmatical sentence spoken to Jean Delay by Gide just before his death, the testimonials of those who saw him during his final illness indicated a very real resignation, a stoical acceptance of a state which he had defined for himself many times during the latter part of his life as a void. All his life Gide had suffered from insomnia, and during the period when he was forced to remain in bed, he seemed never to close his eyes. His mind remained constantly active. He reread the *Aeneid* with extraordinary satisfaction or discussed plans for a scenario he wanted to make from his play *Les Caves du Vatican.* A few years previously he had been astonished and grateful at being able to complete his final work, *Thésée*. In *Thésée* Gide's message reached an unusual degree of serenity and completeness, and with it he felt that he had said all that was important for him to say.

The vast work of Gide is, in a sense, a written confession, initiated by a need to communicate what he felt to be true about himself. He claimed that the central drama of his existence was his love for his wife, a drama which a few months after his death was revealed in his own words in *Et nunc manet in te*. This volume helps to complete the portrait of Gide, of the man who in our century had perhaps the deepest faculty for comprehension, the greatest lucidity in understanding ideas different from his own.

Madeleine Rondeaux was born in 1867 and was therefore two years older than her cousin, André Gide. They grew up together. Despite the deep affection which united them, when they announced their engagement, both families were surprised. They were married after Gide's first visit to Algeria. Madeleine accompanied him there on his second trip. In his *Journal* Gide refers to her as Emmanuèle or as Em. Not until the posthumous work does he call her by her real name. The title is a hemistich from a line of Virgil concerning the lost Eurydice: *Et nunc manet in te*. The work is an attempt to describe the personal drama of Gide's marriage, a drama which throughout his life was constant, secret, central. The love existing between a man and woman was replaced by a sense of purity, by an extraordinary worship. "The spiritual force of my love," Gide writes, "prevented any carnal desire."

No explanation was ever made between Gide and his wife. She seldom left the Normandy country house at Cuverville where Gide's visits became increasingly infrequent. She was pious, meticulous in the running of the large house, and devoted to her care of the poor of the countryside. Between husband and wife the degree of silence grew as the years passed. Madeleine read few of his books, although during the first part of his career, she was an admirable critic and guide. Each of his thoughts, Gide has stated, developed through some relationship with her, because of her. The best part of his nature remained in constant communion with her. The need of expressing himself sincerely originated in her character, which ironically must have caused her great suffering. Gide never rid himself of remorse for having falsified her destiny of woman. In November 1918, at a moment of desperate sorrow over his failure to remain with her, she burned all of his early letters. They were, according to Gide, his best letters, the fundamental document on his formative years, the description of his love for Madeleine. He never understood how she could have been responsible for the literary and personal loss which their destruction entailed.

Gide's love for his wife dominated his entire life, but it never suppressed any part of his nature. Rather it added the element of struggle. Just at the time (1921-22) when his love for Madeleine seemed unique in his life, he felt that she no longer believed in it and preferred to know nothing about his sentiments. In preparing the 1939 publication of his *Journal*, Gide realized that all the deliberate omissions of references to his wife gave an incoherent and mutilated picture of himself. The posthumous volume has remedied this in showing the inevitable drama of such a marriage and the radical differences of temperament between husband and wife. Madeleine Gide appears modest and retiring, traditionalist in taste, austere in her way of living. André Gide is practically the opposite: evasive and always capable of literally disappearing, docile to every event, incapable of refusing any kind of solicitation.

Long before *Et nunc manet in te,* Gide's conjugal idealism was fully exposed in *André Walter.* His early books have been too long considered purely the expression of an esthete. They are much more than that, and the most recent publications will help in forming a new estimate of the earliest writing. Because Gide was not so much a student of doctrine as he was a student of temperament, it is impossible to give a simple, clear answer to any of the major questions one habitually asks about a great writer. Did he live like a monk or like a libertine? This question, for example, would be difficult to answer.

His life seems to have been occupied with an extraordinary interest in life in all of its manifestations and with an assiduous reading of literary texts. He alternated his studies of botany, his walking, swimming, insect hunting, with readings of Goethe, translations of Shakespeare and the writing of books. He rose early, enriched by the ideas which sleep had provided, and full of plans for the day. Everything offered him a subject for meditation: a page of reading, his breakfast, a patch of blue sky, the coloring of an insect or of a flower, the beauty of a child, a noble gesture. In a profound sense, he was a lonely man, but he was seldom alone. He disliked social gatherings where he felt out of place and incapable of saying anything of significance. He claimed that a writer has nothing to gain from such occasions unless he wants to write the work of a Proust. Even more than social gatherings, he abhorred literary discussions.

Gide knew that he possessed nothing of the anguish of a Pascal. That trait he left to Mauriac, and accepted for himself the characteristics of a Montaigne, of a wavering and diverse mind *(esprit ondoyant et divers)*. Every moment of his day was utilized. He remained at all times the writer who profited from every kind of experience, important or trivial. Gide was the opposite of a dreamer or a storyteller. Every reflection and every object was to be captured for future use in the literary work. This way of life was no assurance of happiness. At his first meeting with Claude Mauriac, in 1937, when Gide was already a very celebrated figure, he confessed to the young man that he had gone that day twice to the movies because he had felt lonely and abandoned. During 1938 and 1939, Claude Mauriac observed Gide quite closely and was struck by the youthfulness of his appearance and manner. He had developed certain traits of distrust, certain characteristics of the tracked man under suspicion. He was haunted by a fear of boredom. Claude Mauriac believed that Gide's love for the movies came from that fear. Whatever his message was, it had become through the years indistinguishable from his character. The creation of a literary work and the creation of a personality had been continuing simultaneously for years.

On the first anniversary of Gide's death, February 19, 1952, Marc Allégret presented his film on Gide at the Cinéma Vendôme in Paris. Most of the film had been made during two months of the last year of Gide's life, in his apartment on rue Vaneau. But there are sequences from Gide's life dating from the time of the silent movies. Some of the most exciting parts are Gide's own commentaries on certain of his books, and his conversations with other celebrities. The scene with his two grandchildren for whom he performs a trick with a box of matches was completely improvised and filmed only once. On the occasion of the première of this film, Marc Allégret was asked to describe the characteristics of Gide he remembered best. He had known Gide intimately for many years, and he spoke especially of his seriousness, of his scrupulosity in refusing or accepting, of the depths of his fervor and the intensity with which he spoke to friends and considered their problems.

The film, which bears the simple title *Avec André Gide,* constitutes a precious document on certain aspects of the writer's life and career. It opens with a few solemn pictures of the funeral at Cuverville and Gide's own reading of the opening pages of his autobiography, *Si le grain ne meurt.* There are pictures showing the two contrasting family origins of Gide: Normandy and Languedoc, the north and the south, the Catholic and the Protestant backgrounds. The landscape pictures of Algeria and Tunisia provide a documentation for many of his works, from his earliest, such as *Les Nourritures Terrestres,* to his *Journal* in 1941-42. Among the most curious episodes are the trip to the Congo, the walk with Valéry, the home of his daughter in Brignoles, the speech made in Moscow in the presence of Stalin, the visit with Roger Martin du Gard in Bellème. The most surprising sequence is perhaps the role of attentive and affectionate grandfather. Of all his sentences, the one which has been used the most often against him is his invective against all families: *Familles, je vous hais.* But Gide did play the role of grandfather with his customary sincerity, and Allégret has a perfect right to include the touching scene with the grandchildren as illustrating one of the final roles in the long life.

Gide has probably been the most photographed man of letters of our age, and hence of all ages. As the years passed, his face seemed to take on the appearance of a Mongolian-like mask, with its oblique and prominent eyebrows. One of the earliest descriptions of Gide was inscribed by Roger Martin du Gard in his journal, on the occasion of their first meeting at Gallimard's in 1913. The cloak Gide wore then gave him the appearance of an old starving actor. A defrocked priest, thought du Gard, one with an evil conscience. His voice was, up to the very end, rich in resonance, low pitched, almost solemn. He read aloud with the art of an experienced actor. His facial expression revealed at moments of attentiveness an exceptional combination of emotion and intelligence. His thin, tightly-closed lips contrasted with the trembling of his features. During the last days, when his cheeks had grown quite hollow and his skin a parchment gray, he wore on his head a cotton bonnet. Layers of flannel covered him because his lifelong fear of drafts had developed into a mania. The press notices of his play *Les Caves du Vatican* had been on the whole quite severe. He insisted upon reading them all, claiming that he had grown invulnerable to attack: *Tout glisse maintenant sur moi, je suis devenu proof.* This was far from true. No one solicited criticism more than Gide, and no one suffered more from it.

A possible definition of genius—and one that applies admirably to Gide—is a mind attentive to things which hold no interest for most people. A genius is a man who considers passionately what other men do not see. In the tradition of French letters, Montaigne is pre-eminently this type of genius who seizes every occasion of pleasure, every experience, every meeting for the subject matter of his writing. (*Jusques aux moindres occasions de plaisir que je puis rencontrer, je les empoigne,* wrote Montaigne.) Gide's place as artist is precisely in this tradition, and the magnitude of his work, of his understanding, of his sympathy, places him beside Montaigne. The art of both the sixteenth-century essayist and the twentieth-century moralist is based upon an indefatigable curiosity and a relentless critical spirit. Gide's enthusiasm for whatever came within his vision was usually followed by an admirable detachment from it. Once the conquest was made, he refused to be subjugated by it, he refused to be dominated by his conquest. The image of the minotaur's labyrinth, elaborated in his last important book, *Thésée,* represents any body of doctrine which might constrict or imprison the thinking powers of man. The problem of Theseus, as it was for Gide himself, was that of surpassing his adventures. The one moral error to be avoided at all cost was immobility, fixation. The meaning of Gide's celebrated *disponibilité* seems to be the power of remaining dissatisfied, capable of change and growth.

His *Journal* indicates to some degree the amount of time Gide spent in observing the world. His favorite

diversion was the movies, which flattered his curiosity. The pleasure he derived from reading such an
author as Siménon can doubtless be explained this
way. The *Journal* is a record of his endless observa-
tions and it will always remain the best book about
him. His curiosity was a way of living, an appetite
encouraging him toward life and to an "attentiveness"
(another of his favorite words) toward every manifestation of life. Each time the doorbell rang in his
apartment, he would have to interrupt his work or
rest in order to eavesdrop and discover who was calling and for what reason. *Je suis si curieux,* he would
say, *cela me perd.*

From his avid curiosity about everything, whether
it was the coloration of a leaf or the first book of a
new author, his ideas were engendered. In the mani-
fold forms of attentiveness in which his life seems to
have been spent, there are no traces of misanthropy,
of pessimism, of class prejudice, of fatuous satisfaction with self. But on the other hand—and this is the
inevitable trait of those souls who are attentive to
others—there was little trace of gaiety or happiness.
Gide's lifelong practice of consigning to paper his
most intimate thoughts and his confidences caused
him to be quite reserved in oral speech. In conversation, he preferred to question rather than to answer.
His power of listening was so eloquent that there
was little need for his verbal reply. From a nature
that was dominated by curiosity, which accepted all
contradictions, a will to freedom as well as a sense of
destiny, good as well as evil—his mind grew into one
of the most critical of our age, a mind of infinite subtlety and unexpected boldness.

The many testimonials of his friends gravitate singularly around the impression of authenticity of character which Gide made upon them. To each one he was someone slightly different. He easily stimulated their confidence, although later they were often embarrassed at reading in his *Journal* references to their conversations. What might have been considered indiscretion was used by Gide as part of the truth he sought endlessly. Each friend, in his presence, learned to become curious about himself as well as about Gide. More than an active participant in the conversation, he was a spectator but one whose very presence provided a new meaning to whatever debate was going on. Whenever he was assured of real frankness, he encouraged criticism of himself and his work, almost to a masochistic degree. He demanded time of his friends and a freedom of disposition, a willingness to speak on his favorite subjects which obsessed him. He was especially the friend of those who did not resemble him. Roger Martin du Gard has spoken of the exhaustion and even irritability he felt after spending a long time in Gide's company, but then immediately accused himself of ingratitude because each hour spent with Gide had been an enriching experience.

Robert Levesque has described Gide at the railroad station, where his fear of missing the train urged him to arrive long before the hour of departure. He supplied himself abundantly at the newspaper-magazine wagon on the quai, purchased a letter-opener which he would inevitably lose, settled down in his compartment, with his bags which were never locked, as if the act of taking a train were a liberation and the beginning of a new life. The inseparable notebook for his journal writing was in his pocket or on his lap, and he looked through his morning mail which would be answered the next day from the hotel room. Once the train had left, Gide seldom remained for long in his compartment, or even in his class, for that matter. He wandered through the train, to the despair of the conductor.

The journal entries which Claude Mauriac has just published concerning his meetings with Gide, between October 1937 and the beginning of the war, provide, in addition to a very sympathetic study of Gide, portraits of his father, François Mauriac, of Jouhandeau and of Cocteau. Young Mauriac introduced himself to Gide at the Café du Rond-Point des Champs-Elysées on October 21, 1937. An immediate sympathy grew between the young and the older man. Claude reintroduced Gide to his father. The Mauriacs received him first at dinner in their Paris home, and later, in June 1939, for several days in the large estate at Malagar, outside of Bordeaux.

During the first literary conversation on Claudel and Maritain, Gide reminded Mauriac that he would be compromised at receiving such a visitor. Very often Mauriac's views, expressed in the presence of Gide, amazed his son, who became more aware of his father's personal drama, the official position of Catholic writer he holds in France and his unwillingness therefore to treat in his writing certain subjects obsessing him. Gide constantly brought the conversation back to religious matters, seemingly in order to reaffirm his own position of nonbeliever. *Je ne crois pas; je sais qu'il n'y a aucune raison de croire; c'est pour moi une certitude.*

Gide spoke of the discouragement he had felt over the severe press notices his book *L'Immoraliste* had received. Seven years went by before he was able to write another book. He pointed out to the Mauriacs the lack of success each of his books had at its publication. As the son watched his father talk with Gide, he realized more lucidly than ever that Gide's mystery was his power of reconciling irreconcilables. The period of living so close to Gide provided Claude Mauriac with an admirable opportunity to observe Gide's appetite for work, and to appreciate the man's extensive culture in so many domains: in literature, music, foreign languages. His love for study had always protected him against all onslaughts of discouragement and depression. One evening, for example, he recited from memory eighty lines of Keats. A rich, full life of humanist, certainly, and yet Claude Mauriac wondered often whether Gide was not one of the most lonely of men, whether anyone really loved him.

Since his death, Gide's readers have begun asking of his work the central questions: who he is and what he is offering them. He who spent his life questioning the sphinx is now being questioned in his turn. At his death his interest in the living ceased, and the living now have begun to be interested in him.

The real secrets of Gide are all in his books. They are now being reread from that ultimate perspective which death provides. Every great work of literature is a self-portrait. The sole subject of Gide's books is his own adventure, which he either narrated or interpreted. He never completed this adventure. He never told it all. He once said that at the end of each of his books, he would like to write: "The most important part remains to be said." Gide was capable endlessly of picking up the story where he had left it and continuing it. He was never able to trust completely what he had written the day before or published the year before. Something else had to be added, something new had to be said because the truth moved forward with him each day.

Gide began writing about 1890, at a moment of great peacefulness in Europe. He continued to write during the next sixty years, until 1950, during which time the world changed from the peace of the nineties to the chaos and imminent tragedy of the mid-century. He remained a constant and fervent witness to every ominous development in Europe and the world, from the period when a religion of science and a rational vision of the universe dominated Europe, to the present period of such deep unrest. Gide never lived in an ivory tower, but he was reserved in his judgments on present-day affairs. Essentially a moralist, Gide believed that every change in the world had to begin with oneself. The way has to be tested by oneself first. Our one way of understanding and criticizing and loving is to take ourselves as the means. Whereas the experiences of two men are never identical, there are points of resemblance between any two experiences. By being increasingly honest with oneself, by becoming more and more deeply oneself, one may discover all of human nature. Gide enlarged the Socratic dictum "Know yourself" into "Be yourself."

There is little doubt that Gide hoped to compose a new gospel. With his favorite themes of adolescence, revolt, escape, the gratuitous act, he was able to upset the convictions of his readers, particularly the youthful readers, and yet he never created in them the feelings of terror or dismay which a Dostoevsky or a Lautréamont were able to arouse. He is still read

today by the young, but they no longer weep over
Les Nourritures Terrestres or aspire to be a Lafcadio.
It is impossible to claim any one form of writing for
Gide. He tried all the genres because he was unwilling to restrict himself to any one form, and because
each book, once it was well under way, became irk-
some to him. He would finish it off quickly in order to
move on to a newer work. He had planned, for example, several more chapters for *Les Faux-Monnayeurs*,
but when he wrote the sentence, *Je suis bien curieux
de connaître Caloub,* it appeared to him such an admirable final sentence that he felt freed from continuing any further. His impatience grew always
when he saw the goal at hand. He preferred the search
to the discovery.

At a moment of grateful recognition, Claude
Mauriac said to Gide: "You taught me and several
generations intellectual honesty." As a teacher, Gide
refused to formulate any dogma, but trained his
disciples in a way of learning, in an attitude toward
discipline. Gide's training, if it could be called that,
would culminate in the disciple's choosing himself
rather than any teacher or any one doctrine. Whenever Christianity appeared to him in the form of a
system, of a body of principles, he refused to accept
it. His way was one of detachment and adventure,
which would permit him the practice of what has
been so often called his sincerity. He was never able to
reconcile Christianity as represented in the organization of the Church, with the teachings of Christ in
the Gospels. He was never fundamentally troubled by
any metaphysical problem in religion, and that is one
reason why his Catholic friends, Claudel, Jammes,
Du Bos, Ghéon, Copeau, had no influence over him

when they urged him to be more "Catholic" than "sincere." Problems of ethics worried him far more than religious problems. He was more concerned with justice than salvation. His knowledge of the Bible and his love of the Gospels always gave hope to his religious friends that he would finally submit. But his questions were those of a moralist. He left in the form of a question the problem which remained uppermost: will Faith lead man the farthest toward his goal? The letters Claudel and Jammes wrote to Gide on the religious problem ended by opposing Christian morality to his critical spirit. He remained insubordinate. The wrath of Claudel at such stubbornness is well known. At a dinner with his godson, Paul Jammes, Claudel lit a crêpe and when the flame was high, said, "That is what God is going to do with Gide." This story was told by Gide himself.

His work is not only a written confession. It is at the same time a scrupulously examined code of morals. At the time of his first books, soon after 1890, Gide realized that if he lived in accordance with the accepted moral system of his society, he would live as a hypocrite. The struggle between hypocrisy and sincerity became the central moral issue for Gide, as early as his first book, *André Walter*. Between the simple although rigid laws governing his family circle and his own sincerity, his own purity of a young man, Gide sensed a troublesome dichotomy. He went against the world's morality, not because it was false for the world, but because it was useless and even dangerous for him. In this desire to reject the laws of his society, he was not seeking any indulgence for himself but a form and a rule for his own life, a morality that would be his own, autonomous and independent of any foreordained system.

Early in life Gide learned that advice from someone else is of little use. The extraordinary singularity of each human being makes his particular problem unique. Gide's morality is fundamentally based upon the belief that each man is elected to play a role unlike every other role. Any deviation from that role, in order to pattern oneself on the pre-established rule, represents, in fact, for Gide, a betrayal of oneself. One's role, or one's destiny, to use a more deeply significant term, can be determined only within oneself. Advice from the outside cannot be relied upon. This peculiar separateness of man is a Gidian theme to which Jean-Paul Sartre, many years later, gave his own coloring and importance. In the early books of Gide, where this problem of personal destiny was raised, God was often invoked as being able to guide a human being in his quest for self-knowledge. But as time went on, Gide grew suspicious of religious morality, as the world used it, in creating out of it a highly formalized and complicated body of doctrine. Formalism for Gide, the early Protestant, always appeared empty and vain.

Sentence after sentence in the first books, *Voyage d'Urien, Retour de l'Enfant Prodigue,* and the early entries in the *Journal,* repeat the same belief that each man's way is unique. The Gospel maxim, "He that findeth his life, shall lose it," is closely associated with the conviction that at the end of adolescence one cannot find a set of rules, ready-made for the conduct of one's life. No one book, no one house, no one country can represent the universe. The Gidian hero refuses to shut himself off from any part of the world before he has tested it, and he reserves the right to judge it lucidly. Somewhere between dogmatism and total freedom (literally he moved from puritanism to a momentary licentiousness), Gide fixed his ethical behavior and his constant admonition to observe everything and to try to understand everything. Gide had no hope of substituting for the commonplaces of social morality anything that would be equally direct and simple to understand. What he advocated was necessarily ambiguous in the light of what he wanted to offset.

What appears as conformity to the world's law was seriously castigated in *Les Nourritures Terrestres* and in *L'Immoraliste*. And yet in the two books which followed, *Paludes* and *Saül*, Gide criticized the other excess of giving oneself over to one's instinct. Freedom from the world's conventions must be won, but Gide never underestimated the perils of freedom. In fact, it would be possible to consider all his writings as the study of the dangers of this new freedom. Whereas the freeing of desire is a fairly simple thing, it is extremely difficult to make something out of that state of freedom. It is far easier to follow puritanism as a way of life, than to make out of joyfulness and release of spirit an ethical duty. Gide's strictures against society follow in the wake of an important French tradition, illustrated by the *Contrat Social* of Rousseau and *Le Rouge et le Noir* of Stendhal. The more purely Christian rule of doing nothing that will offend God had gradually changed in the history of French civilization to what might be called the bourgeois rule of doing nothing that will offend your neighbor. The Gidian rule is far more personal than either of these. He is concerned with the peace that can be found within oneself, with a rule of conduct that will not be humiliating to oneself. This personal morality represents a turning away from religious and social morality in order to live in sincerity with oneself. What Gide calls "immoralism" is, therefore, an acceptance of desire, provided this acceptance be accompanied by severe demands.

After the first movement of liberation from all societal constraints, a movement described in *Les Nourritures Terrestres* and *L'Immoraliste*, Gide the moralist advocates a close examination of the new freedom won. He presents in his play *Saül* a tragedy resulting from the misuse of freedom. The very difficulty involved in living with this new freedom is the moral problem of most of his subsequent books: *Les Caves du Vatican, Les Faux-Monnayeurs, Thésée.* After one learns what one's own morality consists of, then begins the long difficult perfecting of this morality, the long vigilance necessary not to slip back into a morality not one's own. Gide's belief about the ideal teacher is deducible from his personal morality. The real teacher will ultimately allow the pupil to choose himself rather than to choose the teacher. The value of any given lesson will therefore be the stimulation it provides to discover oneself.

Gide is no romantic, in the narrow sense of the term, and it is important precisely to distinguish between the Gidian morality of self and the romantic ego. In his volume of essays, *Incidences,* we read the sentence, "The triumph of individualism is in the giving up of individuality." Rather than offering to the public what is peculiarly characteristic and personal (as the typical romantic artist tends to do),

Gide advocates a revindication of self not in order to stress its peculiarity but its universality. There is unquestionably some element of Gide in many of his characters: in Michel of *L'Immoraliste*, in Jérôme of *La Porte Etroite*, in Edouard of *Les Faux-Monnayeurs*, but each one represents a part of Gide he had already renounced. To renounce individuality is to bring about the triumph of individualism. Whereas the Romantic does not exist beyond the portrait he gives of himself, Gide is anxious to know himself in order to move beyond that self. Each of his books is therefore the extinction of one of his selves which will help prepare a more universal Gide. This conviction and his habit of writing combined to make out of a single man with a very personal problem a literary figure of universal validity and significance. From the role of immoralist, of the young man defiant of the fixed moral standards of his day, Gide passed to the role of self-examiner and self-inquisitor, a role lasting until the end of his life, when he reached the final state of moralist.

The multiple aspects of Gide's sensitivity and intelligence have been countless times enumerated and analyzed. His restlessness, his endless quests and curiosity have led him through philosophies, experiences and genres until his very extensive work stands out today as the major source for our contemporary aesthetic and moral problems. Gide no longer appears to us as the diversifier or the wearer of many masks. Both contemplator and contemplative, he is the man of our age who has looked most religiously and most lovingly at himself and at the mirrored features of the universe. Great books renew the myths of mankind. Those of

Gide renew the myth of Narcissus, of that being who
questions himself by means of his sight and the steady
searching of his eyes. To know the form of his very soul
was the objective of the youth who bent down over the
waters of the fountain and excluded from his sight and
from his passion all that was not he himself.

We are familiar with the story of the myth, but we
are usually unaware of its resurgence among us. We
remember Narcissus as that youth for whom a kiss was
impossible because the lips he desired were his own.
He was the boy held not by the world, but by the appearance of the world as it outlined itself in the colorless water. Centered in this mirrored appearance of
the world was his own form with which Narcissus
strove to unite himself. Here the Greek myth reveals
the universal quest of man: union with one's first self,
union with reality and the pure part of one's created
being.

As one book succeeded another, the written words
of Gide became increasingly transparent and revelatory. His books are like crystal works of art, like the
mirror-fountain of Narcissus, that catch partial reflections of the world and of himself. The steady gaze of
Narcissus into the clear water is the myth of man,
whereas the works of the artist are the sacrifice he
makes to the world, of himself and of his self-contem-
plation. In each book Gide tries to recompose his features. Each book is a forcing of himself toward that
form which has been lost in the universe. They are a
series of mirrors, whose beauty lies not so much in the
reflected traits as in the seriousness of the contemplation and the fervent search to unite with the original
self.

At the very inception of his career, Gide wrote a

brief tract on Narcissus (*Traité du Narcisse*). It was
published in the same year that his first book appeared. Today, in the perspective of many years, the
interpretation of Narcissus seems more centrally rele-
vant to Gide's work than his *André Walter*. The influence of Mallarmé and the Symbolists is strong in both
of these early pieces. Sterility and hamletism characterize Gide's first hero, André Walter, in his incapacity
to meet life with action or equate his dream with
reality. But in his statement on the problems of Narcissus, Gide alters the Symbolist pose of immobility enacted by Baudelaire's albatross and Mallarmé's swan.
The sailors who have imprisoned the albatross on the
deck of the boat, and the lake which has frozen over
the white wings of the swan, are symbols of the world
opposing the necessary freedom of the artist's spirit.
But the attraction which Narcissus feels in the calm
water of the fountain has not been imposed upon him
by any outside force. He is free in his self-love and
wills this strange solitary contemplation. There is a
vast difference between the detrimental weight of the
world making impossible any soaring of the spirit and
the long gaze of his eyes which Narcissus directs
downward to the tranquil waters of a fountain. In
each pose—in the incarcerated pose of the Symbolist
and in the self-willed and hypnotic pose of Narcissus
—the artist is alone. But the reason for the pose is
different in each case.

The experience of the Romantic and the Symbolist
seeking to release himself from the bonds of society
and the material world is less metaphysical than the
experience of Narcissus seeking to attach himself to the
profoundest part of his own being. The Symbolist seeks
release in order to create a new part of himself in a

new freedom. Narcissus seeks attachment in order to discover the oldest and most permanent part of himself. One moves toward an unconceived form; the other toward a lost form. Narcissus is therefore religious in his striving to unite with what he feels to be a lost primitive reality, and the Symbolist is still romantic in his striving to be what is unreal and imaginary.

Through his renewal of the Narcissus myth, André Gide has separated himself from the romantic trend which, more than any other, has characterized Western literature of the past 150 years. After his initial treatment of the subject in 1891, he has continued to recast the same problem in all of his major books. Not consciously has Gide recreated the myth in his writings. But the problem of Narcissus is Gide's, and the fervor of its application is religious.

The first important book of André Gide, *Les Nourritures Terrestres,* was published in 1897, but was not read until several years later. This work is a song of love, and especially a song of the thirst of love. Like Narcissus, the singer in *Les Nourritures Terrestres* is contemplating water in the desert of his desire, or that source which might satisfy his thirst.

Echo and the other nymphs who are abandoned by Narcissus are, in the personal experience of Gide, his early puritanism and timidity, Europe and the life of intellection. Africa is both oasis and desert, both fertility and thirst, where the new Narcissus can forget much of his early heritage and lose himself in a new search for his being.

Les Nourritures Terrestres is the second major attack in French letters on the nineteenth century and on the exaggerated roles of science, bourgeoisism, and the nation. The first attack was written in the century itself, in 1873, by a boy of nineteen—Arthur Rimbaud. *Une Saison en Enfer* announces a flight to Africa, where by joining the race of the Negroes, Rimbaud might plunge into a pre-Christian period and forget the morality imposed upon him by his Catholic baptism and the bourgeois conventions of his age. Unlike Gide, Rimbaud was the artist of violence. He renewed, in his flights of self-annihilation, another myth, fully as ancient as that of Narcissus in the history of man: the myth of the phoenix. The work of Rimbaud is a self-immolation. He had to destroy himself utterly in order to rise up again from his own ashes.

These two works are songs of love. Rimbaud's relates the love of violence and self-destruction, and Gide's relates the love of contemplation and of self. Rimbaud, in *Une Saison en Enfer,* portrays himself as the hyena, the convict and the sinner who, Samson-like, causes to crash down upon his own head the world he despised and refused to obey. Gide, in *Les Nourritures Terrestres,* portrays himself as the sensualist who knows the universe through his senses, who feels directly the touch of the earth, of plants, the taste of wine, the longing of thirst and desire, the air of nights and dawns, the ecstasy of sleep. Rimbaud, in his phoenix reincarnation, denounced his century by destroying the artist in himself and by resurrecting himself in Ethiopia as a gun-runner for King Menelek. Gide, in his Narcissus reincarnation, denounced the same century by willfully creating, from a background of bourgeois Calvinism, the artist in himself. The sands, the oasis springs, and the suppleness of young Arabs which he contemplated in

North Africa were the reflections of himself, of the self he willed to become, of that part of him most distant from the earlier Paris self.

He tells us explicitly in *Les Nourritures Terrestres* that the characters he names never existed. Ménalque, who seems to be the teacher of this new fervor, and Nathanaël, who is the disciple being taught, are the two roles of Narcissus: the one who looks and the one who is seen. No characters in the book, and yet it is a book on love. The central dogma in this new religion of love is that of vision. Gide tells us countless times that the act of seeing is more significant than the thing seen. It is the desire which counts and enriches the soul, and not the possession of the thing desired.

This is perhaps the fullest definition we can give of the Gidian term "fervor." Fervor seems to imply an attainment to the bareness of being, to the first elemental part of a man, and also to the fullness of emotion, to the amplitude which precedes any satisfaction or collapse of emotion. Two words, *attentes* and *fièvre*, recur so persistently throughout the text of Gide that they can be taken as synonyms of his fervor in which one being is all beings. To wait, in a state of fever, describes the love of Narcissus. Nathanaël is the soul of Gide to which he speaks in his desert thirst and love, as the fountain is the reflection of Narcissus into which he directs his gaze.

Gide's own soul is his first and his last disciple. When he refers to an imaginary disciple, he relates his efforts to lead the disciple away from all things dissimilar to him: his family, his room, his books, his past. This same kind of seduction was related by Lautréamont and by Rimbaud. With Gide it is less

violent because he has the tenderness of Narcissus
who fears to breathe lest the surface of the water be
troubled. Narcissus learns to judge his own being by
its ability to receive light, and Gide judges all beings
thus. The extreme degree of luminous receptivity is
the measure of love any being is capable of. Light re-
fracted from his face is the joy of Narcissus.

No one exists in *Les Nourritures Terrestres*. Even
Gide himself is just Vision. (*Et même moi, je n'y suis
que Vision.*) And Narcissus also changes his being
into vision. That is why in the ancient myth and
in its modern version of *Les Nourritures Terrestres*
there is no place for the theme of solitude. Because
there is no experience of solitude in the usual romantic sense. To be alone *in* oneself, in the deepest part
of oneself, is vastly different from being alone *with*
oneself. When Narcissus is alone in himself he ceases
being a single person. *Je suis peuplé*, writes Gide
when he becomes aware of the multiple selves of his
being. Hidden and moving within him are all men,
all races, and all moments. The hypnotized quiet of
Narcissus is necessary for Gide to feel inhabited.

The pose of Gide in *Les Nourritures Terrestres* is
absence from the world. Yet all the world is present
in him. He is not alone in his absence, because his
solitary existence has become quietly and fervently
all existence. Narcissus of the myth thus becomes the
artist reincarnated in our age, to an extraordinarily
pure degree, by André Gide. The love expressed in
Les Nourritures Terrestres is the love of the artist:
prepared and protracted and fortified by a very special kind of vision of the world. Little wonder that
young men, gifted in the art of creative work and
thought, have been moved and tormented by this

book. It is about their problem which is a new kind of love evolved by the nineteenth and twentieth centuries.

The modern artist has become Narcissus, and *Les Nourritures Terrestres* is his epithalamium. It is a marriage song celebrating the union of the artist with the world. But the union is consummated by vision and not by participation. The artist is the man who sings of the world without acting in the world. He is chained before the picture of the world, and his sole relationship with it is his dangerous and exquisite power of sight.

The silences of the modern artist are as regular as his speech. When night blots out the picture of the world, his words are interrupted, his work arrested. Between the visible beauty of the world and the hidden depths of the artist's being, a creative relationship exists. But this is broken off and suspended during each period of night when he can no longer see. Narcissus needed the light of the sun, as the modern artist does, in order to pursue his seeing inquest.

As Narcissus is the myth of the love which is generated solely by sight, so *Les Nourritures Terrestres* is the love of the ancient myth regenerated by an ever deepening self-examination. Each instant brings a newer and more visible awareness of oneself. Each instant is therefore different from all other instants. The unpredictable newness of the coming instant underlies the principle of narcissistic love. Because of it, the past is constantly being destroyed for Narcissus; as for Nathanaël, books, after they are read, are rejected and burned.

The desire for love is more real than love. To love, in the ordinary sense, implies the making of a choice. But Nathanaël has learned that he must choose nothing less than everything. And everything is nothing more than what he sees. God is totally in any one part of His Universe. Since God is everywhere, any one being can reveal Him to us. And especially the being which is ourself.

The concept itself of God provides the transition between Gide's first important *Les Nourritures Terrestres* and his second important book, *La Porte Etroite,* published twelve years later, in 1909.

In between these two books, *L'Immoraliste* appeared in 1902. This *récit* is a narrative version of *Les Nourritures Terrestres.* The protagonist Michel is a combination of Nathanaël and his teacher. Michel teaches himself, cures himself, and watches himself throughout the story. His return to health in Africa is equivalent to a new awareness of himself and of deeply hidden desires within his being. He watches the Arab boy Moktir steal a pair of scissors and sees himself liberated from conventional morality. Out of the earlier song of desire and thirst, Gide fashioned in *L'Immoraliste* a circumstantial tale of narcissistic love.

La Porte Etroite is the same narcissistic dilemma, but raised to a Christian level. The title itself, "Strait is the gate," of Biblical origin, gives a clue to our interpretation. This narrow door is comparable to a mirror or a fountain or any reduced area on which one has to live by means of an extraordinary concentration of power. Alissa, in this novel, seeks to learn how to pass alone, without Jérôme, through the narrow door, as Narcissus, in the myth, seeks to inhabit his own solitude and pierce in the reflection on the water the continuous vision of himself.

One-fifth of the book is made up of extracts from

Alissa's journal. This form of writing, used so consistently by Gide in almost every one of his books, is
narcissistic in that it serves as a steadying mirror of
one's thoughts and features. The narrative part of
the story is both explicated and surpassed by Alissa's
journal. There the themes become luminous and
poignant because there they are really seen for the
first time.

The persuasive quality of narcissism in *La Porte
Etroite* is apparent not only in the title and in the
journal form of writing, but also in the use of the
garden setting, particularly on hot summer evenings,
where many of the scenes take place and where the dilemma grows to its highest pitch of intensity. The garden in *La Porte Etroite* is comparable to the desert in
Les Nourritures Terrestres and to the fountain in
Narcissus. These three settings really serve as reflections of the same psychological state. They are limited
and reduced, because they are needed to contain the
form of only one individual, of that unique self which
is André Gide.

Finally, to this list of narcissistic traits, to the
title, to the journal, to the garden in *La Porte Etroite*,
we can add the close blood relationship of Alissa and
Jérôme. The fact that Alissa is Jérôme's cousin makes
for a kind of family reflection of himself, another self
in whom the same traits are either reduced or enlarged. They experience the same inner feelings, even
when they are separated by large distances, as if they
were the same person. And Alissa always more inten-
sively than Jérôme, as if she were Narcissus and
Jérôme were her reflection.

The roles of Jérôme and Alissa are easily reversible.
Gide is in both of them, but more persistently in

Alissa. Jérôme waits. He is Narcissus in the physical quietness of his body. But Alissa looks steadily at the thoughts and experiences of Jérôme, and at the garden site of her solitude. (*Ici rien n'est changé dans le jardin.*) She says that she sees everything through him. (*Je regarde à travers toi chaque chose.*) And this she continues to do even more fully and more amorously when Jérôme is traveling. The narcissistic theme becomes most pronounced when Alissa confesses that her love is more perfect when Jérôme is at a great distance from her (*de loin je t'aimais davantage*). Her solitude in the garden fashions for Alissa a love, not real, but which seems perfect, and turns her into a solipsist, which appears to be a modern term synonymous with narcissist.

The word "happiness" is often on the lips of Alissa. The meaning she attaches to it is difficult to ascertain, and yet in this meaning lies the key to her dilemma and her desires. We can understand best what happiness is not for Alissa. It is nothing which can be saved or guarded; it is nothing to which she wishes or hopes to attain quickly. It is exactly opposed to the happiness which Emma Bovary desires and believes she can have. Fundamentally, Emma is guided by a bourgeois morality of possession, whereas Alissa is guided by a morality of sacrifice. Happiness for Emma depends on an obscure confusion of herself with some other being, and happiness for Alissa seems to depend on an infinite and continuous approach to God. Emma tries to save her life and therefore loses it. Alissa tries to lose her life by avoiding the world and Jérôme and all facile happiness. Constantly she narrows the physical sphere of her world. She eliminates her family, her books, Jérôme, and finally the garden itself. This is the action of Narcissus, of Nathanaël in *Les Nourritures Terrestres,* of Michel in *L'Immoraliste,* of the prodigal son in *Le Retour de l'Enfant Prodigue.* It is Gide's personal interpretation of renouncement which equates salvation. To save oneself is to renounce everything and attain the ultimate state of unencumberedness which Gide defines as *disponibilité.*

Her journal is proof enough that Alissa was not happy in her regimen of renouncement. Michel in *L'Immoraliste* represents immoderate avidity, and Alissa in *La Porte Etroite* represents immoderate virtue. Both destroy their lives. Gratuitous ardor on a hedonistic level, as in *Les Nourritures Terrestres* and in *L'Immoraliste,* can become confused with ascetic severity on a puritanical level, as in *La Porte Etroite.* The religious experience in Gide, whether it be Pagan or Protestant, appears always in the form of search. The usual religious experience implies some direct knowledge of God, some awareness of the absolute. But Gide's experience is exclusively a quest. There is vague sadness at the end of Michel's quest, and profound sadness at the end of Alissa's.

For Narcissus, the fate of continuously seeing attaches him to the fountain site of a garden. Alissa appears attached to the same site for the same intent purpose. She sees herself throughout the years grow dim and unlovely. In her the myth of world-renouncement and self-love become the pathos of solipsism. Had she attained to a religious experience, her solitude would have been happiness. When woman is only Narcissus, she sees not her beauty and her principle as the adolescent boy did, but her vanishing beauty and her losing life.

It was not until 1925, at the age of fifty-six, that
Gide published what he called his first novel, *Les
Faux-Monnayeurs*. Thus he comes to the form of the
novel only after using other genres: the "treatise" on
Narcisse, the dithyrambic utterances of *Les Nourritures Terrestres*, the sober tales of *L'Immoraliste* and
La Porte Etroite. Mauriac has written that the novel
begins where solipsism leaves off. But no single definition of the form is applicable to all novels. Mauriac's
definition applies to his own writings, but Gide's is
largely solipsistic, or, as we prefer to call it, "narcissistic."

The central character Edouard is the novelist, who
is Gide, and who is also Narcissus. Edouard both acts
in the drama and comments on it. He is therefore both
protagonist and chorus. He is both Narcissus and the
reflection. Perhaps the analogy with Narcissus is not
quite so accurate as it would be with the Neptunian:
the single man who is two. But the Neptunian, or the
dual character, is a variation of Narcissus.

Edouard the novelist is alone, standing midway between two worlds. On one side of him is the world
of the young: inhabited especially by Bernard and
Olivier. And on the other side of him is the world of
adults: composed especially of parents, of ministers,
of teachers. The artist finds himself between the world
of the rebels and the uninitiate and the world of the
moralists who stand for security and law. He is the
man outside of life, who suffers from his apartness
from normal living, and yet who is daily destroyed
by life. Tonio Kröger in Thomas Mann's story admirably states this predicament when he says: "I am sick
to death of depicting humanity without having any
part or lot in it." Edouard is the artist incapable of

any facile kind of happiness in terms of human relationships. In the same way, Alissa stands apart from her sister and from Jérôme. And the singer in *Les Nourritures Terrestres* stands apart from Nathanaël and Ménalque.

In *Les Faux-Monnayeurs* the Neptunian character of Edouard is involved in all the various dramas of the novel, and yet he remains aloof from them all. The drama closest to him, and therefore the central drama of the work, is his relationship to Bernard and Olivier. Edouard is unable to hold Bernard, but he does hold Olivier. The experience with Olivier, one which would be condemned by society, is transposed and spiritualized in the novel. By this experience Edouard reveals himself a Neptunian in playing simultaneously the roles of sinner and artist. He is both held by the earth and drawn to heaven. This is no case of schizophrenia, because Edouard remains at all times relentlessly lucid and determined. By being the artist, he wills to attract others different from himself.

The very title of the work, the "counterfeiters," proves that the subject is not schizophrenia but Neptunianism. It is a novel about a man who behaves in one way in the eyes of the world, and who at all times is making plans for another behavior. The artist, the teacher, and the priest, whose vocations demand a fairly fixed pattern of living are most easily Neptunian. They can lead dual and simultaneous existences of good and evil. They can most easily appear one character and be another. Edouard is one man when he is seen by others in the novel, and another man when he sees himself in his own journal. Good and evil seem to be equal forces in *Les Faux-Monnayeurs,* and it is with considerable reason that the doctrine of Manichaeism has been exhumed from its pages. The endless dialogue which Edouard (or Gide) carries on with himself is much more than introspection; it is a dialogue between two different characters who are the same man.

Previous to Gide's work, the novel concerned itself largely with the role of fate, with the conflict between good and evil, with social forces, with the struggle between opposing passions. But it never concerned itself solely with the essence of a single being. This is what Gide tries to do in *Les Faux-Monnayeurs*. In Edouard's temptation to stay with Olivier, to influence him deliberately, and even to make him his secretary, lies the desire to see his own essence more bare. When at this point in the novel, Edouard decides to avoid the temptation and go to London, it is simply a case of Narcissus becoming Huguenot. He is attempting to know a way more difficult than that of his own nature. *Partir parce que l'on a trop grande envie de rester!*

In order to mark his break with Olivier at this time, Edouard buys a new notebook for his journal. The new format and the fresh clean pages, which help him to consummate a painful separation and begin a new chapter in his life, are a facile symbol for another fountain over whose waters the same thirst will be renewed. Edouard (or Gide) always remains the artist who lives by his thirst, and never becomes the protagonist who is defeated by passion or by events in a tragedy or in a novel.

This explains the final sentence of the book: *Je suis bien curieux de connaître Caloub.* There is no end or even climax to the narcissistic pose of Edouard. Events and dramas and sentiments affect him deeply, but they only interrupt momentarily the mirroring of himself in the universe and in the faces of those around him. The last pages of the novel relate the tragic suicide of the boy Boris in his classroom. The pistol shot which kills him is like a stone thrown into the fountain. For a moment the reflection is shattered. Edouard can no longer see himself in the unpredictable death of a schoolboy. But gradually the waters resume their evenness and the gaze returns. There was not sufficient motivation in this suicide to satisfy the novelist and the analyst Edouard. He refuses to incorporate it in his *Faux-Monnayeurs* and his gaze continues to be directed toward that part of the universe which he can still fathom, and which is himself, so different from an ill-considered and brutal suicide. Like Narcissus, Gide is not concerned with progress in morality, but with something which is at once more particularized and more universalized than morality: with progress in man's sincerity.

In 1935, Gide published *Les Nouvelles Nourritures,* which is a recast of *Les Nourritures Terrestres* following an interlude of thirty-eight years. The style is more sober and chaste than that of the earlier book. Gide now seems more intent on formulating conclusions about sensory experience than on describing the experience itself. Yet underneath these more meditative and even philosophical passages continue the same fervent quest and excitement, the same *frémissement,* the same eager self-examination. And there seems to be a larger number of narcissistic images. Gide talks about the white page of his notebook as something which shines in front of him (*la page blanche luit devant moi*); he describes his pose of bending down and looking beyond the present (*je*

me penche par-delà le présent); he has learned to
realize from the "moment" the quietness of "eternity"
(*je sais à présent goûter la quiète éternité dans l'instant.*) These are all exercises of Narcissus on his ab-
sorption with the universe.

Especially, in *Les Nouvelles Nourritures,* the innumerable sentences on the concept of God reveal the
use Gide had made of the term and his increasing personal enlightenment about what the name of God has
meant to him in the past. We remember the opening
sentence in *Les Nourritures Terrestres* of 1897: *Ne
souhaite pas, Nathanaël, trouver Dieu ailleurs que
partout.* ("Do not hope to find God elsewhere than
everywhere.") In the new pages of 1935, God is
described as being diffused throughout His creation,
both hidden and lost in it, continually discovering
Himself in it, to the point of confusing Himself
with His own creation. The meaning which Gide
might have attached to the concept of God during
his lifetime has always been obscured by the facility
and the frequency with which he uses the term.
The meaning of God has always been replaced by
the poetic invocation to the word "God." All the concepts in Gide's mind which are the most vaguely outlined and the most difficult to comprehend—namely,
all those concepts which he enjoys the most—have
been poured into the general concept of God as if it
were a vase of endlessly changing proportions capable of contraction or expansion. The word "God" has
been synonymous for Gide with all kinds of notions
and sentiments, of questions and answers. It is the
word reflecting all other words which has become
"Gidian" in its diversity and constancy. In the *Traité
du Narcisse* it was "contemplation"; in *Les Nourri-*

tures Terrestres it was "fervor"; in *La Porte Etroite* it was "renouncement"; in *Les Faux-Monnayeurs* it was "detachment." These four words, when given a religious connotation, designate the attitude of Narcissus in the profoundest meaning of his self-exploration. The confusions of Gide can never be solved so long as he remains Narcissus. He is looking not at God but at himself, and not even at himself but at a reflection of himself.

The parables which recur the most continuously in the writings of Gide substantiate two of his cardinal beliefs: (1) that a single individual is more interesting than all men; (2) that the only valid adventure for an individual is that one which is most dangerous for him to undertake. This is the meaning Gide attaches to the stories of the lost sheep and the prodigal son, and to the verse: "Whosoever loseth his life shall save it." These three lessons from the Gospels could easily be construed as Christian interpretations of the Narcissus myth. Each one seems to be built around the doctrinal admonition to leave the familiar world in order to engage oneself with the unknown.

In calling nature God, Gide joins himself with the great Romantics, and especially with Rousseau who sought to merge himself with unfathomed and chaotic nature. Romanticism is the major protest man has made against civilization and against reason. The Romantic tries first to establish his uniqueness (Narcissus, the dandy, the artist), and then to experience a quasi-mystical union with nature. But by calling nature God, the Romantic does not thereby convert nature into God. The romantic union is one between man and the chaos of nature and sentiment. Gide is the most recent of the romantic artists and one who subsumes and even transcends the movement by the extraordinary fervor he brings to the role of Narcissus. He tracks down his being, arrests all his movements, and then from the deepest part of his spirit conjures up a mythical past.

THREE

CLAUDEL: *The Spiritual Quest*

Despite the high praise of Charles Du Bos who calls him the greatest genius of the West today, and despite the judgment of Jacques Madaule who compares him with Dante, Paul Claudel still occupies a place in literature and in Catholic thought which is vigorously disputed. In his middle eighties at the time of his death, in February 1955, Claudel maintained not only his full powers of writer but his violent temper as well and his animosities. His detractors are legion. But his admirers come from many varying beliefs, religious and political and aesthetic. He has received homage from such writers as the Catholic academician Louis Gillet and the Communist Aragon, from the Protestant Ramuz and the humanist Jean Prévost, from Alain, Maurice Blanchot, Claudine Chonez. The difficulty of his art, and the need almost of meditating on it in order to follow its full meaning, explain to some degree the long period of neglect. Only since the second World War has there been any marked effort to understand Claudel and to define his position in contemporary art.

He was born in 1868, in Villeneuve-sur-Fère, a small village in Le Tardenois, a locality which lies between the provinces of Ile-de-France and Champagne. As a child he learned to observe all the details of the countryside. He has written of the natural spectacles he watched from the highest fork of an old tree he used to climb. This was the site of his first dialogues with nature and his first impressions from which he has drawn throughout his life. The lycée in Paris, Louis-le-Grand, was for young Claudel a prison, a stifling atmosphere he has described in *Ma Conversion*. Camille Mauclair has recalled the sullen voice of Claudel at the lycée, and his silence he would break only to argue with their famous teacher, Burdeau.

These were the years when, in company with other young intellectuals, he read Baudelaire and Verlaine. But the first great revelation to Claudel, of both a literary and spiritual order, was Rimbaud. He has described in a passage justly famous and justly disputed the seminal and paternal action which the reading of *Les Illuminations* had on him. He first came upon some of the prose poems in the June issue of *La Vogue* of 1886. This reading constituted for him a release from what he called the hideous world of Taine, Renan and the other Molochs of the nineteenth century. *J'avais la révélation du surnaturel,* he wrote Jacques Rivière. Rimbaud was the human means for Claudel's return to his faith. This acknowledgment is couched in such hyperbolic terms that many critics have wondered whether Claudel in his letters to Rivière had not deformed the real facts. A recent critic, Ernest Friche, believes we can accept this claim of Claudel, provided we realize that the conquest of Rimbaud was a revelation and not the imparting of a philosophy or even a system of aesthetics. Certain sentences of *Une Saison en Enfer*, such as *Nous ne sommes pas au monde*, never ceased reacting on Claudel in revealing to him the real significance of his own revolt. Claudel was, not unlike Rimbaud himself, a revolutionary, a Dionysian ecstatic.

The poet has recorded that in the same year of 1886, a second event befell him which was to fix his destiny. On Christmas day, in Notre-Dame, during the service of vespers, he experienced a spiritual awakening, a revelation of faith which was never to be impaired or endangered thereafter. In describing this conversion, Claudel speaks of its suddenness and of the perception he felt of Divine Innocence. This mystical experience was followed by four years of bewilderment and struggle to harmonize the new force in him with his former self. He began a study of the Bible, the history of the Church and its liturgy, and discovered that what he had once studied as poetry was indissolubly associated with religion. He attended frequently Mallarmé's Tuesday evening gatherings and learned from the master and the gentle teacher of Symbolism how to look at the universe as if it were a text to be deciphered. In his later, somewhat severe article on Mallarmé, *La Catastrophe d'Igitur*, Claudel does demonstrate his debt to the older poet, although he groups Mallarmé with Poe and Baudelaire, as poets of the "metaphysical night" of the nineteenth century, who lacked an indispensable key to their art.

At the age of twenty-five, he left for Boston to

serve there as vice-consul for France. This marked the
beginning of a long diplomatic career which took him
to many parts of the globe. In China, where he went
in 1895, Claudel entered upon a period of solitude
and silence and meditation. His studies centered on
the Bible and Saint Thomas Aquinas. Not until the recent book of Ernest Friche, *Etudes Claudéliennes*,
has the preponderant influence of Saint Thomas on
the French poet been pointed out. Friche calls Claudel a Thomistic poet. In an important letter, Claudel
himself confirmed this influence. "I read and anno-
tated the two *Summas*," he writes. "It was a wonderful nourishment and training for my mind. These lessons transformed me and merged with all my creative
activity."

To Rimbaud's doctrine on the power of poetic language, and to Mallarmé's doctrine on the symbolism
of the universe, Claudel added the gigantic synthesis
of Saint Thomas and the religious interpretation of
metaphorical language. At the end of the century,
when Claudel returned to France from China, he was
practicing the patient metaphysical discipline he had
learned in Saint Thomas and which he had fused with
the early examples of Rimbaud and Mallarmé.

As ambassador, Claudel represented France in To-
kyo, Washington and Brussels. His diplomatic career
kept him away from France and literary groups. His
travels helped to make him into one of the most
universal of the French writers. He is as familiar with
the Greek tragedies, with the Latin poets, with Dante,
as he is with the Bible. The repertory of his interests
and studies is unusual for a French writer: Chinese
theatre, Italian painting, Japanese poetry, Spanish culture, Dutch painting, English Catholic literature,

some of which he has translated. The last years of his life were spent in Brangues (in Savoy). He came to Paris for the new productions of his plays: for *Le Soulier de Satin* in 1942, for *Partage de Midi* in 1948, and for *L'Annonce faite à Marie*, in 1955.

As a writer, Claudel never made concessions to his public or to his publishers. The Catholic world in France and outside of France has been slow to accept him. When he presented his candidacy for the Académie Française just before the war, he failed to win the election. Not until after the war, in 1947, was he invited to become a member. His attitude toward the world of letters, and even somewhat toward the world in general, has seemed hostile and almost vindictive. His implacable seriousness has discouraged any sense of humor. In his stubborn peasant temperament, he has been compared to Péguy. And yet Claudel has participated willingly and joyously in every aspect of the Catholic revival in France: in art, Thomism, liturgy. His visible disdain for many of his contemporaries and for the younger writers has not prevented his influence from deeply affecting the lives of some. His early correspondence with Jacques Rivière revealed his exceptional powers of apologist and defender of the faith. The publication, in 1949, of the correspondence of Gide and Claudel was an event of capital importance. This exchange of letters belongs primarily to the realm of apologetics and criticism. Other exchanges of letters in this century have reflected perhaps more succinctly than most literary forms the spiritual problems of the age: the correspondence between Jacques Rivière and Alain-Fournier, between Rivière and Claudel, between Gide and Francis Jammes.

The letters of Gide and Claudel form the most recent dialogue between two opposing voices, a form which is distinctly favored in France. Du Bos once called the great French dialogue that between Montaigne and Pascal, the skeptic and the believer, a dialogue which he says each Frenchman maintains in himself. Such a dialogue as that between Montaigne and Pascal, or between Bossuet and Fénelon, or between Gide and Claudel, is a manifestation of the critical spirit. The Frenchman listening to it prefers not to take sides, not to sacrifice one for the other.

Claudel, the man of severe faith, is opposed to Gide, the man of restlessness and voluptuously felt inquiry. On the one hand, we read an expression of exultant joy, of a peace declared to all men. And on the other hand, we read the narrative of an endless search for happiness, sought in all forms of pleasure. The correspondence reveals, what was already known in its general lines, the tremendous dialectical effort Claudel made, between 1900 and 1926, to convert Gide to Catholicism. Whereas the letters of Claudel show his complete thought on the subjects discussed, those of Gide have to be read in conjunction with the entries in his *Journal,* written at the same time, in order to follow his mind accepting and rejecting almost simultaneously. Claudel is a vociferous catechizer, but his correspondent is reticent and cautious. This dialogue, which ended in 1926, is one of the most vehement and engrossing in the history of French literature. Although not many years have passed since it ended, it can be read now publicly as the most recent example in France of Pascalian apologetics to which the contemporary Montaigne said a seemingly definitive "no."

Gide often gives the impressions in his letters of

playing hide-and-seek with Claudel. And yet his attitude cannot with justice be called hypocritical. If he could write as boldly and frankly as a Montaigne, he was quite timid in speech. The physical presence of Claudel inhibited him. After their meetings together, Gide would write in his *Journal* the arguments he had not been able to articulate.

The Catholicism of Paul Claudel is impressive and majestic. He is a poet speaking with the force of lyricism. He communicates his exultation. The answers of Gide have their own formal beauty, their own careful refinement and reticence. Even after Gide confessed the secret of his life, Claudel continued to exhort and preach. Whenever Claudel spoke from the viewpoint of dogma, there was almost no reaction from Gide. By nature, Gide could not be touched by the scholastic concepts which form most of the intellectual argumentation of Claudel. Claudel's temperament led him to describe the modern world as if he were a medieval man enlightened by scholastic ontology. Gide's temperament was fundamentally suspicious of any such massive construction of the mind. Much of Gide's work, written after his debate with Claudel, was to represent a secularization of the Gospels.

By his strength, by the proportions of his work, by his attitude toward the Creation, Claudel towers above his contemporaries. By remaining outside of all literary coteries, his presence today has been felt as a force isolated and unique. Every object in his writing is stated in terms of its meaning, of its role. The humblest things he can name are signs in much the same way that the characters of his dramas represent their salvation. When he says: "Divine Joy is the one reality," it is not difficult to believe that Claudel's fundamental approach to literature is different from others, different even from the methods of Rimbaud and Mallarmé to whom he owes so much.

It is quite possible that the term "drama," in its fullest sense, never applied to the French theatre until Claudel began writing his plays. Tragedy and comedy, from the sixteenth to the nineteenth centuries were strict forms in France, adhering closely to the Aristotelian precepts and the classical models. Victor Hugo in the nineteenth century attempted to create *le drame* by fusing the comic and the tragic. The formula he worked out was weak. Claudel created a dramatic form which is unique in French and which bears close affiliations with the drama of Shakespeare and Lope de Vega. His drama is not a combination of the comic and the tragic. It is a work of one piece and one texture. It is simultaneously speech of the theatre and poetry of language.

His characters speak with the voices of real men and women who feel that humanity forms one body in that each man is responsible at every moment of his existence for all other men. In each scene of his many plays, we have the impression of following some aspect or other of one of the most difficult and mystical dogmas of all: that of the communion of saints. For Claudel the universe is total at every moment of every man's existence. Every story he undertakes to unravel, he finds to be an anecdote or an element of the same drama of man which is continuously unfolding in the world. Claudel has spoken of the "passion of the universe" which he feels, and of the exultation he derives from contemplating the millions of things which exist at the same time. *Que j'aime ce million de choses qui existent ensemble!*

His greatest play, *Le Soulier de Satin,* is at once one of the most complicated plays ever written and one of the simplest. The three principal characters form one of the most familiar plots in the history of the theatre: an aged husband, a young wife and a lover. Behind the personal relationships of these three characters, Claudel has developed the historical drama of the Renaissance and the destiny of Spain. Even if dates and events are deliberately juggled with, one has the impression of watching the birth of a new era, of seeing a new world emerge from the medieval world of Saint Thomas. Rodrigue and Don Camille are types of conquerors and adventurers of that period. Their quest is as deeply spiritual as it is materialistic. An obvious bond joins them with more modern adventurers, such as Rimbaud and T. E. Lawrence, with travelers like Guillaume Apollinaire and Claudel himself.

In the Claudelian conception of drama, the relationship between man and woman, and between man and God, is an eternal relationship. If salvation is the goal of each human existence, love is the means for reaching this goal. Lovers, in Claudel's plays, appear as potential mystics. In *Soulier de Satin* and *Partage de Midi,* he presents a case of love so total that it would seem to exclude love of God, and yet Claudel believes so deeply in the identity of all loves that he would say, human love as it grows in intensity will end by seeing what it really is.

In these two plays especially, Claudel has reexamined the problem of human passion. The questions about the fatality of passion, asked in such works as *Tristan, Phèdre, Manon,* are reiterated by Claudel: the meaning of passion, the reason for human love, the reason for its particular force, its destructiveness, the Christian attitude toward it, its spiritual meaning. Claudel's answers to these eternal questions, or at least his comments on them, form a significant aspect of his work which has not yet been fully realized or measured. These two dramas in which he considers primarily the problem of human passion are violent in terms of the mystery surrounding the problem.

He calls woman, in *Partage de Midi,* the promise which cannot be held. (*La femme est la promesse qui ne peut être tenue.*) She is not limitless, and yet man's desire, his longing, is infinite. The need for the infinite, which is at the basis of human love, is always being deceived by the limitations of love. It must be remembered that Claudel is not speaking of conjugal love in either play. He is quite literally and with unusual boldness studying the kind of passion analyzed previously in *Tristan, Phèdre* and *Manon.* Claudel's fundamental thought seems to be that a human being cannot be the end or the satisfaction of another human being. The beauty of such human love is all the greater if there is an absence of satisfaction. There are no human means for reaching this satisfaction. As soon as a man is separated from the one he loves, he yearns for death.

In all the many versions Claudel has written for his best known play, *L'Annonce faite à Marie,* he stresses this mystical paradox of human relationships. It is particularly clear in the prologue, the scene between the young girl Violaine and Pierre de Craon, the builder of cathedrals. The bonds uniting these two are as mysterious and as strong as those uniting Prouhèze and Rodrigue of *Soulier de Satin.* Pierre loves Violaine and she represents for him everything he is called upon to give up: woman, happiness, the world itself. His love scene is actually his scene of farewell to the world. This opening dialogue contains the whole meaning of the play and what lies beyond the play, because it analyzes the secret role which every Christian is called upon to play in the world. It is the role of pilgrim, the one who accepts the idea of separation. A kiss usually binds two lovers, but the kiss which Pierre gives to Violaine at the end of their scene, is the sign of their separation. He has guessed the real meaning of her vocation. She is the victim who combines heroism with humility. Her example is the morality of the play and of all of Claudel's plays. If it is true that the world has no value by comparison with life, then the ultimate value of life is in it capacity to give itself. Pierre, as mason, architect and builder of churches, and the other characters in the play, discover their vocations in accord with the seasons and the earth. Violaine stands apart from them all, in that she represents the symbol of eternity within time, of spirit within matter. Her vocation in the play itself adds a further dimension to the characters around her. By her existence she reveals a meaning in those close to her: her father and mother, her sister, her fiancé and Pierre de Craon.

Violaine is the type of mystic who represents for Claudel an analogy with the poet. Although the goals of mystic and poet are different, many of their activities and disciplines bear striking resemblances. For certain degrees of knowledge the poet has to reach a deep inner silence, a freedom of the spirit, a detachment. This necessary stage precedes the real function of the poet who is by definition the maker of something. He is creator not in the sense that God is, who is able to create out of nothing. The poet is creator out of what the world provides. Claudel, coming after Baudelaire's important lesson on "correspondences," has stressed this need of a collaboration between the artist and the world. A poem begins when a relationship is perceived.

The metaphor, according to Claudel's *Art Poétique,* is the new logic of the universe. It is the joining of two things which are different. This is possible because no one thing exists alone. Any one object exists only by its relationship with all other objects. This fundamental belief about the metaphor makes it easier to understand why the work of Claudel always seems the continuation of the same piece or the same poem. The poet's language maintains a constant relationship with the Creator. The metaphorical language of the poet does not explain anything, but in it everything becomes explicable. *Tu n'expliques rien, ô poète, mais toutes choses par toi nous deviennent explicables.* (*La Ville.*)

Claudel feels that the world is constantly asking the poet to find a language by which itself can be expressed. From the universe, man is constantly seeking some explanation for his own existence. In the miracle of the metaphor, a kind of answer to these two questions is reached: a reason for the world and a reason for man. In his doctrine on the poetic word which transmits an image of the relationship of things, Claudel's debt to Rimbaud is obvious. The world is limitless in its relationships, and the poet, in his role of conqueror of the poetic word, becomes reader of the world and decipherer of its relationships. The two most widely separated terms of the metaphor are for Claudel the world and God. In making poetic speech the means of joining these two extremes, he was applying logically the dual revelation which came to him from his early reading of Rimbaud and his religious experience of Christmas 1886. Even in the physical conquering of the earth, in the apparent materialistic drives of Alexander, Caesar, Napoleon, there is a deeply spiritual reason. The ambition of the poet, in his will to know the world, is not unrelated to the ambition of the conqueror.

During the last twenty years of his life, Claudel did not publish poetry or plays. He spent his time writing his reflections and his meditations on Holy Scripture. These works form not only an epilogue to a long career of poet and dramatist, but a continuation of it. The active contemplation which was always an element in Claudel's earlier books simply became the exclusive element in his studies of the Bible.

He had always claimed that Rimbaud had been one of those explorers of the nineteenth century, consecrated to learning something about what the creation is, what it signifies. The basis of Symbolism is a belief that each thing in the world has a meaning which will be revealed to the poet who is able to understand it. Claudel received this belief in the universal symbolism of the world almost as a mission. After learning how to read the universe, he learned how to read the poetry of the Bible in a similar method of deciphering. He brought to the words of the sacred writings the same prayerful attention he once lavished on the material objects of his world. The poet of *Cinq Grandes Odes* and *Corona benignitatis anni Dei* became the fervent and meticulous reader of Isaiah and Saint John.

His most recent book, *Paul Claudel interroge l'Apo-*

calypse, is a clear demonstration of his method and his belief in symbolism as the key to our knowledge concerning Divine Truth. His work is a testimonial against the literal or scientific exegesis of Holy Scripture. In his treatment of the symbols of Saint John, Claudel assumes the role of prophet and man of God whose mission is to speak in the name of God. Such an examination as Claudel undertakes is no mere game of numbers or erudition. His effort is vigorous and consecrated and inspired. This book was composed during the darkest months of the last war, since it was completed in December 1942. The temporal catastrophes were seen as relative from the viewpoint of the real Apocalypse, which for Claudel is a spectacular drama of all times in which we all have our parts. The *Revelation* of Saint John ceases to be the mysterious book of the Bible during the course of this interrogation of Claudel. He transposes it into a work of surprising reality.

The seriousness of Claudel's religious sentiment dominates all else in his work. It lies at the source of each poem and play and essay, and it pervades all the developments. Whether the subject is specifically religious or not, the tone and the lyricism are religious because, for Claudel, the poet is at all times the servant of truth. In a letter to Jacques Rivière, he claims that art is a pale duplicate of holiness (*l'art n'est qu'une pâle contrefaçon de la sainteté*). Claudel is bent upon discovering the deepest meaning of his personal experiences and of all of his varied experiences with the world. Religious art, in the narrowest sense, is concerned with the mysteries of religion, but in its broadest sense, with the mysteries of the world. For Claudel, the divine is constantly intervening in the life of man. This certainty can never be exhausted by words or by poetic inventions.

We learn very early in life that there is a mortal part of human nature which one day will be swallowed up in immortality. The arts have never ceased proclaiming this immortality, and in a profound sense they have never ceased proclaiming it in the service of religious belief in immortality. Approximately at the same time that we learn about the inevitable change our mortal nature will undergo, we also learn that an intense apathy endangers the vitality of every perception we have and of every virtue we may possess. By the creation of art man is able to endow his perceptions with a form of immortality. Most of our perceptions pass by rapidly and disappear into a void. Our incapacity to hold them is cause for sorrow and nostalgia. Art, precisely, sets up the goal of preserving the highest moments of perception.

Many of the most serious of the twentieth-century artists have been concerned with providing their works with an aesthetic justification. In the field of painting, for example, Braque has made theoretical pronouncements of considerable importance. Others, while not contributing any writing as massive as Delacroix' *Journal,* have spoken at times with conviction and acumen: Picasso, Matisse, Rouault, Masson, Severini. In literature, the achievement of Marcel Proust is the masterful way in which he combined his novel with the analysis of its origin and its meaning. Joyce, Mann, Gide, Valéry have all striven to propose a work and at the same time the aesthetics of the work. The five great odes of Claudel open with one entitled *Les Muses,* inspired by a frieze of the nine muses the poet had seen sculptured on a sarcophagus. The ode is a kind of poetics dealing with the poetic act, with its birth and its function.

On many points the theories of Claudel converge with those of Proust, and behind him, with the tenets of Impressionism and the theories of Ruskin. These artists and theorists believe that each time a new original artist arises, the world is recreated. He is able to confer immortality on what has no duration, a man's perception of the world. Aesthetic truth is not the same as scientific truth. It is not based on direct observation or exact notations. The reality of the world for an artist is his vision of the world. It is a particular universe not seen by other men until it is put in the form of art. The public is ignorant about art or indifferent to new artistic creations. But each work will create its own posterity, and finally that work will reveal the temper and the soul of the period in which it was created.

Universal love is expressed everywhere, not only in nature, but in the creative works of art, in paintings, poems, cathedrals. Real things of the world cannot be possessed save in the form of eternity which art creates. In the making of the poet's metaphor or the painter's metamorphosis, the artist is the man who changes the names of things and the forms of things in order to establish a greater contact with them, a purer contact of intimacy. The modern artist, whether he be Claudel or Proust, Rouault or Picabia, is greatly concerned with the relation existing between the recreation of art and the reality of the world. Metaphor and metamorphosis are signs of the sovereign freedom of man's mind to substitute one element for another, to substitute what we usually call reality for its spiritual state.

Each man watches existence move by him in a series of scenes and pictures. Most of them disappear and sink into oblivion. Our personality is constantly being formed by time and eroded by time. A profound distress comes to us from our incapacity to hold on to scenes of happiness and perception. The objective of art is the elucidation of those scenes which are habitually so elusive and fleeting. In his very act of creation, the artist explores the meaning of those original impressions and fugitive sensations. The difference between works of art is not so much the divergence of technique as it is the qualitative difference in the ways the world appears to various artists. Art alone is able to show us how the universe appears to someone else.

The problem of modern art, and especially the Christian viewpoint of modern art, is central in any study of the writings of Paul Claudel. No single figure, not even the painter Rouault, has called forth such contradictory judgments from his critics. Whichever view is held, Claudel as the greatest contemporary Catholic poet, or Claudel as leading example of the monstrous incommunicability of modern art, the dimensions of the judgment are gigantic as are the dimensions of the work itself. Some of the more recent evaluations of Claudel have pointed out that the fate of his work, which suffered first from public indifference, and then from public hostility, and thirdly from a marked division of praise and blame, testifies to the present state of Christianity which today has lost its full vitality, its full self-consciousness.

It would be difficult to find another contemporary artist whose religious belief or philosophy is as much the object of controversy as the principles and forms of his art. Claudel has been equally attacked on the score of his Catholicism and on the score of his art. Lasserre, one of the most vehement critics of the French poet, states that Claudel rejected the heritage of the Renaissance and embraced an archaic medievalism. He thereby, according to Lasserre, repudiated all philosophical reflection and progress, and separated himself from the central tradition of French literature. Frédéric Lefèvre, one of the earliest ardent defenders of Claudel, claims on the contrary that the humanism of the Renaissance was reactionary and Claudel's main glory is that of having resurrected medieval humanism.

The controversy over Claudel, when often the very principles of modern art are at stake, is particularly significant when both sides are held by Catholic writers. Henri Massis, who follows strictly the theories of Pierre Lasserre, believes that the aesthetics of Claudel are not in agreement with the principles that his art is trying to demonstrate. Massis finds in the subjective lyricism of Claudel an incommunicability and a disorderliness which are contrary to the spirit of order and discipline and hierarchy consistent with the Revelation in which the poet believes. The original apostolic fervor is sacrificed, for Massis, to the hermetic closed quality of the work. This attack is obviously leveled at the school of Symbolism as well as at the specific art of Claudel. In the solution of such a controversy, granted that a solution may be reached, it would be necessary to consider the difficult and tortuous rhetoric of Claudel as the poet's expression of man as he is, of man as contradiction, torn between the demands of the flesh and the spirit. It would represent Claudel as the modern poet who has achieved a synthesis of the aesthetics of Rimbaud and of Saint Thomas Aquinas.

It is difficult to dissociate the work of a Christian poet, such as that of Claudel, from the teachings of the Church on art. These teachings through the century are not dogmatic as are the teachings on morals and theology. They emphasize different points in different periods because of the characteristic art of the period. But the great doctors of the Church and the mystics appear in agreement that there are, generally speaking, two ways to God.

The first is usually referred to as the "way of signs." Nature and all the myriad parts of the physical universe are, in this sense, signs. Our sensibility in seeing and hearing them, yes, and in smelling and feeling them, confers on them an intimacy which may be religious. All the manifestations of art created by man represent a further and more complicated development of this same communion between man and the world capable of being apprehended by his senses. Art is the stylization or the extension of nature by means of an emotion expressed significantly. Liturgical art differs from other forms of art only in being consecrated and used in the manifestation of something the artist considers a mystery in the world. The Christian dogma implicit in this belief is that of God as Creator of the universe. The world created by God may be an instrument of sanctification. The very nature of man, which moves from the physical to the spiritual, parallels the nature of the universe and its spiritualization in art. Nature is as full of signs as the

Bible is, whether we are looking for a symbol of the human soul or a symbol of Christ's mystery. There is no more separation between the sensible and the intelligible than there is between the body and the soul. This "way of signs" is based upon a belief that God is immanent in His universe and in His creatures. Saint Francis of Assisi expresses this immanency of God in his poem usually called *Canticle of all creatures,* in which he addresses his brother the wind and his sister the moon. Dante uses the figure of the beloved as guide to the summit of Paradise—Beatrice, who is the Christian counterpart of Diotima in Plato's *Symposium.* Giotto's celebration of the world in his paintings and Rouault's studies of clowns and prostitutes illustrate the "way of signs" and the immanence of God in His creation. Claudel stresses the importance of the "immense octave of creation" in the drama of his conversion.

The other way to God leads beyond signs. In this far more ascetic way, nature is avoided, art is rejected and even liturgy is rejected. The belief upon which this way is based is the transcendence of God. Saint John of the Cross is the great doctor of this way which leads beyond the sensual world and the power of the intellect. This second way, when it is really reached, lies beyond the first, but it is often lost sight of for its caricature, usually referred to as Jansenism or a pessimism such as Pascal experienced at times. Man is called upon to remain in the "way of signs," where nature, art and liturgy may guide him, until he is able to move into the second way without encountering any of the specious forms of the "way beyond signs."

Catholicism during the nineteenth century in Europe developed into a particular form in the dominant social class, the bourgeoisie. It was a Catholicism far more moralistic than spiritual, far more Jansenistic than purely Christian. It must be remembered that the Jansenistic spirit is on the whole hostile to art. The ideal of the bourgeois Christian was an ideal of personal perfection, of personal success, rather than a love of God, a love of the sensible world and the creatures of the world, a desire to understand history and great works of art. During the first fifty years of the twentieth century, some of the leading Catholic writers: Bloy, Péguy, Bernanos, Mauriac, have attacked in their novels, and polemical writings particularly, the ideals of the Catholic bourgeoisie. It will be evident in time that they participated in a profound revolution of Christian values, to which the achievements of a poet like Claudel and a painter like Rouault contribute monumentally. Claudel's closeness to his peasant ancestry and his imperviousness to any Jansenistic influences help to explain the quality of joyous praise his entire work reflects and the precedence which the spiritual takes over the moral. He calls himself a *rassembleur de la terre de Dieu* and the earth he calls a text which teaches jubilation.

Both the Catholic writer emphasizing a polemical message, like Péguy and Bernanos, and the Catholic artist (Claudel and Rouault) have revealed an exceptional desire to illuminate for the contemporary world the mystery of that dogma which is primarily concerned with jubilation. It is the mystery of the communion of saints which teaches the universal solidarity of all the souls who have been born and who will be born. In this mystery, suffering and evil are given a mystical meaning by the supernatural hope which envelops the world and which is constantly struggling to efface the memory of sin. Claudel sees history in the image of a single unbroken sentence unfolding throughout time until it reaches its final period.

Claudel's parable on Animus and Anima may well have been written to explain the lesson of analogy or relationship. It is the marriage of the mind and the soul. Anima brought a good dowry to her husband Animus. But he is difficult in his vanity and tyrannical ways. Anima does not like to oppose him because she did not go to school, whereas he knows a great many things. He has numerous bad traits. He is unfaithful. He spends his time at the cafés while she cooks. One day, by chance, he hears her singing. An unusual and wonderful song. He pleads with her to sing it again, but she refuses, and this time she does not give in. He tries to trick her and pretends to leave. But he hides behind the door. Then he hears her sing again and realizes that the song is addressed to his wife's Divine Lover. Animus is the part of us which divides and separates and analyzes. Anima is the part which unites and makes us one.

Her song is the poetic word which Rimbaud had talked about: a veritable instrument of discovery for the creation of a new being. The state of poetry is that state of pure receptivity. The poet hence becomes a medium and poetry a magical means of seizing the ineffable. Poetic language is no longer an expression. It is a sign. A poet is put into a state of communication as his words come to his lips almost obsessively. Claudel had before him the example of Rimbaud, and especially of Rimbaud's poetic failure.

The parable of Animus and Anima is Claudel's version of the struggle of opposites for existence, a struggle which has been explained in some form or other in every period of history, by every major thinker. Father d'Arcy uses Animus and Anima to explain Eros and Agape. The terms lend themselves to many pairs of opposites, both general and specific: male and female, romantic and classical, life and death, egoism and self-sacrifice, the conscious and the unconscious, the limited and the unlimited, Dionysos and Apollo. Denis de Rougemont, in *L'Amour dans l'Occident,* analyzes the dark romantic passion in the poetry and music of *Tristan* as a memory of joys of the unconscious and as a conflict between Dionysos and Apollo, between egocentrism and self-sacrifice.

This celebrated pair, Eros and Agape, or Animus and Anima, appear under countless names. The interpretation of Jungian psychoanalysis defines anima as the center of the irrational and the unconscious, the abode of the dark passions and instincts, the archetypes of both aggressive and seductive forces. Anima, on the conscious level, when freed from the control of reason, is usually referred to as Romanticism. Whatever hope it feels in the force of love, on this level, declines into melancholy and the murkiest forms of mysticism. On the highest level, as interpreted in Claudel's parable and in Henri Bremond's *Prière et Poésie,* anima seems to signify poetic or mystical knowledge. Animus is the surface self (*le moi de surface, le "je" qui s'agite à la circonférence de l'âme.*) Anima is the deep self (*le moi profond, qui s'unit aux réalités; qui reçoit les visites de Dieu*).

In this parable of the two selves or the two parts of the soul, it is obvious that harmony does not always exist between animus and anima. The temptation of animus is the love of self which may weaken the love of God. And the temptation of anima is, in the romantic sense, the excessive emancipation of the deep self and the resulting contempt of self. Love, when it becomes a frenzy, sings the *Liebestod* which is the song of the death instinct. When ideally married together, the deep instincts of life and death should produce happiness.

Claudel's visit to Notre-Dame on Christmas day 1886 prefigured the important precept of his faith that man has to will to go to God and find his joy in that encounter. On this point, he is opposed to anything pantheistic or subjective in religion. The divine is outside of us, existing whether we believe in it or not. A life of action and expression is necessary in religion. The creation of the poetic word is the poet's action. A poem is a testimony, an apologetics consented to not merely by the reason of the poet, but by his sensibility and his entire being. The unity of the world is perceived by the experience of love which provides us with an imperfect and often tantalyzing contrafaction of unity. Everything has its meaning in the world and everything can be sung of by the poet. At our birth we enter into a secret pact with all beings and all objects. The mission of the poet is that of pointing out our relationships with all the realities of the world.

Claudel's Catholicism has an impassioned fullness and vitality we associate with the Middle Ages and which had to a large extent disappeared in Europe with the early Renaissance. It is a belief in the Church as representing an interpenetration of all of man's needs. Differing needs but not contradictory. The *Odes* of Claudel express a joy in contemplation of the world and in spiritual contemplation which has its best counterpart in the French Romanesque and

Gothic cathedrals. When the moral and theological system of Christianity left its manuscripts and pulpits, it showed its symbolized face in Gothic architecture to the multitudes. When the four animals of the Evangelists appeared in stone, a new world of animate forms invaded the capitals of columns and the tympanums of doors. The Church became a storehouse of wealth, a theatre for the people, an ark large enough to house all the inhabitants of the city on market days, feast days and days of penance. The cathedral combined all the tender human myths with the Christian belief in the supernatural. Gothic sculpture became an image of freedom in its depiction of angels and prophets, of birds and vine branches, of strawberry plants, clover, thistle, watercress, fern.

The appearance of Claudel's poetry in the twentieth century is not unlike the appearance of the Gothic cathedral in the thirteenth. They are comparable in their depiction of the ever dying and ever renascent forms of the world. In them, symbolism and theology are bound up with life. The mediocre types of churches which have been built during the past century and a half testify to the spiritual defection of modern humanity. The poetry of Claudel is a reminder that artistic creation at its best is concerned with human realities and that sacred art, if it is painfully deficient in architecture, reaches paradoxically its height today in writers who are not always fully accepted by the Church: Bernanos and Claudel, and in painters like Rouault and Matisse.

The basic assumption of the Christian faith is the belief that each individual soul is the creator of its own destiny. This kind of creation is not unrelated to the aesthetic creation of the poet. Christian life has to be lived in a very real way if it is to support a vital and creative sacred art. This happened during the few centuries when the Gothic cathedrals were built. But today the writings of Claudel reach a very small segment of the Christian world. The question of sacred art is always a question of spiritual renascence in the world, of which today there are only scattered and fragmentary examples. But the fact that the art of Claudel is being gradually recognized by the Church is significant. The Church has always preached that she is the last universal community where all the authentic works of man will be welcomed and preserved. The theological doctrines about Christ stress the close relationship in Him between divine truth and human truth. Any artistic creation which renews the expression of human truth is bound therefore to testify at the same time to divine truth.

Perhaps the greatest lesson which Claudel has bequeathed our age is the belief that the truth of art always tends naturally toward the sacred. To this extent, the term "renascence of sacred art" is justified. The chapel of Matisse at Vence, in Southern France, illustrates this contemporary hope. The conversation between the aged bishop of Nice and the aged painter, who was not a practicing Catholic, revealed a similarity of inner spiritual life in the priest and the creative artist. The synthesis between art and faith which was so remarkable in the Middle Ages, and which is just beginning to reappear, depends upon the inner life of man, on a certain quality of his soul, on silence, poverty, solitude, nobility.

The sanctuaries recently erected at Assy, Audincourt and Vence appear as original and new as the odes of Claudel, when they were first published, and as the clowns and Christs in the paintings of Rouault. The same kind of accusation has been leveled against these particular examples of Christian art as against modern art in general. Judgments of men who speak with authority in matters of sacred art have been colored with harsh words, such as subversion, ignominy, aberration. These judgments are directed not only against painters like Matisse, who is a nonbeliever, but against Rouault as well, who belongs to the great tradition of Christian painting, of stained-glass makers and medieval illuminators.

Through the nineteenth century there was no meeting and no discussion between a church prelate and a major painter. There was no interchange between the Church and a Delacroix, a Corot or a Cézanne. Yves Florenne designates as the greatest religious painting of the nineteenth century that of the Chapel of the Holy Angels in Saint-Sulpice and claims that it was a pure accident! Sacred art is one of the last symbols of the freedom and the universality of the Church. The creation of art, when it is significant, is always extreme, but the Church lives habitually in accord with the extreme. It is curious that she has kept at the portals her two patriarchal artists today: Claudel and Rouault.

There is no one authoritative treatise on aesthetics from the Christian viewpoint. In the twentieth century, men like Thomas Gilby and Jacques Maritain have tried to cull from the voluminous writings of Saint Thomas Aquinas a sufficient number of precepts which might form the basis of such a treatise. The *Art Poétique* of Claudel, and all of his writings, for that matter, substantiate and illustrate what perhaps can be called Aquinian aesthetics.

For the Thomist, the problem of the aesthetic revolves around our knowledge of the concrete. The concrete is the field of experience, the center of poetic knowledge as opposed to rational knowledge which is always general and abstract and conceptual. Our deepest desire is to know the real, and in this sense the aesthetic experience may be the quieting in us of a persistent craving. The world itself, in its very immediate reality, provided Claudel with an inexhaustible supply of impressions, pictures, customs, colors, words. He is the type of universal artist interested in every culture, every mythology, every landscape. All instances of human life and activity, all aspects of nature, all laws and all forms of knowledge are open to the poet. But the only material the poet uses is the word, in which Claudel claims there is a secret virtue which the poet alone is able to master or at least use to its fullest capacity. The word, as used by the poet, is not the conventional sign as used in prose and ordinary speech. It is a rhythm, able to recall the thing it stands for, able to make that thing present and real, able to restore it to its existence. The poet's function for Claudel and the Thomist aesthetician is the calling up of the world to its primitive reality by means of the human voice, of the words in rhythm spoken by a poet's voice.

The poet's art parallels therefore the fundamental continuity and development of the world. At each moment in time the world is renewed. The artist works in an extraordinary perception of this principle of perpetual change, development, renewal of the world. We often have the faulty impression of leading our own lives in our own way. The truth is that our lives are always crossing others, that no one thing or being is isolated from the others. We are part of an intricate pattern, of an inexhaustible set of correspondences. The creation of a metaphor is the poet's new design or composition in which two opposite existences or things are joined.

If Thomistic doctrine states that our deepest desire is to know the real, it also states that a thing may be more loved than it is known. Saint Thomas believed that although we can love God perfectly, we know Him imperfectly. This problem of love-knowledge is central in Thomistic philosophy and in Claudel's aesthetics. God's will alone is able to give existence to concrete things. They are created by love, which is God's work. And then they may be experienced by love, which is the artist's knowledge of them. At this point, the philosopher is careful to point out that it is not the mind of man that knows, but the entire person who knows through the mind. Perfect knowledge, characterized by wholeness, exists only in God. Man's union with God in beatific vision would be the only perfect union of love, but the dynamics of love in its desire to effect a union with the thing loved, has relevance to the experience of poetry. Claudel writes that the world is still intact and virginal as it was on the first day of creation. Man is able to know the world because he is a part of it. He himself creates the agreement, the concord which is the object of his knowledge.

The relationship of the poet to his poem is comparable to the relationship of God to his universe. The basic assumption in Claudel's aesthetics is the universe seen as the mirror of God and man as the mirror of the universe. It is not difficult to move from this point to the belief that the revelation of the meaning of the world which the poet gives is expressed in the arrangement of words. The poem is not the abstract essence which may be derived from the words. The poem is the concrete reality of the arrangement of the words. The new meaning of the world lies precisely in the specific creation of the poet which is his arrangement of words.

Here the parable of Animus and Anima seems to apply to the poet's recreation of the world. The surface self, the animus, is constantly composing words into clear, simple, intelligible notions. But these are not the words of the poet. They are the words spoken by anima, from the deepest part of her being. They are obscure to the poet himself until they are uttered. They are characterized by a greater totality, a greater wholeness than the words of ordinary speech.

PART II

PART II

FOUR

FATE OF THE NOVEL:
From Radiguet to Sartre

Since the publication of Proust's novel in the twenties, many efforts have been made to renew and reinvigorate the French novel. Some of these efforts have been noteworthy, but on the whole the achievements of the novel do not appear as significant as those of contemporary criticism or poetry. The effect of the novel in its greatest instances: Proust, Joyce, Balzac, Dostoevsky, is dynamic. It can alter the order of an existence. It is the youngest of literary forms and the one which best characterizes modern literature. It still lacks a mode of criticism comparable to that mode which can be applied to poetry or to tragedy. Even in France, where the critical spirit is perhaps more active than elsewhere, the aesthetics of the novel is a baffling study. And yet the novel has enjoyed a tremendous vogue in France and has attracted those readers who in earlier periods would have enjoyed more abstract and philosophical writing.

Before writing his two novels, Raymond Radiguet practiced with poems (*Les Joues en feu*), composed in accordance with a type of preciosity which is difficult to define or describe. They bear some analogy with the early poems of Cocteau and with the paintings of Marie Laurencin. One might place them midway between the Cubists and the art of the *Fauves*. They are written with so few words and they combine so ingeniously a formal elegance with licentiousness that the term "classical" or "post-classical" would not be inappropriate to apply to this youthful art. Radiguet first excelled in a form of wit which the French literary tradition has always esteemed. It is the skill in using a word which will say one thing and imply another. It is almost the practice of the metaphor, the uniting of two seemingly disparate and contradictory terms. Radiguet once acknowledged that his models were La Fontaine and Malherbe. His poems, not so successful as those of Max Jacob and Apollinaire, belong to their tradition—it is Cocteau's also—which banished the mysteriousness of Symbolism in order to rediscover the more direct spiritual quality of things, their bareness, their provocative freshness. Contemporary with the Cubist movement in painting, this art of poetry was a worldly, sophisticated heritage from earlier periods when French intelligence had enjoyed great freedom and suppleness within the formal limits of madrigals, anagrams, sonnets and songs.

Radiguet was born in 1903, at Saint-Maur, just outside of Paris. As a young boy (he was only twenty at his death) he came into Paris frequently. Cocteau befriended him and believed in his vocation of writer. Radiguet wrote his poems on bits of paper which he kept crumpled in his pockets. He had to iron them out with the palm of his hand and then, because of his extreme myopia, raise them to his eyes in order to read them. Cocteau was the first to realize the originality with which Radiguet was investing old formulas. The boy wandered through the studios of the Paris painters and examined their pictures by placing, monocle-fashion, a pair of broken spectacles over his eyes. Although he claimed to be eighteen, he was only fifteen when he first appeared before Cocteau. He had been sent by Max Jacob. The servant announced him to Cocteau with the words: *Il y a dans l'antichambre un enfant avec une canne.* Since Saint-Maur, where Radiguet lived with his parents, was on the Marne River, the poets and painters of Montparnasse and Montmartre used to call him *le miracle de la Marne.*

He read quantities of second-rate books in order to compare them with masterpieces. He claimed that since the mechanics of masterpieces are invisible, one has to study those mechanics in books which pretend to be masterpieces but which are not. Radiguet's first novel, *Le Diable au Corps,* was published in 1923, and his second, *Le Bal du Comte d'Orgel,* after his death, in 1924. The notion that there were no adolescent novelists had to be revived, and Radiguet was instantly acclaimed the "Rimbaud of the novel." It was not difficult to acknowledge his exceptional gifts and it was obvious that he had thought considerably about the art and the technique of the novel. The principles of his art were as austere and controlled as his personal behavior was erratic and unpredictable. More deeply and more subtly than other books of the early twenties, Radiguet's two novels, and especially *Le Bal du Comte d'Orgel*, depict the new *mal du siècle* which had broken out during the years following the war. *Le Diable au Corps* involves a study of the sense of limitless freedom which resulted from this very freedom. Radiguet himself defined *Le Bal* as a novel in which the adventure element is the psychology. *Roman où c'est la psychologie qui est romanesque.* The analysis in the novel is not carried out in order to reach its own truth, but rather for what it reveals about the hero who is analyzing himself and others. It is a means to provide his portrait of the hero rather than to judge him.

Le Bal bears a close affinity with the seventeenth-century *Princesse de Clèves* of Mme de La Fayette. It appears that Radiguet did not conceal from his friends his deliberate intention of using the model of the classical work. Both novels are stories of a wholly admirable woman who loves in different ways but incompatibly two men. In Radiguet's novel the passionate love which Mahaut feels for her husband diminishes through the course of the book until it becomes a conventional attachment. The purity of her heart, from beginning to end, testifies to the significance of her love. Yet it is this very purity of heart which leads her close to great peril. Mahaut is the wife of Count Anne d'Orgel. They participate in the worldliness of Paris society, quite comparable to the court life background of Mme de La Fayette's novel. The third character, François de Séryeuse, is a friend of Count d'Orgel. The love he feels for Mahaut and her love for him exists at the beginning of the book and does not change. By the last scene, Mahaut and her husband are seated in the same room, but they are actually on two different planets.

Radiguet exercises control over his characters at some distance from them. He is almost too much their master. Their own speeches reveal what they discover about themselves and then Radiguet intervenes to tell us what is really transpiring. The importance of the book is perhaps in its philosophy of love. When we learn that Mahaut is deeply in love with her husband, we have a first intimation about Radiguet's fundamental pessimism, because Count d'Orgel is a shallow character who obviously is not in love with his wife. At the moment in the story when Anne d'Orgel discovers that Mahaut and François are cousins, he forces them to embrace. They are embarrassed, but they perform the ritual of the kiss and laugh over it. With such a scene, Radiguet's belief that love, rather than joining two beings, separates them, becomes clear. Behind the remarkable chastity of the novel, lies a concealed sensuality which is totally reckless. Radiguet himself has said about his novel: *Roman d'amour chaste, aussi scabreux que le roman le moins chaste.* By the end of the story, we realize we have passed through many peripeteia all of which transpired within the hearts of the characters. Radiguet discovers the sentiments of Mahaut and François by looking at them steadily and directly. He releases their thoughts and their gestures in methodical fashion as if he were performing a series of tricks. The book has an acrobatic sense of proportion in its brevity, its swiftness and the chastity of its concealed fire.

The ball, referred to in the title, is to be a masked

ball. It does not take place during the novel, but the characters are planning to attend it. Their costumes obviously will symbolize the parts they cannot play in real life or the parts they do not realize they are playing. D'Orgel himself, for example, has no conception of the jealousy he feels for François de Séryeuse. Passion, whether recognized or not, tends to mechanize its victims. The adolescent hero of Radiguet's first novel, *Le Diable au Corps*, wore a deliberate mask of virile maturity during the course of his love experience. Physical suffering, even sadism, and cynicism characterize *Le Diable*, but all that is absent from *Le Bal*, where the attitude toward love has deepened at the expense of appearing more hopeless, more tragically pessimistic.

La Princesse de Clèves may well be the model for *Le Bal du Comte d'Orgel*. Gide has pointed out that the Radiguet novel was strongly influenced by *Les Pléiades* of Gobineau. It is not extraordinary that a novelist, at the age of twenty, leaned heavily on other works. Proust learned how to write by composing his *pastiches*, and Mallarmé's first poems were cast in Baudelairian form. What is extraordinary is the deftness and the precision of Radiguet's writing, its competency which is executed almost as if it were a wager. The sentences have a colorless purity and create an effect totally different from that of the far more romantic and diffuse novel of Alain-Fournier, *Le Grand Meaulnes*. This latter held an important place in the French novel during the twenties and thirties (it was published in 1913), but today it seems to be losing out in favor of such works as *Le Bal du Comte d'Orgel* and *Les Enfants Terribles* of Jean Cocteau. Radiguet and Cocteau are close in their common dis-

like for the pretentious, the loquacious, the tiresome.
Their purely descriptive passages are more swift and
condensed than the swiftest in Stendhal. They are
most skillful in their depiction of brief moments,
brief encounters. They are interested primarily in
taking candid camera shots of man's adventure. Pictures which will relieve the monotony of a too familiar story.

The theme of love in Radiguet is at all times comparable to the high moral conception of love in the
tragedies of Racine or in the novel of Mme de La
Fayette. And yet, it bears analogies with the theme of
love in the work of Cocteau, for whom love is never
a moral problem, but rather a willfulness to explore
and a curiosity. Passion for Cocteau is almost always
the capacity of being enchanted, of being be-
witched. I suspect that the meaning of love is more
dramatic and more tragic in Radiguet, but very often
his treatment of it in *Le Bal* resembles a strange fas-
cination for the perilous, for the properties of an object like that snowball in which the pupil Dargelos
had concealed a stone. In their will to avoid the
monotony of the novel and the inherent heaviness
of its form, both Cocteau and Radiguet created semi-
mythological characters who do not have the same
need of speech and action of ordinary creatures. It
is enough to see them briefly, in a brilliant setting.

It is claimed that the new element of poetry which
so often participates in the form of the modern novel
is generally expressed in the "atmosphere" of the
story. The French writer has always had traditionally
another use for his treatment of the poetic. This trait,
which is almost an idiosyncrasy, is illustrated in Raymond Radiguet's second novel. It is poetry conceived

of as a source of truth, as a means of knowledge. What is poetic in Racine, for example, is quite different from what is poetic in Shakespeare. The poetic in Mallarmé is not the poetic in Hopkins. I am trying to say that there is an important idiosyncratic element of the poetic in French art which is not materially poetic. In *Le Bal*, Radiguet actually refers to the type of poetic beauty which comes from the description of atmosphere and from the analysis of imprecise states of feeling, and he announces that another kind of poetry is to be found in the notation of the precise and the direct. It is a form of art which sustains and deepens intelligibility, exemplified in the best pages of Baudelaire, Rimbaud and Claudel. The art of Stendhal, whose novels have been exceptionally enjoyed in the twentieth century, has some of this poetic element which is a concentration or a denuding, a swift precise expression of critical judgment. Stendhal sees more than he feels, but he remains in the tradition of the French moralists, of Mme de La Fayette, of Choderlos de Laclos, and in the category of French artists, where we would place Radiguet, who give primacy to the senses and the reason of man.

On all sides one reads that the French novel today is undergoing an eclipse or a crisis. It is quite true that the form of the novel has not, during the past twenty years, been so renovated or rejuvenated as, for example, the form of the American novel. There are few examples in the recent French novel of inventiveness, boldness, originality. On the whole, it has continued to depict a banal society and a familiar world of objects. An exaggerated belief in "realism," in a painstaking faithfulness to reality is perhaps one of the major causes for the decadence of the novel. The French reader finds in most of these novels the same daily life which he is able to observe himself in Paris or in the provinces. Few writers have dared to depart from the usual form of the French novel: a well-written story, a clearly organized plot, recognizable characters, a familiar society, minute details which are true to life and observable. The critics—and they have been very harsh on the contemporary novel—are still calling for the writer who will purify and recast the form, who will do for the novel what Mallarmé did for poetry.

The hopes of some of them are fixed on Raymond Queneau, who, more than others, more even than Sartre and Camus, seems to be affecting the fate of the novel. The writing of Queneau's *Les Temps Mêlés,* for example, is a departure from the usual realist technique. The first part of the novel contains twelve poems which sustain the rest of the work. The second part is a monologue which puts into action the pure sentiments of the first part. The third part is a dialogue which serves to transform into events the figures and the passions of the story. The innovations of the novel are linguistic and technical, whereby Queneau transforms words and deranges syntax.

The Existentialists have read widely in the American novel, especially Dos Passos, Hemingway, Steinbeck, Faulkner; and a staggering number of American novels have been translated in the last fifteen years. Interest in the American novel is not limited to the contemporary. In 1941, *Moby Dick* was translated by Giono and commented on by him. Giono's admiration of *Moby Dick* is somewhat explained by the general inadequacy he felt in French realism. What struck him in the Melville story was the totality of the work, which seemed to be the creation of an entire world. He saw it as an enigmatical work that can be read on several levels. One may see in it an adventure story or the story of a man in love with a forbidden monster. Giono calls it an example of *le véritable réalisme*.

Another example of a novel, this time English, whose technique is opposite to that of realism and whose translation appeared in the early forties was *The Waves* of Virginia Woolf. Here was a novel almost without anecdote, almost without characters in the usual sense, from which almost all psychology had been excluded. The French critics saw immediately that the problem of time was uppermost in Mrs. Woolf's art, in her passages on the fortuitous moments in the lives of everyone which reveal ecstasy or the secret meaning of death.

The almost passionate interest with which American literature is being read in France points to a possible fuller mutual understanding. Before loving a country, one first loves its literature. The young Frenchmen have been struck not only by the tragic stories in the American novels, but also by the example of so many writers who have died young and who before dying left brilliant testimonials of their experience: Nathanael West, author of *Miss Lonelyhearts*, killed at thirty-six, at the wheel of his auto; Scott Fitzgerald, author of *The Great Gatsby*, who died at forty-five through nervous exhaustion and perhaps despair; Thomas Wolfe, who died at thirty-eight. Thanks to these translations, the French can see better that the American does not dispose of a long solid cultural tradition which the Frenchman has. They understand better the artistic solitude of a Melville and a Hawthorne, and the despair, described by Dos Passos in his article on Scott Fitzgerald, the American feels at not knowing for whom he writes.

The gifted critic Mme Claude-Edmonde Magny published in 1948 a book on this subject, *L'age du roman américain,* by which title she means that this age is best characterized by the American novel and cinema. She has been impressed by the fact that the American novelists read preferably such European authors as Joyce, Kafka, Proust, Mann, whose complex architectonic works are vastly different from their own books. She sees the American writer not only as a scapegoat of a society, a kind of sacrificial victim redeeming the subconscious of other men, but also as the man who is going to recreate a "church," a community that will be sacred. Her elaborate analysis and interpretation of Faulkner is the central chapter in her thesis of the reconstruction of a community. In Faulkner's case it is a community of sinners all of whom assume the same guilt. She points out a relationship between Faulkner and Melville, Graham Greene and Bernanos, all of whom are men reconstructing a church in this particular sense which Mme Magny gives to a church.

Ever since Balzac, in the middle of the nineteenth century, the novel has taken unto itself many forms: history, criticism, psychological analysis, sociology, politics. Of all literary forms, it is the most omnivorous. It has recently added to its powers lyricism itself and forms of the personal essay. These additions have caused such changes in the form of the novel that it no longer resembles in any faithful way the typical

nineteenth-century novel. The new novelist, Queneau
or Samuel Beckett, no longer feels compelled to nar-
rate a story or to delineate closely his characters or to
describe a social background. Especially since the
second World War, the novel appears to be more a
document on man than a story about a particular
man. It often corresponds to what the French call a
témoignage and might well have appeared in another
century in the form of essays or maxims or *pensées*.
Philosophy and literature are closely related in the
work of the two serious novelists who have perhaps
reached the widest public today. The novel, still in
progress, of Jean-Paul Sartre, *Les Chemins de la
Liberté*, illustrates his philosophical treatise, *L'Etre
et le Néant*, as Albert Camus' *Mythe de Sisyphe*
theorizes on the theme of the "absurd" in *L'Etranger*.

Man is looked upon and studied by these new novelists as if he were at some distant point in the universe, a metaphysical object far removed from the
artist himself. For Sartre, for the early Camus and
for some of the younger novelists influenced by Existentialism, man exists without his traditional beliefs
in God, or in a rationally conceived and functioning universe, or in humanity capable of progress. The
universe as he sees it is not merely tragic, it is mute
and absurd. The contemporary hero feels no con-
straint in speaking of his terror before such a picture of the universe, of his loneliness, of his sexual
obsessions. The books of Jean Genet represent the
extreme in frankness, in a confessional-kind of literature where no private secrets are held back. Genet
has been compared to Villon and Verlaine. He has
been severely castigated by Mauriac and fervently
praised by Sartre. What is unquestioned is the beauty

of his language. He is probably the greatest stylist writing in French today. The effect of his books is ultimately one of lamentation, of passionate incantation. His thefts for which he has been imprisoned many times, and which he celebrates in *Miracle de la Rose,* are stimuli for his eroticism. It would seem that the writing of his books, *Querelle de Brest, Notre-Dame des Fleurs, Pompes Funèbres,* is another stimulus, another means for provoking his eroticism.

The American novelists most admired in France during the late thirties and the forties had, with the exception of Faulkner, eliminated almost all the analysis of the inner or psychological life of their characters. They rarely went beyond stating objectively and dispassionately what the characters did and what the characters saw around them. The American novel introduced a new repertory of characters: the strong silent man of Dashiell Hammett's *Maltese Falcon* and *The Glass Key;* the tramp, the unemployed and the drunkards of Steinbeck's novels and Chaplin's films. Hemingway's high-class art of reporting or showing without analyzing or describing is quite evident, for example, in Camus' *L'Etranger.* French critics in many cases paid earlier and more sophisticated attention to contributions of American art than American critics. In a very special way, they have heeded the Hemingway myth of the man aggressively virile, opposed on all sides by society or fate. The books of William Faulkner have for the French a Biblical or apocalyptic quality. They see in them the massacre of the innocents, the unending series of terrifying punishments visited on men which are out of proportion with their faults or their misbehavior. This is a familiar thesis found in Sartre's

essay on *The Sound and the Fury* and in Claude-
Edmonde Magny's *L'Age du roman américain.* The
work of Faulkner is looked upon today by many of
the serious French critics as the principal literary
testimonial to the deficient state of modern spirituality.
They see in his novels a composite of Balzac, in Faulkner's effort to write a new *Comédie Humaine;* of
Proust, in his analytical powers; of Joyce, in his
capacity to reflect the universal conscience; of Eliot,
in this newest depiction of a wasteland.

The French discovery of Faulkner was followed by
the still more recent rediscovery of the Marquis de
Sade. By the new editions of some of his writings, and
by the critical and biographical books devoted to him,
Sade is beginning to occupy a position of importance
in contemporary French thought. There is unquestionably a degree of *snobisme* in this rehabilitation
of the marquis, as there was with the vogue of Existentialism and with the popularity of Henry Miller in
France. But there is also considerable seriousness.
Such an astute critic and potentate in the domain of
literature as Jean Paulhan has pointed out that Sade
was an important influence on such writers as Lamar-
tine, Baudelaire, Swinburne, Lautréamont, Nietzsche,
Dostoevsky, Kafka. It is true that the Surrealists, in
the twenties and thirties, had revived interest in Sade
in a semi-clandestine way. They had been somewhat
guided by Apollinaire's belief that Sade, who had been
obscured by most of the nineteenth century, would
end by becoming a leading figure for the twentieth.
The approach to Sade of such critics as Pierre
Klossowski and Maurice Blanchot and Simone de
Beauvoir refuses to limit him to the category of por-

nographic writer. The fantastic proportions of his universe make him into a visionary or a poet. Freud has indoctrinated the modern world to such a degree that what was once scandalous in Sade, no longer seems so. The criminal is now looked upon as a philosophical martyr. The vast system of perversions found in the writings of Sade, contributed by its action, concealed but powerful throughout the nineteenth century, to the formulating of psychoanalytical practice and the creation of new myths destined to important roles in twentieth-century literature. These books expose an anarchical vision of human behavior whose fundamental pessimism it would be difficult to exceed. In their most intense vision, humanity, after liberating its desires and homicidal instincts, is seen disappearing in a deluge of blood.

Only about one-fourth of Sade's writing, most of which was composed during his twenty-seven years spent in the prisons of Vincennes, the Bastille and Charenton, has been printed. His philosophical system, if it is ever fully revealed and clarified, will doubtless establish his quasi-theological theory of evil. His denial of the existence of God led him quite naturally to the denial of the existence of his fellowman. His bad conscience of a libertine preserved this double denial of God and his neighbor. And yet he seems to be establishing a religion of evil not in order to deny all concept of crime, but to acknowledge crime as consequent on the existence of a god of evil.

The importance which Mme Simone de Beauvoir ascribes to Sade in her enlightened essay, *Faut-il brûler Sade?*, and Gilbert Lély's authoritative biography, serve what is currently called in France "Sade's revenge." They are interventions in his favor, efforts to see in his atheism an absolute which exceeds the frivolous impiety of other libertines of the later eighteenth century. They see him as a precursor of the *poètes maudits,* and place him at the head of a lineage of blasphemers who reached Luciferean proportions: Lautréamont, Nietzsche, Jarry.

The unity in Jean-Paul Sartre's novel, *L'Age de Raison* comes from the protagonist Mathieu. The novel is conceived as a series of scenes representing the world closing in on Mathieu from all directions in order to lay bare, irritate and stimulate his precious belief in human liberty. From the opening scene where Mathieu meets on the rue Vercingétorix a drunkard to whom he has the choice of giving or not giving a few francs and thus expressing his total freedom in creating his immediate future moment, to the final scene where he is left alone in his apartment after Daniel's departure and where he assures himself that the past experiences have propelled him into the age of reason, every episode would seem to contradict his liberty. Sartre's work is a metaphysical novel constructed on the paradox of the world inflicting its complexities and constraining bonds on a hero, and the boundless inner liberty preserved by the hero.

L'Age de Raison is much more than a further example of Naturalism. Its subject is the condition of man in the universe. The anguish of his existence is reminiscent of that already described by Pascal and Rimbaud, although Sartre never gives it the vibrant poetic tone of his predecessors. The single fact of existence engenders the problem of liberty which provides the entire work with its metaphysical focus. Of all the characters, Mathieu speaks the most of liberty and thinks about it the most directly. He considers his existence a condemnation of liberty. In leaving Marcelle, at the end of the novel, he realizes that there is no real reason for his leaving her. Life around him is seen as superfluous and absurd. Much of the art of the novel is devoted to the stifling universe in which Mathieu finds himself, to the closed world in the center of which his precious concept of liberty seems to be his astounding lucidity. There he is powerful and free, as Daniel is also. As Mathieu is seen emerging out of the abundant confusion and engulfing power of the world, Daniel is seen descending into it. Each protagonist in his action preserves his personal consciousness and his awareness of the continual presence of death. Sartre, both philosopher and novelist, has projected himself into Mathieu, teacher of philosophy and thinker, and into Daniel, closer to the artist, who descends from his angelic aloofness into the confused pattern of human existence.

The bulk of the second volume of Sartre's essays, *Situations*, published in 1948, is given over to a long piece entitled *Qu'est-ce que la littérature?* No other work of Sartre illustrates better than this his remarkable intelligence, his learning, his polemic power. He affirms violently and dogmatically. Sartre is concerned in this work with the literary movement of the last thirty years, with its metamorphoses and its development which may now be threatened. Sartre is a skillful, almost diabolical dialectician. He openly scorns the philosopher-critic Taine, but in the fifty pages where he reviews literature of the last three centuries and avoids the error of the seventeenth-century writers who paid no heed to the economic, political, religious, metaphysical factors in a writer, he is employing a method quite similar to Taine's. Sartre admires very few writers. His hostility to Flaubert is well known. He compares Mallarmé's work to an icy silence (*Ce silence de glace, l'oeuvre de Mallarmé*). He disapproves of Valéry's abstractions and Proust's bourgeoisism. Sartre wants a writer to participate in his period (*s'engager*), not in order to preserve it but to help in its process of change, to precipitate its evolution. Nothing, he warns, assures us that literature is immortal. The chance for literature today is, he believes, the chance for Europe, for democracy, for peace.

The principal character of Jean Cayrol's *Je vivrai l'amour des autres* (1947) is a *clochard* or tramp. *Gibier de Potence* (1949), by Jean-Louis Curtis, is the story of a *voyou*, of La Place Blanche and the black market after the war. In such novels as these, the traditional and specifically French formulas, such as the psychological emphasis in *Adolphe* of Constant, and the documentary emphasis in *Germinal* of Zola, appear markedly diminished. Yet the novelist of today is still primarily concerned with the nature of man's experience. The nineteenth-century novelists, on the whole, believed that man is formed and explained by his environment. Many of the more recent twentieth-century novelists believe that man is formed and explained by forces outside of his control. In this shift of belief from evolutionary forces to psychological forces, the entire meaning of such a term as environment has altered. Whereas it once referred to the home, the city and the social class of a fictional character, today it refers to political, religious and sociological ideas, and to the various neuroses of other characters in the life of the principal character. In order to follow the art of the new novelists, one has to accept the fact that the method of presenting a character is far more indirect than it was in Flaubert's day, and that the narration of plot is less sharp because of the new importance accorded to seemingly slight situations. Of all literary genres the novel has the fewest formal constraints. It has no codified aesthetics comparable to the aesthetics of a poem, or a play, or even a short story. Yet its objective has never ceased being the description of human reality, of the varying relations between man and society.

FIVE

MAURIAC'S DARK HERO

Mauriac's province, which was Montaigne's also, plays a much more significant part in his novels than that of a mere setting. The somber and somewhat sad city of Bordeaux and the countryside around Bordeaux, composed of pine forests, vineyards, stretches of sand and large isolated houses, have helped to form the sensitivity of the novelist. He is no regionalist writer in a narrow sense, but the physical and spiritual qualities of his province exist in close alliance with the characters of his novels. The province is part of the poetry and part of the drama in each of the books, to the same degree, so difficult to measure, as in the novels of William Faulkner about the deep South. Mauriac does not sing directly about his province, as Barrès did about his. He is always concentrated on the landscapes of the soul, but this first landscape reflects the romantic wildness and solitude of Les Landes.

The childhood of Mauriac was completely provincial in accordance with the most sober of traditions, and was dominated by piety and devotion to family. He was one of five children. His father had died when the boy was only a few months old, and his mother had full responsibility in bringing up the family. The house was lovingly but austerely governed. Evening prayers in common and numerous religious practices were a fixed part of the day's routine. François was a sickly looking child who feared each day that his lessons were not sufficiently learned and was seized with terror in the presence of his schoolteachers. Many of these childhood memories are transposed in his novels, but when M. Mauriac began his autobiography, of which only a few pages appeared, *Commencements d'une Vie,* he found the literal transcription of these memories too painful to execute.

He studied at a Catholic school where, even during the winter, the pupils rose at 5:30 in an unheated dormitory and where some degree of heroism was necessary for the simple act of washing. At the four o'clock recess period, he was usually vanquished in the disputes which would arise between himself and his sturdier comrades and he feared that these physical defeats prefigured a life of anguish and violence. It is little to be wondered that the need to write and to express himself was felt very early. The evenings became for the boy the most precious part of the day, when he acquired the taste and the genius for solitude and when he practiced writing in a journal and composing his first verses.

The purity of his childhood and early adolescence was dominated by a deep love for his mother. She wondered at his preference for solitude and study, but respected his temperament which was already formed. Until twenty, Mauriac lived the ordinary existence of provincial adolescents: a repressed life, largely expressionless. The city of Bordeaux impressed itself on his sensibility: midnight masses in the Cathedral of Saint André, the large sinister-looking houses, the monotonous suburbs and, beyond them, the flat Landes: vineyards, pine trees, cicadas, wild birds, heather, ferns. *L'histoire de Bordeaux*, Mauriac writes in *Commencements d'une Vie, est l'histoire de mon corps et de mon âme*. Mauriac is the Bordelais whom Bordeaux prevented from visiting Rome or London. As a child, when he was preoccupied with the gravest problems, such as "the state of grace" he was in or others were in, when he was compressed within himself and lacking any expansion of spirit, he felt between him and his city a complicity and a strong alliance. The oldest sections of the city had their particular odors for him, and at Christmas time, in the noisy crowded rue Sainte Catherine, he watched the girls selling the fresh sour-tasting oysters which had come from the *bassin* of the Garonne, as if he were an integral part of the scene and the entire life of the city. When he entered alone the nave of the cathedral, he knew a happiness which he felt must be comparable to that of an insect burrowing into the earth.

Mauriac's obsession with Bordeaux has not prevented the exercise of his critical faculties. He both hates and loves his city and its inhabitants. He has always lived close to the bourgeoisie and observed, from his earliest years on, its vices and virtues. One of the major conflicts of his mind, which has been used in many of his writings, arose from his watching the sedate, prudent and circumspect race of the bourgeois during Mass. The striking paradox, for example, of the midnight Mass at Christmas, with its Gospel asceticism: "He was born in a manger," and the rich bourgeoisie dressed in their fur coats, has disturbed Mauriac and motivated many of his pages. He has never ceased to worry over the close proximity of the celebrated Bordeaux truffles and the Communion table.

The award of the Nobel prize to François Mauriac, in November 1952, was recognition of a long literary career and a long participation in contemporary French thought and problems. Since 1944, Mauriac has become a leading journalist, with his bi-weekly articles in *Le Figaro,* and has made as many enemies as Gide, who received the same prize a few years previously.

The enemies, or detractors, have been saying for some time that Mauriac's career is over and that his conception of the novel is outmoded. Serious critical attacks have been made against him by Sartre and Claude-Edmonde Magny. Yet Mauriac has published two recent novels, *Le Sagouin* and *Galigai* which stand up favorably beside his most successful. M. Mauriac has become a very eminent personality in Paris. His Catholicism has always been a meditation on the Christian life as it participates in daily problems of politics and morality. A large portion of the public who read his *Figaro* articles take him as a guide on the complicated issues of the day which he analyzes. His early departure from a première of Cocteau's recent play, *Bacchus,* was commented on in the press the following day and instigated a polemical discussion. Few writers have participated in more controversies of political and moral order than Mauriac. His discussions about the art of the novel, and especially about the problem of the Catholic novelist, constitute a significant part of his writings.

Mauriac never denied that originally he had the ambition of writing a new *Comédie Humaine,* another work of gigantic proportions that would be the story of a family and of a period, in which the same characters would continue to appear from book to book. But this early ambition was replaced by what became his permanent ambition, to write a single book, a masterpiece, which is always the current book he is working on. Each book of his, according to Mauriac, is therefore born from the failure of all the others. Early in his career as a writer, he renounced the temptation to write another *roman-fleuve* in which he would describe his entire period from the outside, from anything which might be a purely historical viewpoint. In this determination, Mauriac has often acknowledged the decisive influence of Proust. With the example of Proust's novel before him, Mauriac willed never to put into his stories what he had not rediscovered in himself. Proust had been able to absorb the whole society of his time. Mauriac's world is much more limited and restricted. It is a tiny provincial world which today is almost extinct.

He left Bordeaux at the age of twenty, and since that time has lived in Paris where he has participated in many aspects of the social and political and literary worlds of the capital. But he has not drawn upon these experiences in the composition of his novels. Like Proust, he prefers to rediscover in his own past rather than to observe immediately. What he discovers in his memory is the confined Jansenistic world of his childhood: its piety, its repressed sadness and even anguish, its provincial setting. Whenever he borrows details for his novels from his immediate experience, they appear to him additions to the real substance of the writing. That substance is a special element of the bourgeoisie, now undergoing a process of transformation and perhaps even of disappearance. It is a single city, with one or two landscapes around the city: vineyards and pine forests; a single religion, or rather a religious atmosphere of which almost nothing remains today, even in strictly Catholic circles.

In each of his stories, Mauriac achieves a remarkable harmony between the characters and the landscape which they seem to reflect. The storms which descend from the skies over Bordeaux are closely related to the inner storms of the heart. The same wind stirs the tops of the pine trees and the deepest parts of the soul. The fires which so often sweep through the forests and the Landes resemble the human passions. Mauriac remains always at the center of his novels. His characters live in him. He reveals himself only in his fiction because from his so-called *Journal* his intimate self is absent.

Human solitude is Mauriac's most deliberately explored theme. For twenty-five years, between *Le Désert de l'Amour* of 1925 and his recent play of 1950, with its subtitle, *Le Pays sans chemins*, he has been writing about the subject of incommunicability which creates precisely the desert of love. It is the same book endlessly recommenced on childhood and adolescence, on love which is an attachment to a being who avoids becoming attached. Mauriac himself has said that *Le Désert de l'Amour* would be an appropriate title for his entire work.

He believes that a novelist has to invent his own

laws, those which will serve his particular art alone. Such novels as Tolstoi's *War and Peace* and Hemingway's *For Whom the Bell Tolls,* are totally different from the type of Mauriac's novels which has its principal antecedents in Racine's tragedies. In Mauriac's art, as in Racine's, a human destiny is revealed at the time of a significant and usually fatal crisis. In answer to the reproach made so often to Mauriac that he judges his creatures as if he were God, he replies quite simply that Molière judges his miser, Racine his character Narcisse, Shakespeare his Iago. And he adds that the Christian novelist pays little heed to this habit of judging since his particular judgment is of no consequence by comparison with grace which, although it is invisible in his work, is always present in it. Mauriac points out that if God appears absent from the novel of Proust, His existence is no more denied in it than that of the human soul.

Mauriac's meditations on the moral and religious problems of man have been closely associated with his meditations on the role of the writer, and more especially on the function and the responsibility of the novelist. The work of the writer is for Mauriac the justification of his life. He would consider that his novels contain the essential truth about his life and his mind. His pages of fiction represent a closer approximation to truth than any purely factual rehearsal of his life. In every page of his novels, the novelist is at the bar defending himself and his ideas and pleading for the justification of his existence.

The novelist draws upon the memories of a lifetime. Rather than being dispersed or effaced, each memory is recorded permanently within him: each face he saw, each word he heard, every anecdote that was told him, every accident he witnessed. The rooms, the houses and the gardens, which serve as the background for Mauriac's novels, are inevitably monotonous because they were all observed by him in Bordeaux and in the family estates outside of Bordeaux. Friends and neighbors of Mauriac have been startled in recognizing in his novels their own rose garden or their own living room. But they were even more astonished at reading the somber dramas which unfolded in the familiar setting. The secret of the novelist was the discovery of the hidden monsters in the seemingly inoffensive characters who lived in the houses and walked about the gardens. Against the background of decorous conventionality in a Bordeaux household and the logically patterned gardens, Mauriac has projected characters of illogicality, of passion and complexity. These are his creatures and his creations. He is concerned with the deepest motivations within them, with their suppressed desires and the unspoken dream fantasies.

If therefore the content of Mauriac's novels is somber and passionate, the actual form of his writing, like the symmetrically ordered gardens of his settings, is lucid and classically direct. The chastity of his style permits him to say anything he wishes about his characters. The disorder of crime and chaotic mental states in the novels of Mauriac is offset by the sense of order which controls his writing. The total absence of melodrama in his style permits the violent drama of the characters to take on its full objectivity. The simplicity and understatement of the sentences help to increase the torment of the creatures, which in many cases is unarticulated.

Mauriac believes that behind each novel there exists to some degree a part of the novelist's own life, a personal drama either directly experienced or imagined. Thus the writing of the books becomes a deliverance of personal suffering or passion, of suppressed anger or desire. And the characters in the books almost resemble scapegoats, mystically loaded with the sins which had been committed or imagined by the novelist. The literal defect in the life of a novelist, when it is transplanted, may easily grow to monstrous proportions. The novelist's art is a transposition and not a reproduction of the real.

François Mauriac occupies a very special place among the Catholic writers of contemporary France. His work, completely innocent of didacticism or proselytism, is devoted to the study of evil, sin, weakness, suffering. Sanctity is not one of his themes. He has confessed that he always fails in the depiction of virtuous characters. Pietistically minded Christians as well as non-Christians have found it difficult to accept this trait in Mauriac. Gide at one time chided Mauriac for the preponderant place he gives to evil in his novels, for the compromise, as he defined it, which permits Mauriac to love God without losing sight of Mammon. Gide continued his argument by saying that if he were more fully a Christian, he would not be able to follow Mauriac quite so easily.

The major attack on Mauriac's conception of the novel (whereby Mauriac believes the novelist comparable to God, having full knowledge of his creatures, although never denying them freedom of will) came from Jean-Paul Sartre, in an article written before M. Sartre enjoyed the fame he does today. (*La Nouvelle Revue Française*, February 1939.) The Exis-

tentialist argues that the Christian writer, because of
his belief in man's freedom, is admirably suited to
write novels. Dostoevsky would be a leading example.
But Mauriac, according to Sartre, sees the whole of
his universe at all times. His dialogue, like that of a
play, is always efficacious and moves rapidly ahead.
Whereas the characters of Dostoevsky, Faulkner and
Hemingway do not know what they are to say next.
They are freer than the creatures of Mauriac. And
M. Sartre concluded that God is not an artist and
neither is François Mauriac! This criticism of Sartre
greatly limits the art of the novel. Mauriac is a descendant, not from other novelists, not from the realists Balzac, Flaubert and Zola, but from Pascal,
Racine and Baudelaire, whose sense of tragedy demanded a certain aloofness of attitude and an abstraction or purgation in style.

In the majority of cases, the Catholic writer in contemporary France is the convert, either from Protes-
tantism or Judaism, or the man who returns to the
faith of his childhood: Bloy, Péguy, Psichari, Maritain, Du Bos, Rivière, Claudel. But Mauriac has never
been separated from Catholicism. He has never had
to explain or prove a change of mind and a new adherence. Like Montaigne and La Rochefoucauld, to
whose lineage he really belongs, Mauriac has steadily
contemplated human behavior from a single position.
He, like his moralistic predecessors in the history of
French thought, has watched, not the exterior man-
nerisms and superficial garb of men and women, but
the secrets and frustrations which grow in the dark
of their subconscious and encumber their inner life.
A text from Saint Paul's Epistle to the Romans illustrates the essential dilemma of the Mauriac character:

"For the good that I would I do not; but the evil which I would not, that I do." (7:19)

One of the constantly reiterated themes in the writings of Charles Péguy is the important position which the sinner occupies in Christendom. *Le pécheur est aussi de chrétienté.* The novels of Mauriac illustrate this significant and dramatic role of the sinner. It was particularly after the publication of *Les Anges Noirs,* in 1936 that the criticism of Mauriac's themes grew almost into a storm of protest. Was it not a sign of morbidity and unhealthiness, his detractors questioned, that the world of evil depicted by this novelist was so uniformly black and despairing? Does not this perpetual preoccupation with sin and perverseness indicate a connivance or a compliance with them? His work has often been called a scandal and Mauriac has been asked repeatedly to defend and justify himself.

His answer is always the same. He is interested in the problem of evil, and finds nothing exceptional or outrageous in his characters. The newspapers alone furnish sufficient proof that in every city every day crimes are committed which are not more strange or more monstrous than those in his novels. The novelist simply isolates one of those cases and analyses its genesis and its development. A novel is a steady floodlight focused on one of the lurid stories of passion which the journalists dispatch with flagrant irony and disinterestedness. Mauriac has called his novels a matter of "lighting."

The characters of Mauriac represent that kind of human nature, formed and conditioned by a long background of orthodox Christianity. Even if in many of the characters there is only a nominal or hypo-

thetical adherence to the Catholic faith, the deepest
part of their natures reacts to the forces in them and
around them as if Christianity, acknowledged or un-
acknowledged, governed the beginning and the end
of human existence. In such natures as these, the
struggle between good and evil is clearer and more
dramatic than it would be in others. It is true that the
Calvinist as well as the Catholic may experience a
kind of terror when he has committed sin or when
he is alone with his passions, but it would seem that
the Catholic, more than other Christians, feels a more
metaphysical or historical terror in the presence of sin
and in the memory of sin. Every sin committed by
others affects him in some way and augments his
personal drama. There is a profound solitude in many
of Mauriac's characters, but the solitude is controlled
by an ancient knowledge of sin. They are immobil-
ized, not so much by their own personal experience
of sin, as by some ancient sense of responsibility for
the sins of mankind. The Catholic is more attached
than other men to the imperfections and the failures
of the world. Every day, even if he performs his religious obligations in the most perfunctory manner,
even if he does not perform them at all, he ties himself up with the sins of the dead, he fills his solitude
with the terror which comes from the sense of solitude created by the alienating force of sin. The barrenness of the Mauriac scene is in constant complicity with the barrenness of his creatures' hearts, but
it would be difficult to discover in any literary tradition a more cosmic sense of evil.

The general climate of Mauriac's novels may appear unhealthy to many readers because it is dominated by the more somber aspects of passion. The

sexual problem, never blatantly stated, is at the center of each of the books. The drama takes its origin in the most secret of all meeting places within a human being: there where religious aspiration, or at least religious conditioning, collides with sexual desire. In most of Mauriac's characters, this sexual desire is repressed and continues half hidden, half forgotten, until it breaks out in some tense abnormality. The problem is always there, waiting in the dark, so to speak, but its presence is felt in all the actions and decisions of the characters, as well as in their periods of loneliness and in their attitudes of waiting. Although Mauriac seldom gives any direct expression to the sexual problem, he is concerned with the degree to which it adumbrates and even controls all other problems. Concupiscence ties up the soul with the body, and becomes in itself an indistinguishable commingling of spiritual aspiration and passionate urgency. Mauriac finds in the sexual origin of each life, not an absolute determinism, but a bent and an inclination which constantly threaten the possible sanctity of human life. Each one is tested to a degree proportionate with his nature, because of this dark origin of the flesh. This is the world of evil, for Mauriac, whose site is the heart. The other world in his novels, of Bordeaux and Les Landes, serves only to delineate more sharply and more poignantly the ancient world of the heart.

As early as 1923, in his novel *Génitrix*, François Mauriac attained to a full expression of his art. Condensation of style, starkness of passion, the isolation of a lonely provincial house are the characteristics of this book as well as of every other major book of Mauriac. He is complete and identical in each novel.

He returns always to the same problem and the same setting, more rigorously perhaps than other artists whose works are repetitions with variations: Molière, Dickens, Henry James. Such an artist usually succeeds five or six times in creating works of remarkable fusion between temperament and subject matter. They willfully repeat the same story until it emerges clear and perfected. *Génitrix* appears as one of the earliest finished masterpieces of Mauriac. The quality of writing, the sense of tragedy and the moral preoccupation in the novel are all integrated in more subtle proportions than in many of the first books.

The opening passage of *Génitrix,* the first five or six lines, indicates with extraordinary precision the involved relationships of three characters, who turn out to be the three main characters of the novel. I know of no other novel whose initial sentences plunge the reader more persuasively into the central drama, or by which the reader's attention is more dramatically or more instantaneously fixed on the psychological problem around which the entire novel is to evolve.

Elle dort.
—Elle fait semblant. Viens.
Ainsi chuchotaient, au chevet de Mathilde Cazenave, son mari et sa belle-mère dont, entre les cils, elle guettait sur le mur les deux ombres énormes et confondues.

She is sleeping.
—She is pretending. Come.
At the bedside of Mathilde Cazenave, her husband and mother-in-law whispered while she watched through half-closed eyes on the wall their huge mingled shadows.

The tone of the opening lines pervades the entire first scene, which serves as prologue to the work.

The young wife, Mathilde Cazenave, is dying. She is morally alone, and physically alone in the large house of her husband's family. Her husband Fernand, and his mother, Mme Félicité Cazenave, have abandoned her at this supreme moment. She is the outsider, deeply hated by her mother-in-law who dominates her son with the tyranny of a matriarch. The miscarriage which Mathilde has just suffered is a triumph for the mother-in-law, who reminds her son as they talk together during the evening that the baby would have been a girl and therefore would not have perpetuated the name of Cazenave.

Mathilde realizes that her mounting fever is fatal and that her death has been planned by Félicité who saw no need of keeping someone in the sick room. Her life history passes before her and especially the failure of her marriage. Hers has been a life without love. Death comes gently to her because she had never been consumed in love. The scene is speechless and Mauriac executes it with brevity and with a tone of abstraction as if he, the creator, watched his creature die without being able to help her. The few simple facts of the case history and the condensed poetic rhythms re-enact the solitude and the desolation of the prologue.

Ce corps allait être consumé dans la mort et il ne l'avait pas été dans l'amour. L'anéantissement des caresses ne l'avait pas préparé à la dissolution éternelle. Cette chair finissait sans avoir connu son propre secret.

This body was going to be consumed in death and had not been consumed in love. The annihilation of caresses had not prepared it for the eternal dissolution. This flesh was ending without having known its own secret.

Then the real drama begins, during the hours when Fernand watches beside the body of his wife and begins to feel for the first time in his life a sense of suffering for someone else. Mathilde has had to die, in order for him to feel united with her against the enemy in the house who had willed their separation. Mathilde's absence becomes a real presence from this time on. Fernand's silence, which characterizes the first scenes between him and his mother after the funeral, are really filled with the inaudible conversation he is carrying on with Mathilde. Once his new character is formed, the second part of the drama breaks out with the series of violent scenes between himself and Félicité. Mathilde grows into the triumphant presence in the house. She alone counts now, as the son and his mother flay one another with their words and their accusations. This second part ends with the paralysis of Mme Cazenave and her death. The intermittent flashes of tenderness which Fernand shows for her during the last months of her life are due, he tells her, to Mathilde's influence, and this represents for the aged woman the greatest defeat and humiliation. At the burial scene, again in the space of five or six lines, Mauriac recapitulates the entire drama and shows the progress in Fernand's character and the new relationship among the three characters. He leans over the grave opened to receive his mother's body, in a desperate effort to catch sight of his wife's casket.

Nul ne comprit qu'il cherchait seulement à discerner, entre toutes ces formes dans l'ombre, la boîte où ce qui fut Mathilde redevenait poussière et cendre.

No one understood that he was really trying to distinguish among the shapes in the darkness, the box in which Mathilde's body was becoming dust and ashes.

The third and final part of *Génitrix* is the justification of the title. Up to this point, Fernand Cazenave had existed in terms of his love and hate for his mother, but now that she has gone he gradually ceases to exist as a human being. During her lifetime she had been the sun goddess, the creator of life, the provider and sustainer. With her extinction Fernand has no longer an orbit in which to revolve. *Le soleil maternel à peine éteint, le fils tournait dans le vide, terre déorbitée.* The old servant in the household, Marie de Lados, who represents fidelity to the faith and to the race, a humble counterpart to the matriarch, assumes now the dominant role of humanity in the house. Félicité was the solar principle, the Paganized concept of *Génitrix*, race-founder, cold and invulnerable. Marie is the earth principle, the obscure repository of the seed, the toiler, whose hands are centuries old and whose life unfolds in the dark. She is not the matriarch who creates and strikes down. She is the mother who reproduces and perpetuates, and she introduces into the Cazenave house, where two women have died and where one man lives in a kind of death, a young boy, Raymond, her grandson. The old servant creates around him the new center of life.

The final scenes of the book are as tragic and bare as all the preceding ones. Enraged at Marie when she tries to seat her grandson at the master's table, Fernand orders them both out of the house. Then for a few hours he knows the experience of total solitude, of total silence which represents the fullest tragedy in this novel of silences and empty rooms. But at the very end, Marie returns to the master's room and stands at the doorway holding a lamp. He calls to her. With the last sentence, therefore, the absolute tragedy ends, and a new history begins.

Génitrix is dedicated to Mauriac's brother, a physician, and the inscription refers to the characters as "patients." But there is always hope for the sick. Even in the creation of the character Félicité, Mauriac reserves a spark of hope. No human life ever closes off irremediably the hope of eternal salvation. Every act of monstrosity and every deformation may be redeemed. Natural love, no matter how far it may be warped, no matter how insidiously it may destroy the object of its love, is never totally cut off from its participation in divine love. The profoundest meaning of *Génitrix* is to be found in the original title which Mauriac had planned to use: *Il n'est qu'un seul amour.* ("There is only one love.") The phrase occurs in the text itself, in connection with the matriarch, in a scene of rage, during which the novelist felt that even the hatred of Félicité for Mathilde concealed an origin of pure love. *Peut-être n'est-il qu'un seul amour,* he writes, and thus testifies to the belief that all manifestations of love, even sinful and harmful forms, rise up from the same unique source. The heart does not cease loving as the body grows old. The ever increasing lethargy of the house is an objective correlative for the aging bodies of Fernand and his mother. But the passion in their hearts does not decrease. It continues, only to grow more and more deviated.

Two years after *Génitrix,* Mauriac published in 1925 *Le Désert de l'Amour,* which may well be the

supreme example of his art. Both the tragedy in the
novel and its form are more measured, more elliptical,
more skillfully fused than ever before in his work. *Le
Désert de l'Amour* is an example of classical art, if
one accepts Gide's definition of classicism as it appears in *Incidences: le classicisme tend tout entier
vers la litote. C'est l'art d'exprimer le plus en disant le
moins. C'est un art de pudeur et de modestie.* This
precept applies as strictly to Racine's art as to
Mauriac's, and one can't help wondering if the fate of
Mauriac's writings will be comparable to Racine's in
being the least accessible of modern French art forms
to other nations. The French have a strong predilection for litotes in art and a permanent tradition in
their literature for a sober condensed casting of the
gravest psychological problems: Scève, Racine, La
Rochefoucauld, Baudelaire, Valéry, Mauriac.

The construction of the novel permits a rapid narration. The opening scene takes place in a Paris bar
where the hero, Raymond Courrèges, aged thirty-
five, is observing his features in a wall mirror and
realizing that the first signs of age are more apparent
on his life than on his face or body. A woman enters
the bar whom he recognizes. She is Maria Cross,
whom he had known about twenty years before in
Bordeaux, and with whom he had fallen in love
when he was eighteen and she twenty-seven. The
meaning of the title is already apparent from this
initial scene. Maria Cross is the woman whom Courrèges considers responsible for the hardness of his
character. He has known many women but has never
been able to fall in love with any of them since his
first wild passion for her. Before he speaks to Maria in
the bar, his mind goes back to the two years of his

youth, between sixteen and eighteen, when he was tormented by his love, and the main part of the novel begins. This is a study (only one among many in Mauriac's writings) of adolescent passion, of the incommunicability of sensuous love, of the strange law by which men fall in love with beings who do not love them. Mauriac says, as Racine did before him, that we do not choose those whom we love. They appear in our lives and we are incapable of not loving them. Hence, the desert of love, the solitude and the barrenness of love.

The story unfolds in a setting of family life which represents, on a first level, the desert of love. Between Raymond and his father, Dr. Courrèges, there exists an abyss of misunderstanding: Raymond feels hostility toward his father, who, in turn, is incapable of expressing to his son any of the paternal tenderness which he feels. There is a similar estrangement between the doctor and his wife and between the other members of the family. This is the background of family incommunicability against which Mauriac sets the dual passion of father and son for the same woman. The love of the doctor for Maria Cross is composed of longing and tenderness. It is middle-aged love, far more idealistic and patient than the son's love for Maria, which is violent and sharp. Two remarkable scenes illustrate the divergence of these loves: Raymond's attack on Maria and his abortive attempt to seduce her; and the doctor's professional visit to Maria when she is ill and the deep love he feels when he examines her body, in his physician's capacity.

Maria's personal drama is more subtle and intricate than that of the two men who pursue her, each according to his own temperament and age. She is characterized essentially by languor. Her most familiar posture is on a bed or divan where, half-dreaming, she tries to fix more clearly the lines of her thought and the forms of her desire. The sensuality of her nature, which is strong intermittently, changes constantly into a maternal kind of tenderness. She is the type of woman who arouses sensuality in men, and then wishes to treat them as children. She prefers the doctor's letters to his visits. After attracting Raymond and desiring him, she finds his advances brutal. As soon as she feels herself desired, she becomes indifferent. The characters around her chose her. She did not choose them. This thought, which Mauriac finds in the mind of Maria Cross, is a further description of the desert of love. *Ah! l'importunité de ces êtres, à qui notre coeur ne s'intéresse pas, et qui nous ont choisis et que nous n'avons pas choisis.* Her passion is idle and languorous. She is consumed in a desert solitude as if she were a modern counterpart, although far less dramatically presented, of Racine's Hermione and Phèdre.

The dramatic quality of Racine's heroines is transposed in Mauriac's art to the adolescent heroes, as in the case of Raymond Courrèges in *Le Désert de l'Amour.* The passion of adolescence is at once the most violent and the most ephemeral. In describing the development and urgency of Raymond's passion, Mauriac has made an admirable use of a tramway in Bordeaux. There Maria and Raymond see each other first and continue to meet daily many times before daring to speak. The tram symbolizes the brevity of these meetings, their chance, their irregularity (Raymond is still a schoolboy and Maria a young woman

ALBERT CAMUS

PAUL VALÉRY

ST.-JOHN PERSE

JEAN COCTEAU SELF-PORTRAIT

JEAN-PAUL SARTRE

who has had a child), and their anonymity. The fact that Maria Cross is ostracized by the society of which his family is a part, intensifies Raymond's attraction to her. There is a kinship between Maria's loneliness in Bordeaux, her role of pariah and languorous courtesan, and the insistent sexuality of the adolescent which cuts him off from the world, as it does every adolescent, especially from the family world in which he had lived as a child before the sexual need clearly pronounced itself.

This theme of the great isolating power of sexuality, apparent notably in adolescence, is one of Mauriac's most persistent themes. It is more overtly developed in *Le Désert de l'Amour* than in other books. The novel seems to derive its form from the sharpness and the relentlessness of the passionate instinct in Raymond Courrèges. His character grows around the new force in him. The central part of the study, which drains and reflects all other parts, is the hero's increasing assurance of his maleness and of his indifference to everything in the world that his body was not created to penetrate. The sentence I have just paraphrased, which concludes the sixth chapter, is an illuminating example of the psychological import of the Mauriac theme and the purified form into which it is cast. *La nuit d'été battait en vain ce jeune mâle bien armé, sûr de son corps, indifférent à tout cela que ce corps n'était pas créé pour pénétrer.* After using the tramway as the symbol of the strangeness and the stark anonymity of the first meetings and longings of Maria and Raymond, Mauriac uses an exterior scene of nature as prelude and prediction for the central scene of attempted seduction. A violent rainstorm ravages the garden outside Maria's house. Raymond crosses it to come to her and can hardly contain the pent-up energies and desires which urge him to perform an awkward and frustrating scene. His passion is wasted like the garden itself and this defeat marks the beginning of his life of hardness, of his desert life in love.

At the end of the novel, after the rapid narration of Raymond's adolescent love, we are back again in Paris, at the chance meeting between him and Maria Cross. He is now a mature man, closer in many ways to his father, and he tests in himself the effect of this woman's presence and words. The fire is still strong and real within him. All his attempts to overcome and forget his passion with minor passions have failed. Raymond concludes—and this represents the psychological and moral conclusion of the book—that everything serves such a passion: that virtue irritates it and debauchery enhances it. His easy conquests, all that he had had in the world, were of no value by comparison with what he had not been able to possess. And thus, the theme of the desert of love joins with that of the mother love, through this second study of the oneness of passion. The son perpetuates the father in *Le Desert de l'Amour* by his fidelity to the unknowable love, as the son perpetuates the mother in *Génitrix* by the unaccountable power which comes to him in his struggle against the matriarch.

Mauriac's dark hero (Jean Péloueyre in *Le Baiser au Lépreux*, Fernand Cazenave in *Génitrix*, Raymond Courrèges in *Le Désert de l'Amour*) illustrates an entire aspect of Pascalian psychology, which still remains, especially in France, the chief source of psychological inquiry in the Christian tradition. According to this aspect of "Pascalism," the human heart is the microcosm of the universe. Each individual heart is the reflector of the universe, the container of immensity. Mauriac studies in his hero's heart its tragic precision and uniqueness. Dostoevsky's writing is very close to this conception of the heart, but Mauriac's art is more concentrated, more precipitous, and therefore more Pascalian.

Mauriac as a novelist combines in a subtle and almost indistinguishable way the roles of Freudian analyst, in his study of the secret disorder, and of the theologian, in his study of the origin of sin. Throughout the Mauriac novel, the deepest part of man is imperiled. It is the dramatic representation in characters of Pascal's wager passage, and one cannot tell which state will win out: grace or damnation. The typical novels, such as *Génitrix* and *Le Désert de l'Amour,* are inconclusive, because the novel, as Mauriac conceives of it, is the story of the peril (or the disorder) in which the dark hero finds himself, and the novel stops at the moment when the peril may come to an end.

Jansenist by temperament, both Pascal and Mauriac carry on in their writings a constant dialogue between appearance and reality. Pascal, abstractly as moralist and philosopher, and Mauriac, concretely as psychologist and novelist, depict the mysterious dignity of sin and the blindness of men who do not love what they think they love. If Mauriac appears Jansenistic by inspiration, he is not so doctrinally because of the freedom of his characters. In them he sees the constant unpredictable interplay of nature and grace. The leading trait of Mauriac's dark hero is perhaps his nostalgia for a lost purity. His hero's soul, no matter how perverted it has grown, is always considered by

Mauriac in its quality of eternality. He is concerned, as Pascal was, with the existential character of the soul, with the wretchedness of the soul without God. Once Mauriac defined himself as being the metaphysician working with the concrete. His excessive use of the word "drama" is a clue. In Mauriac's mind everything becomes a drama: love, passion, family, poverty, nature, evil, religion, grace.

Pascal and Mauriac appear as two lawyers pleading before God for the case of man. The somberness of Mauriac's world recalls that of Proust, but there is nothing of the pleader in Proust. Mauriac believes that each man bears within him much more than himself. An out-and-out sinner is a myth. A man represents an accumulation of inherited tendencies. He is all his ancestors at once, as well as himself. The divisioning and bestowal of grace come from an unknowable system of economics where unpredictable correspondences occur. At the end of each of the two novels we have considered, the dark hero stands, not alone, but in an intricate relationship with his ancestors. He represents them as well as himself before God. But his will is not entirely bent to God, because in that case the devil as well as the novelist would lose his rights over the man's soul.

SIX

LITERATURE AND CATHOLICISM

At all periods of its history French culture has brought to Catholicism a very remarkable understanding. It is not exaggerated to say that without a solid understanding of Catholicism, much of French civilization and literature will remain obscure to the foreign student. François Mauriac has recently commented on the art of Graham Greene and particularly on *The Power and the Glory*. Although he recognized all the theological themes of the book, Mauriac said that the religious atmosphere puzzled him. He felt that he was entering upon Christianity through some back door. The French writer, he claims, has a far different approach. His immediate and distant past have given him a familiarity with Catholic problems. His very education taught him, even when he was without firm religious convictions, to take sides with Port Royal or with the Jesuits, with Bossuet or with Fénelon and Quietism. Although Mauriac greatly admired the almost secretive way Graham Greene treats the religious problem in his writing, which almost corresponds to the subterranean radiation of grace in the world, he confesses to feeling disoriented and even ill at ease in the world of the English novelist.

During the twenty-year period between the two world wars, French literature was given over to a very serious self-examination and self-criticism. Catholic critics, especially, had seemed severe in their analyses and reproaches. Henri Massis, as late as 1941, in a book called *Les Idées Restent*, bitterly attacked Gide, Proust and Valéry for having alienated French intelligence from its real goal, for having undermined the moral precepts of the nation. Claudel has not been sparing of harsh epithets of criticism, in calling the contemporary atmosphere in France morbid and depressing. In time, and in some degree of perspective, such criticism, especially that of Massis, will seem unwarranted and intolerably severe. During the same years, a strong renaissance of Catholic literature and a rehabilitation of Catholic thought were taking place. The study of medieval philosophy, especially Saint Thomas, received a new impetus from the teaching of Etienne Gilson, at the Collège de France, and from Jacques Maritain, at the Institut Catholique. Eminent ecclesiastical figures, such as Monseigneur Verdier, participated actively in the Christian Socialist movements. In the art form of the novel, Catholic thought and sensibility were to play a particularly important part after 1930.

Georges Bernanos died in 1948 and was at that time claimed by the astute and learned critic André Rousseaux as the sole contemporary writer upholding the Catholic tradition in France. It is true that the novels and essays of Bernanos are being read and commented upon more than those of other writers who seem to belong to this tradition. Bernanos was a man of prodigious vitality whose character was marked by opposing traits of violence and tenderness, gaiety and vituperation. Those who approached him saw in him the man of his books. He is remembered especially for his passages of invective and strong polemics. He has often been called the pamphleteer of modern France, the successor of Léon Bloy. The work of Bernanos constitutes a major testimonial of our time. His works will gradually reveal their essential meaning, which is doubtless of a prophetic order. His books are warnings, especially on modern man's loss of liberty, of many kinds: political, economic and humanistic. The extremely dramatic character he confers on belief in Christ will alienate the nonbeliever, as it has done for the work of Léon Bloy.

Bernanos is perhaps today the supreme example of a literary presence in French literature. He recalls and even reincarnates one aspect of French civilization, the baptistry of Rheims and the adventure of the Crusaders. Nothing in his work can really be understood unless it is seen from a Christian perspective, as engaging a real man behind a fictional character and, behind him, a nation, and behind it, the entire world.

Bernanos, like Malraux, writes from an historical viewpoint. His works were written for our time and yet far surpass our time in their attempt to explain it. He was the first to see in the priest the real hero and martyr of the modern world. And he, in the tradition of Léon Bloy, assigned to Catholics their real function of worriers and disturbers of the peace, of consciences never at rest. He hurls his priest into all possible dramas of life, sexuality and death. The background of his stories is the present period in history when the world does not accept miracles and when the Church refuses saints and when the individual soul rejects the idea of perfection. Little wonder that Bernanos, as well as Mauriac and Greene, have been difficult sons of the Church.

For Bernanos, the supernatural is not just one element of life reserved for miracles. It is the light of the divine which remains in the most humble creature. It is the source of every human life and therefore the source of every story. Nothing can exist independent of its presence. The common vocation of humanity is to bring about human perfection by placing it in contact with the divine. The universe of Bernanos, like that of Kierkegaard and Léon Bloy, represents a reaction of Christianity against naturalism. But in this universe of the novelist, God is often manifested as a paradox and as a scandal rather than as a supernatural light. Each age creates its characteristic type of man. For Greece, the sage; for Israel, the prophet; for the medieval world, the saint and the knight; for the classical age, the *honnête homme*. Bernanos believes that the modern world has created a type of man who is mediocre in intelligence and satisfied with himself, the tepid Christian, the complacent priest. This mediocrity he associates with Satanism and judges it far more pernicious than earlier more melodramatic manifestations of the devil's presence. No one has stigmatized the middle class more violently than Bernanos. He calls them *la canaille bourgeoise* who applauded the conquest of Ethiopia, the Munich pact, the Vichy government.

The architecture of *La Joie* is, even more than that

of *Sous le soleil de Satan,* the expression of a temperament. We read what pours out from the heart of Bernanos. His particular vision of the world impels him to write, and he is guided by enthusiasms and indignations. The book is a study of a young girl, Chantal, who finds herself surrounded by a strange world of beings: by Fiodor, a Russian chauffeur, who stalks her and watches her; by her father, a millionaire professor, who lives in ostentatious surroundings; by a mad grandmother, a psychiatrist, and a priest who has lost his faith. In their midst, Chantal, invulnerable in her truthfulness, harbors within herself the secret of sanctity. Her simplicity is her only ruse, and all the members of the household: servants, relations, doctors, try in vain to discover whether Chantal's secret is madness or holiness. The most striking parts of Bernanos' novel are the long dialogues between Chantal and her father, Chantal and the psychiatrist, Chantal and the priest. There are elements of drama in these dialogues, but Chantal lives in so separate and unique a world that the art of the dialogues consists chiefly in two differing and implacably opposed statements on holiness and worldliness.

For the past hundred years, the religious problem in French literature has been more profoundly reflected in poetry, although it has often been poetry not rigorously, not doctrinally Catholic. For this period of a century, when the Catholic spirit has not been universally persuasive in France, when it has been put to many tests and undergone many attacks, its particular expression in poetry (and especially in the three poets who seem to testify to three cardinal aspects of its problem) is the most valid, because it is at once bound up with the eternal spirit of Catholicism and with the specific drama and dilemma of modern man.

Charles Baudelaire is the source of modern poetry, and the poet in whom the spiritual problem appears both in its most agonized and most transcendent form. The creation of beauty for Baudelaire contains the promise of a spiritual deliverance. He was haunted all his life by a sense of tragic dualism and a need to discover a way to effect a unity and harmony between these two opposing forces of good and evil. The foundation of Baudelaire's aesthetics, as well as the foundation of his personal moral problem, is stated in his *Journaux Intimes,* when he says that as a child he felt two contradictory sentiments, the horror and the ecstasy of life. The opening sentence of *Mon coeur mis à nu* states the same idea: "Everything is in the vaporization and the centralization of the self." Honest with himself, Baudelaire never claimed to have known the mystical form of ecstasy, the result of assiduous prayer and religious ardor. His ecstasy was more sensational, more voluptuous, and at the end of it he sought not love, nor truth, but some revelation of beauty, beauty the source of the unknown. His way is mystical in only the broadest sense. It is really a poetical mysticism. He calls the principle of poetry, human aspiration toward a superior beauty. Its manifestation is in an enthusiasm, a rapture of the soul.

This instinct or aspiration toward beauty makes us, according to Baudelaire, consider the world a "correspondence" of heaven. Our yearning for another life is the proof of our immortality. By means of poetry, we half see the beauty of the purely spiritual world. Swedenborg had helped Baudelaire formulate this theory. The notion of analogy leads one to the doctrine of "correspondences," which, in its turn, leads to the theory of Symbolism. Nature is a temple, each part of which has a symbolic meaning. The poet is the one who finds in nature a "dark profound unity." Baudelaire's book, *Les Fleurs du Mal,* reveals a constant search, impeded by velleity or impotence, to get out from himself and master his fate. He certainly believed that artistic creation contained the possibility of his salvation. When he speaks of religion in his *Journaux,* it seems to be a last recourse of a desperate man, not an experience which engages his entire being. He was always skillful at forming resolutions and incapable of following them out. His destiny was that of a seeker, a voyager, moving toward the unknown, the different. He made no arrival. He was unable to change his original condition. His was the ambition of the poet-priest, capable of changing the world, of recreating the world by the word. His system was one of analogies and correspondences, where the poet appears as decipherer of hieroglyphics, as reader of the book of creation. All the elements of Baudelaire's great ambition, which have guided subsequent poets, were felt and practiced by him as a means of uniting his life with that of the world, of discovering behind the individual and the ephemeral, the universal and the eternal. Baudelaire's is the myth of a lost paradise, of an Orpheus no longer able to enchant the animals and bewitch all nature.

The second case history in modern French poetry and infinitely more mysterious than that of Baudelaire, is Rimbaud's. His life as poet was a dazzling brief period of four or five years. Ever since it terminated, it has been examined by countless critics and historians, each anxious to arrive at a solution, an explanation of the adolescent destiny. There seem to be as many solutions as there are critics, but all agree on the essential mystery of this life, a mystery of a spiritual order, and one that may well contain the clue to modern man's spirituality or search for a spiritual absolute.

Rimbaud has been defined by all the opposites: Catholic and Pagan, visionary and rascal, Surrealist and Marxist, the devil and God. He has been compared to Julien Sorel, to Villon, Faust, Prometheus, Icarus, Peer Gynt, Adam, the two Saint Theresas, the four Evangelists, Ezekiel, Isaiah, Orestes, the Messiah. Rather than using any one of these names, or discovering a further prototype, let us consider him the modern poet, the almost purely intuitive poet who repudiated the logic of philosophers and doctrinaires. He was the visual poet, the *voyant*, aggressive and revolutionary by temperament, who had alienated the conventional approaches to God and to love. He willed to make himself into a magus, a magician, a *voyant*. But the magic he learned to control was poetry. Although he scorned the trivial exercise of writing poetry in the usual way.

For Rimbaud, the true poet has not yet arisen. We do not yet know what a poet is. But he tells us that the first study of a man is to know himself, the true self, to cultivate himself. In this process of self-knowing, poetry depends on the discovering of the hidden self, of the other personality that we are. *Je est un autre* ("I is another"), wrote Rimbaud, and I suppose that no sentence of modern times has elicited so much commentary. In this work of a poet, man finally reaches the unknown, according to Rimbaud's formula, which is reminiscent of Baudelaire.

The world we live in is conventional and fabricated. We have to reach another realer world. One would not have to go farther than this to sense the deep spirituality of all of Rimbaud's formulas. His poetic experience was always close to the mystical, although I do not believe it ever became that, literally. The poet he defined as the re-creator of the world. Before engaging upon such a destiny, his life was characterized by a denial of everything, by insults, insolences, vagabond voyages, seductions. From today's perspective, it is possible to see this violent period as a *chasse spirituelle,* a name given to a Rimbaud manuscript which has been lost. If Rimbaud was not the illuminated mystic, he was the hallucinated poet who created a whole new world in his *Illuminations,* only to find that it was really a subjective world and the confession of the deepest part of himself. What he thought was self-exploration and self-knowledge was, in part at least, nostalgia for some lost purity, for some original innocence.

The precise way in which Rimbaud helped Claudel, in revealing to him his mission of a religious poet, will always remain a mystery. Deep within a poetic work which seems largely to be composed of revolt and blasphemy, Claudel discovered traces of a religious drama which spoke directly to him and to which he owed his return to Catholicism. In his preface to the work of Rimbaud, he tries to analyze systematically the phases of Rimbaud's drama which had taken on such limitless importance for him. Rimbaud's violent period, Claudel interprets as the necessary mutation of genius, the sentimental reaction to his world. The visionary phase, the *voyance* of Rimbaud, Claudel calls the way of the spirit. The magnificent images of the literal *Illuminations* were preparation to seeing truth. The final phase Claudel calls that of belief where, as in the last pages of *Une Saison en Enfer*, Rimbaud greets beauty and its radiant simplicity. Claudel believes that Rimbaud accomplished a mission in the world, that of a violent reaction against positivism. His theory of Rimbaud being a Catholic poet has been developed by other subsequent critics. The value of this interpretation, which I do not myself share, has been to invest Rimbaud's poetic imagination with a profundity that it deserves.

The most ardent admirers of Claudel have not hesitated to compare him with Dante. The reading of Rimbaud and the religious experience he himself underwent at the age of eighteen changed the world for Claudel. These were revelations whereby he saw the world as the work of God and worthy of the song and praise of the poet. This was the genesis of his great theme of joy, the one reality for Claudel, the one requirement for the making of an artistic work. Without it, he believes that man has nothing to say. But a conversion is only a beginning. A new Catholic has to learn two things, a way of renouncing the world, of giving up all passions except the Divine Passion, and the way of acquiring spiritual powers—*membres spirituels,* as Claudel calls them—with which to reconstruct all of one's former knowledge. There are many ways to do this, ways dependent on the individual's temperament and aptitude, but they have to include the two pivotal forces of love and knowledge.

Claudel has not been reluctant in describing the stages of his spiritual development which in many instances resemble those of an authentic mystical experience. In China, his *Vers d'Exil* described his boredom and disgust with his early suffering; the solitude he needed, and the Presence he finally came to. There, he studied attentively the two *Summas* of Saint Thomas, which encouraged his love for syntheses and unifications. Mallarmé had taught him something of the symbolic structure of the universe and Rimbaud something of the creative power of language. These two lessons were gradually illuminated by medieval philosophy. He discovered that religious symbolism and poetic symbolism are the same, and that in addition to the logic of a syllogism, there exists the logic of analogy and metaphor. Aquinas had called the universe "a general sacrament which speaks to us of God, of all good and all beauty, principle of the ideal which the artist tries to reproduce, supreme end of all that was, is and will be, sovereign rule of all that we should do."

Such a text was for Claudel both a discovery and a confirmation of what he had learned through the poets. Saint Thomas completed the work of Mallarmé, in providing Claudel with a theocentric aesthetics according to which the universe is the mirror of God. The world for Claudel, with his faith of a medieval artisan, is a textbook which can be read and must be read. It speaks to us of two things. First, of its own limitation, of its own "absence," as Mallarmé would say. And secondly, of the presence of its Creator. Claudel contrasts the sorcerer's book, *le grimoire* of the Symbolist poets, with the Word, the *Logos* in which everything has been uttered. He was not, in any profound sense, the disciple of the Symbolists, and yet his work represents the accomplishment and the culmination of many themes of

Symbolism, especially those whose purpose was the understanding and the demonstration of the poetic act.

By temperament Claudel belongs to the race of revolutionaries and conquerors, poets such as D'Aubigné and Rimbaud, but also close to Mallarmé in his will to define poetry in its essence. From Mallarmé, Claudel learned especially his lesson on the metaphor, the essential element of his poetics. He learned that a metaphor is a relationship between two objects. It may even be a relationship between God and the world. The poet's role is to apprehend, to seize the metaphors which exist in the world. This means naming each object and restoring it to its rightful place in a new ordering of the universe, in a new lexicon of the world. Each time that Claudel states that with each new breath of a man, the world should appear new to him, as fresh and virginal as it appeared to the first man, with his first breath, he is reiterating Mallarmé's belief about the metaphor, about the endless metaphorical richness of the world. By naming an object, the poet gives it its meaning, as God had originally done when He created the world by naming it. The total word, or the total poem, is, therefore, the universe. Each poet bears in himself a picture of the universe, a subjective maze of images which have relationships with one another. Mallarmé follows an instinctive quest in naming various objects and seeking to understand their metaphorical meaning. Claudel goes farther in willing this quest as if it were a religious obligation. Symbolism, under the initial guidance of Mallarmé, was a spiritual way of understanding and celebrating the universe. It became later in the art of Paul Claudel a more frankly religious way of discovering in the midst of endless variety a secret unity. In his *Art Poétique* of 1903, Claudel states that the metaphor is the logic of the new poetry, comparable to the syllogism of the older logic. Things in the world are not only objects to be known, they are means by which man is being constantly reborn. He had not altered his basic belief when, in 1925, he commented on Mallarmé's *Igitur* and called the world not a sorcerer's handbook, *grimoire,* but the Word engendering all things.

Our civilization seems to have lost the meaning of a bond between man and the universe. Through the centuries this relationship had been expressed in painting, tragedy, poetry, religion. The symbolic form, used by the imagination of poets and theologians to interpret this relationship, had been weakened by the rational spirit which has been so persistently encouraged by the development of science. The conquests of science have not been successful in protecting and strengthening this necessary liaison between man and the world in which he lives. Against this background of thought, certain writers, like Sartre and Camus today, have judged as fables the relationships between man and the universe instituted by religious belief. They declare the universe a meaningless void in which man is condemned to live without those images capable of relating him to everything which transcends him, to the seemingly absurd fate of suffering and death.

Man limited to himself has become the theme of much of our contemporary literature. In the stories of Kafka and in the thrillers of Graham Greene, he appears as a traveler lost in a strange world with which he has nothing in common. Writers have tried to define man within himself, limited to his own existence, and violently aware of his limitations and stifled by them. In periods when the cosmic relationship of man was too systematically defined, as at the end of the medieval period, this relationship was greatly weakened by its conformity. Positivism, at the turn of this century, seemed to have destroyed the meaning of the sacred. And yet such a cosmic poet as Claudel was able to rise up at just that time. Malraux and Saint-Exupéry questioned whether man is not accomplishing his mission when he faces the absurd and the perilous in the world. Mauriac and Bernanos ask the same question about man facing the supernatural.

In a century inspired on the whole by a positivistic spirit and attitude, literature has become a dialogue between man and all that is inhuman, and a dialogue between man and the supernatural. The Catholic novel today, perhaps even more than "existentialist" writing, shows man to be an ambiguous reality. The possibility of choosing against God is an indication of the greatness of man's freedom, although the fact of choosing against God limits and immobilizes this freedom in a low stage of its development.

In such novelists as Greene, Waugh, Bloy, Mauriac, Bernanos, a similar definition of man's freedom occurs. This freedom is expressed in a willingness to have no other right than that of choosing God. It is primarily a question of transforming man's fate into a vocation. He is "called" to rise above the level of fatalistic determinism to the exercise of his freedom. The Catholic novel, then, will, in some way or other, point out the supernatural vocation of man. Whether he succeeds or fails, the story in human terms is tragic.

The "thriller," used by Graham Greene, is a contemporary form of writing calculated to arouse in the reader some of the strongest and most fundamental emotions. In this sense, it has a distinct relationship with Greek tragedy. The world is a jungle. Men, within the conventions of the thriller, are able to consecrate themselves to good or to evil. The thriller is based on the conviction that the character of human destiny is tragic. The form of the thriller has come into prominence today perhaps because of a belief concerning the essentially antitragic contemporary world. It is antitragic because of the absence of virtuous exaltation, of the powers of pure enthusiasm which seems to be generated by belief in the sacred. Tragic man originally meant "greater-than-man." The real problem of suffering is whether there exists a good reason for suffering. Precisely, this loss of the meaning of tragedy will tend to make life intolerable. The present-day interest in the thriller, as exemplified in the writings of Graham Greene, comes not so much from a desire for escape as an attempt to discover the real nature of man. The thriller is able to release some of the intimate feelings and powers of man which have been stifled by the modern antitragic period. This form of fiction allows men who have lost sight of the meaning of their destiny, to recover metaphorically some vision of their tragedy.

In the modern novel, not only in Catholic writers, but in Existentialists as well, the doctrine of fate has been substituted for the traditional psychological motivation. The universe of Graham Greene is not obviously permeated with the supernatural. His human-

ity has something of the Existentialist anguish of man
facing the limitlessness of his freedom, the weakness
of his will and his responsibility in an absurd world.
The world of Georges Bernanos is characterized by
the scandalous appearance of holiness and damnation.
Whereas the power of Satan in Graham Greene's
work is manifested in his perfected incognito (Gide
has written that we serve the devil best by believing
he does not exist), he is clearly incarnated in the
writings of Bernanos.

The Augustinian tradition in Catholic theology has
emphasized the degradation of sinful humanity, but it
has never neglected the possibility of man's triumph
and the reversibility of good works. In the characters
of Greene and Bernanos, in differing degrees, there is
evident the slow and sometimes terrifying progress
of Divine Love seeking to make its way through a des-
olate world. In ancient tragedy, the sinner was unconscious of the full meaning of his deeds and of his
fate. But in the characters of Greene and Bernanos,
as in those of Dostoevsky, tragedy has become specifically Christian because the sinner knows the import
of his acts and knows where they are leading him.

The literary expression in novels and poetry given
to Catholicism today can hardly be studied without some knowledge of what it means to be a Christian in the contemporary world. The Christian is
both very old and very young, by his dual participation in time and eternity. By comparison with the
Sartrian man, about ten years old, and the Marxian
and the Nietzschean man, both about one hundred
years old, the Christian is 2,000 years old. If Christ
really lives in him, the Christian is the type of perfect

man, the center of history, the reason why the world was created. The Christian does not expect any other Messiah. What he has to do, through the centuries which began with the Incarnation and which will end with the end of the world, is to use the virtues and powers which are divinely his. Péguy warned Christians against speaking in just this way, with such pomposity and assurance. If the message of Christianity is not heeded universally today, the Christians themselves are to blame. They have not been very skillful in solving the problem of the relationships between man and the world of history and the world of science.

What is the Christian meaning of history? Marxists particularly have accused Christians of turning their backs on life, of repudiating what is now called collectivism. This complaint can be justified. The Christian is torn between his nostalgia for the kingdom of God and his conscience urging him to participate in the temporal unfolding of history. But this conflict does not date from our period. Roman magistrates accused the earliest Christians of undermining the Empire, of stressing the individual conscience to the detriment of the state worship. The same remarks have been used by Marx, Lenin, Mussolini, Hitler. The Christian will always, to some extent, be unassimilated, falsely nationalist, falsely revolutionary. He will always be a public danger, in the sense that his mind is more fixed on eternity than on the imperious and pressing needs of any society or race or class or clan. He will always be tempted by the desert. God's love has made him a captive, and the very weight of that love draws him out of the world, toward invisible things. He belongs to that other society of the saints, and he is always repeating as did the earliest Christians, "May this world pass and may grace come!"

Even if he does not fully realize it, the Christian is always secretly an anchorite fleeing the world. Certain phrases from the Gospels have branded themselves in his soul and he can do nothing about them, sentences about the insignificance of gaining the world if he lose his soul, about the kingdom of Christ not being of this world, about the need to lose one's life in order to save it. Saint Paul taught that "the world rests in evil." The lives and writings of saints and ascetics for centuries have underscored this Christian impulse toward retirement and pessimism. But that is only one aspect of the Christian revelation. The other, equally important and forming the great paradox, is the central mystery of the Christian faith, that of the Incarnation, by which God became man and dwelt among men in this world of iniquity. If the Christian excluded himself from the world and history, he would betray Christ as the incarnate word. The Christian's position is not easy to hold, because he belongs both to heaven and earth. He must first fill himself with the spirit of God and then cause it to live in the midst of sin and matter. Supernaturalism and naturalism are his two worlds, in neither one of which he is allowed to live exclusively. Supernaturalism alone would separate him from the world, and naturalism alone would separate him from God.

The great lesson of the Incarnation has become the pivotal theme of contemporary Catholic literature. It teaches that the supernatural destiny of the Christian is, to a large degree, ordered and governed by the particular condition of human life he knows. Time itself is a kind of determinant for eternity. Péguy has written in one of his most moving passages that we lead a life temporally eternal. *Nous menons une vie temporellement éternelle.* The tree of grace is deeply rooted. *L'arbre de la grâce est raciné profond.* This is why the Catholic believes he has chosen everything by joining the two kingdoms of God and the world. To a Catholic the Marxian solution which states that materialism will lead to a society without class distinctions and where the exploitation of man by man will be abolished, seems oversimplified, unwarrantedly optimistic. History is made by men, and like them, is a complex of good and evil. In it there are forces of disintegration and selfishness which lead to its ruin, and also forces of generosity and love which transform the world and are constantly saving it. The same kind of struggle is going on in the heart of each man. The Christian believes that the powers of truth and justice are always deeply working in the world, even if at times they are not visible and not felt. History is as ambivalent as man. The artist who works more in darkness than in light will be more apt to depict man as unaware of the forces of good working in him. This is true of many contemporary French Catholic artists.

If the Incarnation is the central doctrine of the Christian faith, two other doctrines are placed as extreme poles of the faith, protecting and defining it. First, the Creation, which plunges us back in history long before the flood, affirming the dependence of the world on God who made all things. And the other, the resurrection of the body, which forces us to look way ahead into the future toward a cosmic optimism that exceeds all our powers of imagination and which leads us to believe that, thanks to our body, the material universe may be saved. Saint Paul, on this doctrine, said, "Nature will be delivered from the bondage of corruption." This text contradicts the overfamiliar opposition of body and soul, flesh and spirit. Existentialism has called attention to the Christian belief in the abjection of man. Pascal, long before Sartrian Existentialism, wrote of the old opposition of nature and grace. This Catholic tradition in which the body is considered evil has been exaggerated by Catholic literature. For some time, Catholic literature has been one of original sin and concupiscence. One wonders if Claudel, of all the authors referred to in this chapter, is the only one close to the Dominican interpretation: grace does not destroy nature, but perfects it and raises it. Despair is not the ultimate secret. Claudel believes in a theocentric humanism. Nothing is more exultant than this conception of the universe. When the Word became flesh, it assumed the universe.

PART III

SEVEN

THEATRE AND CINEMA

Americans visiting Paris since the war have been struck by the number of plays in production and by the richness of their variety. It is not unusual to see forty plays advertised simultaneously at the height of the theatrical season, many of which are new plays while others are revivals of fairly recent successes or are taken from the classical repertory. Parisians have always loved the theatre and continue to love it. It is for them a manifestation of contemporary life and contemporary criticism. Events in society and politics are often magnified in the theatre where they may take on the form of polemics, a favorite genre of the French. Each year the Folies-Bergère changes its elaborate spectacle, and each year the more modest musical reviews of the boulevards change their show in order to keep up with the times, with the political figures, the world events, the scandals. The same stars reappear year after year. Parisians prefer aging politicians and aging dancers. Their taste is classical

187

in that they like to recognize the same traits on the stage and welcome back the favorites at the beginning of each season. This applies even to the American Josephine Baker, who first danced in Paris in 1925. Her costume that year was a string of bananas around her waist. In 1950 she was still dancing and singing, although she then wore gowns with trains five yards long.

This last decade and a half of the French theatre began under the German Occupation. The theatres in Paris during those difficult years became the site of a subtle plotting against the enemy. The Germans, on the whole, preferred the opera and the movies. For four years the theatres in Paris were extremely prosperous and produced difficult plays which helped to bind the French together and to consecrate their threatened tradition. The trials of each day and the constant surveillance of the enemy performed paradoxically a service to the arts of the theatre. In the 1943-44 season alone, three new plays of exceptional quality were produced: *Sodome et Gomorrhe* of Giraudoux, *Les Mouches* of Sartre, and *Antigone* of Anouilh. During the Occupation and since then, the theatres of Paris have produced plays of Claudel, Supervielle, Audiberti. On the whole they have not been plays of character study. They tend to concentrate on an event which excites men. The new plays seem to prefer cataclysmic events to the hero who dominates or fails to dominate the events. This characterizes the theatre of Sartre, whose *Huis Clos* (*No Exit*) revealed his free and supple genius, and of Camus, whose *Caligula* was a revelation, but whose recent plays, *L'Etat de Siège* and *Les Justes* have been unsuccessful.

The dramatic genres are impurely mixed in the plays of the last decade. Giraudoux mingles the pathetic with the ironic in every scene. Claudel joins the sublime with the realistic or the trite. Anouilh and Roussin are constantly converting the comic into the tragic, and this applies to so many of the contemporary plays that the terms comic and tragic have lost any well-defined meaning. As in London and New York, the spectacle, the physical production, has been so lavish that it has often submerged the text. In an attempt to rival the movies, spectacular productions have saturated the theatre. With the result that it has been, ever since 1945, and increasingly so, an expensive and often ruinous enterprise. The theatre has always made excessive demands on its actors, and these last years have been no exception. The great actress Moréno, when she was playing *La Folle de Chaillot,* said at an intermission: *Voyez-vous, l'essentiel, c'est de durer.* At that time, when she was over seventy, she was making a film during the day, playing *La Folle* each night, and between times writing her *Memoirs.*

One of the great accomplishments of the contemporary theatre in France is the reconciliation it has made with poetry. The pure poetic language of Claudel, Gide, Giraudoux, Camus and Montherlant is far different from the speech of the realists and naturalists of the preceding period. What would have been an avant-garde movement in another period is the central movement today. It would be difficult in 1957 to startle the theatre-going bourgeois. Revolutions or radical changes have always been rare in the history of the theatre. The past decades have not been fertile in new dramatic tendencies. *Les Bonnes,* a play by Jean

Genet, irritated many, but did not disappoint the few who were held by the play's originality. *Les Epiphanies* of Henri Pichette, in his early twenties, was the boldest theatrical adventure of the forties. It is really a poem in several voices, admirably interpreted by two of the most gifted young actors: Maria Casarès and Gérard Philipe. It was played on the smallest stage in Paris, Les Noctambules, the former theatre for chansonniers in the Latin Quarter. In the course of the decade, the French theatre lost four great figures: Christian Bérard, the most remarkable of the contemporary stage designers, whose set for Cocteau's *Machine Infernale* in 1934 is still remembered; Jean Giraudoux, who reinvented the lyric theatre in France; André Gide, far less associated with the theatre than Giraudoux and Bérard, but whose plays and adaptations have been performed especially during the last ten years; and finally, in August 1951, Louis Jouvet.

At the turn of the half-century, in 1950, three generations of writers were actually represented in the Paris theatres. To the oldest generation, born about 1870, belong Paul Claudel, who died in 1955, and Gide, who died in 1951. To these very celebrated names should be added that of Alfred Jarry, who died in 1907. Jarry's play, *Ubu-Roi*, produced in 1895, was the forerunner of the avant-garde theatre of the following generation. The imbecile vain character, Ubu-Roi, is already a classic figure in the French theatre. Some critics have not hesitated to compare the play, because of its fresh comic style, with Aristophanes, Shakespeare and Molière.

The "case" of Claudel is the most striking for this

oldest generation in terms of the theatre. One of his plays is world famous today, *L'Annonce faite à Marie,* which went through three versions, in 1892, 1900 and 1912. Two of his plays, *L'Otage* and *Le Pain Dur,* have been playing in smaller theatres, and two of the major plays, *Partage de Midi* and *Le Soulier de Satin,* have received productions in the largest theatres.

In 1906, one hundred and fifty copies of *Partage de Midi* were privately printed. But further publication was withheld by Claudel until 1948, when he reissued the text and gave permission for its performance. Ten years previously Jean-Louis Barrault had asked Claudel for permission to put on *Partage de Midi;* but the poet had refused, saying at the time, "You will play it after my death." He was present at the rehearsals and introduced many changes in the text. But in speaking with the actors about himself in connection with *Partage de Midi,* he would say, "the author of this play." It is well known that the play is the literary expression of an episode in Claudel's personal life.

The drama concerns only four characters. Their speeches are long, but sober and bare. Each scene resembles a musical composition of two or three or four voices which reproduce a great variety of moods and tempi. In reading the play, the language seemed sufficient unto itself and one almost resented the idea of a theatrical representation. But the Barrault production was something of a revelation. The text came to life in a new way, and now it will be impossible to read the play without hearing the voices of the four actors at the Marigny and seeing them move about the stage. The production was not overstylized. The

language of Claudel controlled and dominated all
the movement, as if the actors had only to understand
it and recite it in order to discover their action and
their moods. The play remained at all times a majestic
verbal quartet of which each motif was audible and
in harmony with all the other motifs. Ysé, the
heroine (admirably played by Edwige Feuillère),
pursues in the three men around her, her husband
and two lovers, an assurance or stability which no
one can give her and which she will find only in
death. She is the dominant character of the play and
incarnates the principal idea, defined in Claudel's
own terms as "the spirit desiring against the flesh."
Mésa, the leading male character (played by Barrault), is precisely the one whom Ysé desires the most
and who is for her the most inaccessible. He incarnates not only the lover who comes to a woman for
the first time but also that secret force in a man
which he is eternally unwilling to yield to human
love. The action of the play transpires between the
moment of noon (*partage de midi*) when each character makes a decision separating himself from
his previous life, and the moment of midnight (*partage de minuit*) when the tragedy occurs and death
comes to join Ysé and Mésa.

Claudel's greatest play, *Le Soulier de Satin*, was
written in 1930, twenty-five years after *Partage de
Midi*, of which it is in reality an elaborate amplifi-
cation. It was not played until 1943, when Jean-
Louis Barrault, by cutting the text considerably, made
an acting version for the Comédie-Française, which
took four hours in performance. It was revived in
1949, and with it Claudel seems to dominate the contemporary theatre. *Le Soulier de Satin* is a long poem

which possesses a tremendous dynamics. In the tragic meaning it gives to human existence, it stands as a summation of twelve centuries of Catholicism in France.

In February 1951 Gide died, just after the première of his *Caves du Vatican,* a play adapted by himself from his novel of the same title. Gide, in recent years, had been associated with the theatre through his translations and adaptations of Kafka's *Trial* and Shakespeare's *Hamlet.* One of his early works, *Le Retour de l'Enfant Prodigue,* was recently presented as a play by a group of young actors in Paris. Gide wrote three full-length plays: *Saül, Le Roi Candaule* and *Oedipe,* which until now have not received the attention they deserve. *Oedipe* was performed at Avignon in 1949, in a striking new production by one of the leading theatre directors in France, Jean Vilar. After Gide's death, Vilar revived his production of *Oedipe* for Paris at Barrault's Théâtre Marigny. In this very carefully delineated and intellectualistic production, Oedipus, played by Vilar himself, is fully recognizable as the predestined tragic hero, but he is also, in the Gidean sense, the champion of the gratuitous act. Gide's Oedipus is more impertinent than the Greek model, and the drama combines with elements of parody. Dramatically speaking, the scenes of Oedipus' revolt against God are more interesting than those of his final submission to fate. The play, because of its production by Vilar following the death of Gide, took on the solemnity and significance of a final testament. The text is concerned with the conflict which Gide had studied the most assiduously throughout his long career: that existing between a religious disquietude, which denies that life has suf-

ficient meaning unless it appeals to something supernatural, and a humanistic acceptance of the condition of man in the universe without any aspiration toward the divine.

It is somewhat paradoxical that at the end of a long
life largely given over to reading, meditation, writing
and in part to lecturing and the direction of a literary
magazine, Gide should be involved in the theatrical
productions of his plays. No literary work of our age
has reached more directly and influenced more profoundly the public for which it was written than the
work of Gide. That is one aspect of his achievement
and probably one that gave him tremendous satisfaction. He remained, even through the last years, a remarkably present writer. His is not a lucid work, but
it is a mirror in which every kind of reader can see his
own individual torment, especially the youthful audience Gide has never ceased holding and upsetting.
This effect of presence and urgency which Gide has
had on his readers was not secured for any length of
time by either Barrès or Malraux, the two writers, a
forerunner and a successor, with whom Gide has
been compared in terms of the extent of their influence over the young.

The last photograph taken of Gide was at the Comédie-Française, at the première of his *Caves du Vatican*. It is the photograph of an old man in a tuxedo,
smiling at the official glory and recognition of the
moment. The theatre has always attracted the French
writer, and Gide was no exception. In the theatre itself, Gide welcomed the homage of Paris, the general
approbation he had never received before. It might
almost be regretted that he had outlived the period

when his work appeared revolutionary and even shocking.

The generation after Gide and Claudel has made many important contributions to the history of the French theatre. This generation, born in the 1880's, gave four or five of the most imaginative experimental directors the French stage has ever known, most of whom are now dead. The oldest and perhaps the most gifted of them all was Jacques Copeau, founder of the Vieux-Colombier, an experimental theatre in the highest sense and a training ground for many who were subsequently to found their own theatres. Charles Dullin of the Atelier, Gaston Baty of the Théâtre Montparnasse, Georges Pitoëff of the Mathurins, Jouvet of the Athénée, perpetuated and embellished the work of Copeau.

The four outstanding playwrights of this middle generation all started writing in other forms and turned to the theatre only after achieving fame in some other literary connection. The last to turn to the theatre was the novelist François Mauriac, who saw his first play produced at the Comédie-Française in 1938. *Asmodée* is a well-constructed play which has continued in the repertory. In the four or five plays he has written, of which only the first, *Asmodée*, and the most recent, *Le Feu sur la Terre,* have been really successful, Mauriac has remained faithful to the earliest themes of his novels. Although he has lived in Paris for some years now, Mauriac remains as a dramatist what he was as a novelist, the provincial from Bordeaux or the country around Bordeaux, tormented by the religious problem. In the column he has written for many years in *Le Figaro,* Mauriac has commented on all the major events and problems of the contemporary world, and has become thereby a kind of spiritual director of a vast number of Frenchmen. His messages and judgments are guided by his deep faith of a Catholic, and his plays, also, but far more obliquely, reflect his moral and theological convictions. The title of his most recent play, *Le Feu sur la Terre,* refers to a literal fire which destroyed some forests of Les Landes and thereby impoverished some of the wealthy landowners. But the subtitle of the play reveals the real subject matter: *Le pays sans chemins,* "The land without roads," which refers to the passions of a family group and the violent drama resulting from the love of a sister for her brother.

Like Mauriac, Henri de Montherlant was a well-known and highly regarded novelist in the thirties. And like Mauriac, he turned to the theatre in the forties. In 1942, *La Reine Morte,* the first of his so-called costume plays, was revived by the Comédie-Française. *Le Maître de Santiago,* of 1948, illustrates admirably the classical origins of his style, and the type of character he enjoys depicting: the man who refuses the exterior trappings of life and isolates himself in a literal and moral asceticism. Le Maître appears haughty and disdainful, almost a character from Corneille. *Malatesta* was published some time before it was performed by Jean-Louis Barrault at the Marigny, in 1951. Both vanity and cynicism are in the character of Malatesta, who is caught in a position of inferiority. To these historical plays, which in part resemble the blood tragedies of the Elizabethan theatre, Montherlant has added a few plays in modern dress and setting, such as *Fils de Personne* and *Celles qu'on prend dans ses bras,* where the text is as classically stripped and bare as in the others. The pure elegance of style in Montherlant's plays rivals the vigor and clarity with which he describes human life and motivation. He claims, with a certain amount of justification, that in his plays he shouts out loud the secrets that are usually whispered. *Dans mon théâtre j'ai crié les hauts secrets qu'on ne peut dire qu'à voix basse.*

No contemporary playwright receives such a varied press as Montherlant. In 1948-49, at the moment when the revival of *La Reine Morte* at the Comédie-Française was being lavishly praised, Montherlant presented a new play, *Demain il fera jour,* a continuation of *Fils de Personne,* which has excited more serious hostility than any other of his works. It is a drama on the theme of cowardice and fear, which Montherlant must have known himself was going to arouse public opinion. And yet the tragic sentiment in the play is so pure that it recalls Greek tragedy. It has been called "tragedy in modern dress" (*tragédie en veston*). Giraudoux, in his *Electre,* treats a Greek theme from a modern viewpoint. Anouilh, in his *Antigone,* has transposed a Greek theme into a modern tragedy. And Montherlant, in *Demain il fera jour,* in the play's spirit and expression, has composed a modern Greek tragedy. It is Greek especially in the simplicity of its action and sentiments. It may well be more purely Greek than the other contemporary plays on specifically Greek subjects. The father at the beginning of the play refuses to allow his seventeen-year-old son to join the Resistance movement. (The date of the action is 1944, in Paris.) But on receiving a threatening letter denouncing him for appearing pro-German, the father revokes his decision and sends his son into the Resistance group, where, on his first mission, the boy is killed.

Throughout 1952, Henri de Montherlant refused to give permission for performances of his newest play, *La Ville dont le Prince est un Enfant*. The title is taken from a verse of *Ecclesiastes:* "Woe to thee, O land, when thy king is a child, and thy princes eat in the morning!" The setting of the play is a boys' school directed by priests. It reveals with sobriety and concision a drama, a moment of intense crisis and solution which take place within the walls of the school. The boldness of the theme could easily have lent itself to vulgarity, but the seriousness of Montherlant's style and the dignity of the sentiments avoid any complacency with scandal.

Jean Giraudoux, like Mauriac and Montherlant, began his career as novelist, but it seems today that his fame will ultimately rest on his plays. Mauriac and Montherlant represent the rigorous, severely classical style of the French theatre, and Giraudoux remains closer to the tradition of preciosity. The precious writer is always close to the confusion of the world, both its confusion and profusion. The verbal fantasies of his writing are brilliant and elusive. Concerning preciosity itself, the term which has been associated with Giraudoux' style and sensibility, he has offered a formula which, better than most, describes his work. He claims that preciosity is a malady which "consists of treating objects as if they were human, and humans as if they were gods, and gods as if they were cats or weasels." He goes on to say that preciosity is a malady which "provokes not study in libraries, but personal relationships with the seasons and small animals, an excessive pantheism and a great politeness toward all created things."

It is impossible to speak of Giraudoux' career as dramatist without speaking at the same time of the actor who deserves the praise of revealing the talent of Giraudoux: Louis Jouvet, who died in August 1951, in his own theatre where he was rehearsing the leading role in an adaptation of Graham Greene's *The Power and the Glory*. *Siegfried* was Giraudoux' first play and an adaptation of his novel, *Siegfried et le Limousin*. His second play, *Amphitryon 38*, was an even greater success, and from then to Giraudoux' death, Jouvet trained a group of actors for the plays of the dramatist-diplomat, actors such as Valentine Teissier, Madeleine Ozeray, Pierre Renoir and Jouvet himself.

Jouvet had been trained under Jacques Copeau in the Vieux-Colombier. His first role under Copeau's direction was Doctor Macroton in Molière's *L'Amour-Médecin*, in 1913. He also played Philinte in *Le Misanthrope* with exceptional success. He was much more than a mere actor; whenever it was needed, he was stage-hand, *régisseur*, decorator, *metteur-en-scène*. In October 1934, he took over the Athénée which remained his theatre until his death. The theatre is in the heart of Paris of the boulevards, quite unaccustomed to the quality of the literary works Jouvet was to choose.

After *Siegfried, Amphitryon 38, Intermezzo,* he produced for Giraudoux the richest play of the new series: *La Guerre de Troie n'aura pas lieu*. It is a brilliant text of wit and intellect for which Jouvet found the right lighting, the right actors, their expressions and their intonations. In his own magnetic appearance

of Hector, he was the incarnation of a thought which
had given itself over to the power of the theatre. The
title itself indicates the theme of Giraudoux' play, a
theme of predilection for him, that of war, or rather
peace, elaborated on by the poet who was also dip-
lomat. The great problems of our contemporary age
were treated by Giraudoux from a certain perspective
of time and place. *Ondine,* the one play which
studies solely the problem of love, transpires in the
pure domain of fable. Like Racine, Giraudoux draws
his characters from literary memories: Hector, Judith,
Amphitryon, Electra, Delilah. But he treats them as
friends and intimates. The philosophical conclusions
of his plays are often deeply pessimistic. In *La Guerre
de Troie,* war is presented as something hateful but
eternal. It is hated by man but is a result of his nature.
And even if men agree to avoid war, destiny will force
it to break out since it is the favorite amusement of the
gods.

Jouvet was playing in Rio de Janeiro in 1942 when
he received word from Giraudoux that *La Folle de
Chaillot* would be ready for him on his return to
Paris. At the same time, Giraudoux told Christian
Bérard, who was to do the sets for the new play, that
the first act set was the terrace of the Bar Francis.
It was a real bar, on the Place de l'Alma, known to
Giraudoux and Jouvet. The role of the Madwoman
was written for Marguerite Moréno, the last of her
great parts. Giraudoux himself died in 1948, and
Jouvet, the last of the quartet responsible for the pro-
duction of the brilliant satire comedy of *La Folle de
Chaillot,* died in 1951, stricken at rehearsal in the
Théâtre de l'Athénée. The cot in his office became
his bier, and thousands of Parisians climbed the back-

stage staircase to pay him their last respects. Jouvet, who was born where Rimbaud was born, just outside of Charleville, was the only intellectual French actor today who was popular with the masses.

The collaboration between Jouvet and Giraudoux marked an epoch in the French theatre. Each strove in his own way for a perfect synchronizing of the creation and the production of the dramatic work. Each sought in the other the precise resonance that was wanted. The Giraudoux-Jouvet entente must have concealed generous concessions, in the name of friendship and art, for that final harmony which they reached on so many occasions.

The first important play of Jean Cocteau was *La Machine Infernale,* of 1934. It was produced by Jouvet and the settings were designed by Christian Bérard. The beauty and freshness of the production are still remembered. The first act represented the ramparts of Thebes. The second act was a countryside. In the third act the bed of incest appeared in the form of a funeral pyre or sacrificial altar. The sets revealed the genius of Bérard. He had understood Cocteau's atmosphere of phosphorescence and the symbolism of the infernal machine which counts out the time granted to man to enjoy his illusions, and which, when the time is over, explodes and destroys. Cocteau is obsessed by this belief in supernatural surveillance and intervention. In *Les Chevaliers de la Table Ronde,* of 1937, he continued with the same problem. Oedipus pursues the secret of his birth as Galahad pursues the quest of the Grail. The hero is protected by his Fate which paradoxically lays traps for him. Between the two plays of *La Machine Infernale* and *Les Chevaliers,* Cocteau wrote his *Essai de Critique Indirecte,* where, in the passage on Chirico, he develops some of his principal ideas. "Poetry," he writes, "is a calamity of birth."

Cocteau has become an enigmatical figure in our day, a sphinx whose influence is probably more far-reaching than is realized. In the *entre-deux,* the period between the two world wars, when the Surrealists were studying their so-called "disorder" of the human spirit, and Gide and Claudel were continuing with their particular forms of humanism, Cocteau turned inwardly to that study of self which other men will call wearing a mask. He became one of the solitary men of his age, who had neither the faith of a Claudel nor the animation of a literary movement which guided Breton and Eluard. And yet Cocteau always maintained some faint allegiance to the two beliefs in order and disorder, to Catholicism and Surrealism.

When the five years of the second war were ended, it became apparent that Cocteau had been adding steadily to what has now reached the proportions of one of the major corpora of the period. Since 1945, he has published a new poem, *La Crucifixion.* He has done two new ballets (*Le Jeune Homme et la Mort* and *Phèdre*), two new plays (*L'Aigle à deux têtes* and *Bacchus*), six new films (of which *Les Parents Terribles* and *Orphée* are perhaps the most remarkable) and two new books of personal essays, *La Difficulté d'Etre* and *Journal d'un Inconnu.* Taken together, these last two volumes represent a summation of his wisdom and perceptive genius which may one day place Cocteau in the unpredicted category of French moralists.

In the last week of 1951, Jean Cocteau's new play, *Bacchus,* was presented by Barrault, at the Marigny.

With its religious theme, involving a bishop and a cardinal in Germany at the time of Luther, it bore certain resemblances to Sartre's new play, *Le Diable et le bon Dieu,* and to the new play of Thierry Maulnier, *Le Profanateur.* With these three plays, God became, as a *chansonnier* put it, the leading character in the Paris theatres. Whenever the religious problem is treated in France, it is fairly certain that a controversy will start. *Bacchus* provided the excuse. Within a week after the première, journalists were referring to *L'Affaire Bacchus.*

The play begins with a debate on the meaning of revolt and grows into a description of the rebel. A tradition in a small German town gives a man absolute power for one week each year. Hans, the village idiot, is elected to this role of Bacchus and he turns out to be a simulator, a hater of leaders and priests and the rich. He begins to prepare the ideal city as if he were a disciple of Rousseau. His adversary is a cardinal, a cynical, intelligent man sent from Rome to investigate heresy.

The debate between Bacchus and the Cardinal is really the eternal debate between the young and the old, between the idealist and the rationalist, in a sense between Rousseau and Voltaire. As is usually the case, the idealist begins the revolt and the rationalist ends the revolution. The brilliant second act shows the struggle between the Cardinal with fifteen centuries of theology and politics behind him, and a very lonely, very vulnerable youth.

But the controversy over the play began with a letter of François Mauriac to Cocteau, published in *Le Figaro Littéraire* of December 29, 1951. Mauriac had been present on the opening night and had left the

theatre before the final curtain. His exit had been
generally noticed and he explained at great length in
his open letter his sadness over the play. He said that
he had been watching what he calls Cocteau's "number" for almost half a century, and that his new play
illustrates the current phrase that God is dead. He
upbraided Cocteau, as one might a child, for his
mockery of the Church in the character of the maud-
lin bishop, of the cynical cardinal and in the speeches
of Bacchus-Hans.

On the last day of the year, in *France-Soir,* Cocteau
answered Mauriac, in a letter every sentence of which
began with the phrase: *Je t'accuse.* Cocteau claims
that his play is in honor of the Church, that his cardinal wants to save the soul of a young heretic. Two
sentences of the play, censured by Mauriac, were
revealed by Cocteau to be historical. The one on the
devil: "The devil is pure because he can do only evil,"
is taken from Jacques Maritain. The other, spoken
by the cardinal in the play, "A man who thinks is our
enemy," is a sentence of Napoleon's and means "a
man who does not think as I do is my enemy."
Cocteau especially objected to the tone of hatred he
sensed in the letter and accused Mauriac of respect-
ing only one French tradition, that which consists
in killing the poets.

The third generation of contemporary French playwrights were born at the turn of the century or soon
after. They produced their first plays in the forties
with the example before them of the Resistance movement, with the new or renewed belief that literature
must be "engaged," must come from direct participation in actual events and problems. The Existentialist

leader, Jean-Paul Sartre, and the quasi-existentialist Albert Camus dominated the decade of the forties. Almost each year has seen a new play, characterized by a passionate dialectic and a sobering voice of mankind, which has been applauded and denounced as only Paris can applaud and denounce a new literary work: 1943 and 1944, *Les Mouches* and *Huis Clos* of Sartre; 1945 and 1946, *Le Malentendu* and *Caligula* of Camus. In 1947, *Les Bonnes* of Genet, a play only loosely associated with Existentialism, was far from being a success. In 1948, Camus' *Etat de Siège* was a distinct failure, but *Les Mains Sales* of Sartre revived belief in the new theatre of the Existentialists. It is the kind of play in which the art of the theatre and the play of ideas meet. The dialogue is steady, irritating, almost monotonous. It is a case of conscience, revealed immodestly, while the public watches the degrading of mysticism or idealism into politics. The disillusionment of the character Hugo in the play is one more lesson on the intransigency of youth.

Les Justes of Camus, produced in 1950, belongs also to the cycle of French tragedies dealing with cases of conscience: *Caligula, Les Mouches, Antigone, La Reine Morte,* and *Sud,* Julien Green's first play, of 1953. *Les Justes* has greater beauty of language than the plays of Sartre, but the play is not convincing as drama. The style of Camus is closer to that of Montherlant, but the warm humanism of Camus is opposed to the inhumanity of Montherlant.

Younger than Sartre and Camus, since he was born in Bordeaux in 1910, Jean Anouilh is one of the most prolific and gifted of the younger French playwrights. Today he is just over forty and has written fifteen plays, all of which reveal a very sure sense of the theatre. He has one theme which reappears in various disguises and forms in all of his work: the opposition of youth, in its strength and purity and love, to the hypocrisy and cynicism and corruption of the other kind of living. This opposition represents for Anouilh an implacable antinomy. The conclusion of the play is usually tragic because society seems to have in most cases the final word and the final triumph. The tragic plays of Anouilh, those he calls *pièces noires* (as opposed to his series of *pièces roses*), testify to a painful negation of man's fate. The conflict between Creon and Antigone illustrates the central dramatic conflict in all of Anouilh's work: the conflict between order and truth, or what might be called the conflict between the spirit of obedience and the spirit of examination. Creon is the politician, bent upon maintaining the regime by organizing it. Antigone is the anarchist, bent upon preserving the purity of her love and her solitude. This same quest for solitude is as evident in *L'Invitation au Château* (*Ring Round the Moon*) as it is in *Antigone*.

There are other theatres in Paris, such as Les Nouveautés, Les Bouffes, La Michodière, which have a tradition of lighter plays, those which make fun of the excesses and the vices of the day in a direct and usually comic fashion. André Roussin, born in 1911, in Marseille, is one of the most popular of the younger playwrights. He was an actor for about ten years with a theatrical group in Marseille, called Le Rideau Gris, which presented plays of such different authors as Supervielle, Cocteau, Shakespeare. He was in New York in 1938-39 with the troupe Les Quatre Saisons, directed by Barsacq. His first play was done in 1934. A few years ago his comedy, *Les Oeufs de l'Autruche,* with the lead taken by Pierre Fresnay, the most universal perhaps of the French actors, promoted Roussin to a place quite close to that of a literary writer.

For more than twenty years the French studios have produced films the best of which have received international recognition. The French are jealous of their cinema and have tried to protect it from contamination with Hollywood. A few of their stars have a "type" and a personality recognized by the world today. A Jean Gabin, for example, is as celebrated as a Dietrich. He appears in many films in essentially the same role of deserter or criminal, a goodhearted outcast who is photographed against an empty wet street in Paris or in the provinces, whether the director be Carné, Renoir or Duvivier. He has become for the French and for other nationalities a symbol of condemned humanity.

The history of the French cinema extends from *La Passion de Jeanne d'Arc* of 1928, a silent film directed by Karl Dreyer, in which Renée Falconetti gave an unforgettable interpretation of the martyred saint, to the films produced just after the turn of the mid-century. Among the best of these is *La Beauté du Diable* (1951), a work on the Faust legend, directed by the justly celebrated René Clair and performed by one of France's veteran actors, Michel Simon, and by one of the youngest, Gérard Philipe. An early success of René Clair, *A nous la liberté* (1931), appearing a few weeks after the première of Chaplin's *City Lights,* contained one of the most brilliant episodes of the early films, the Inauguration scene, in which political bosses, generals, professors, capitalists raced after 1,000-franc notes scattered by the wind.

Only two French writers have been significantly associated with the making of films: André Malraux, whose *Espoir* far exceeds the form of the documentary in the deep sensitivity it shows to the fate of the Spanish loyalists, and Jean Cocteau whose career as cineast equals if not surpasses his careers as poet, critic, dramatist, novelist, designer.

Cocteau is opposed to what he calls the "poetic film." Whatever poetic elements finally exist in the films should have come of themselves, he believes, and without the solicitation of the cinematographer. He expresses this thought in his own particular way when he claims that the magical and the poetic (*le merveilleux et la poésie*) should attack him from ambush. He has been associated only indirectly with the making of three films which are somewhat erroneously called Cocteau films: *Le Baron Fantôme, L'Eternel Retour* (a work on the Tristan theme starring Madeleine Sologne and Jean Marais) and *Les Enfants Terribles,* an adaptation of Cocteau's novel, in which Nicole Stéphane plays the Electra role of sister and Edouard Dermithe the brother.

Cocteau's creative freedom and suppleness were the most remarkably expressed in his first film, *Sang d'un Poète,* of 1931, and in *Orphée,* of 1950. The production of *Sang d'un Poète* was made possible through the generosity of the Vicomte Charles de Noailles. It was a unique example in film history, when the director was totally free to do what he wanted, to assume full responsibility of theme, text and photography. Cocteau began shooting the film in

1930, without any preconceived notion of method or technique. Throughout his career Cocteau claimed that each film demands its own technique. In *Sang d'un Poète* he learned to use what he called the "ink of light" (*l'encre de lumière*) for the drawings and signs which crossed the white screen. An attitude of indifference to the usual rules and a love of risk have characterized his various cinema undertakings. He once said that *Sang d'un Poète* and *La Belle et la Bête* were really made for *aficionados*: "In these films I don't kill the bull according to the rules. But this scorn for rules does not exist without a scorn for danger which excites a great many people."

In this first film, which Cocteau made as one writes a novel, without need of sacrificing anything of the complexity or the delicacy of the inspiration, he created a work of deep significance to him personally. He used in it, for example, an episode from his own childhood, that of the school boy wounded by a snowball, which he had once before used in his novel, *Les Enfants Terribles*. Such scenes have encouraged the writing of many exegeses of the film, among which is one by Sigmund Freud. Cocteau has always disclaimed any desire to mystify in this film, and in all of his work, for that matter. The camera itself, he believes, registers in advance of the film director, around the characters and the objects of the film, all the mysteries which man is unable to decipher. The camera director is therefore comparable to the spring or well discoverer, or comparable to the magician. The two French words designating these functions are almost the same: *sourcier* and *sorcier.* Without willing it in a deliberate or pedantic way Cocteau expects from the poetry of cinematography the same kind of revelatory power he demands of poetry itself, of the novel, criticism, plays and graphic art.

Some of the elements in *Sang d'un Poète* have been called *trucages* or magical tricks: the plunge through the mirror, the beating heart, the living statue, the poet's walk in the corridor. Such *trucages* are more successfully performed in *Orphée*, thanks to the film's and Cocteau's technical progress during twenty years. The film of 1931 stands today as a kind of manifesto, as a license permitting the magical and the esoteric to take place in our time. Its most violent symbol is the factory chimney which collapses at the beginning and which reaches the earth at the end, with the word *Fin*. The film is the dream world in its pure state, without the excuse of a coherent plot. The only key is the science of dreams, illustrated by the theme of the child endlessly bleeding on immaculate snow, or the theme of the mouth in the hand which caresses the body of the artist before it is drowned in the washbasin.

In the film Cocteau made in 1949 of his play *Les Parents Terribles* he accomplished a kind of paradox. He used the text of his play without adapting or transposing it, cast it with the same actors who had given hundreds of performances of it and who therefore acted it in the film as they would have on the stage. And Cocteau made of this enterprise one of his most successful films. One of the major points of the play is the closed-in effect of the room or apartment of the family, of the *roulotte*, as the mother calls her home. The art of the camera was able to make even more pronounced this closeness of cohabitation or claustration. The mother wants to keep her son for herself and is jealous of any intruder. The most dramatic scene is the son's confession to his mother that he has fallen in love and wants to marry the girl. In the play production he comes up behind his mother and puts his head over her head and clasps her shoulders. The public can therefore observe simultaneously the two conflicting expressions, the one above the other. In the film, the actors take the same position, and then the camera moves closer and closer until finally it frames the speaking lips of the boy or the agonized eyes of the mother. The director Rossellini made a similar close study of facial expression in his adaptation of Cocteau's play, *La Voix Humaine*. It is a thirty-five minute film, largely devoted to the inner suffering visible on the face of the Italian actress, Anna Magnani.

The dialogue of *Les Parents Terribles* has the mechanical quality of Cocteau's earlier play, *La Machine Infernale*. At the end of the film, the *roulotte* turns into a real gypsy wagon and you can hear it rolling on the cobble stones and you hear the voice of Cocteau, always a strangely metallic voice on the microphone. This same voice is audible in *Sang d'un Poète*, in the opening scene of *Orphée*, and throughout *Les Enfants Terribles*.

Orphée, released in 1950, is a summation of all of Cocteau's cinema successes, and the only esoteric poem on the screen today which has reached anything like a large public. Cocteau used three well-known French stars: Maria Casarès, who plays the part of the princess; François Périer, who plays her chauffeur; Jean Marais, in the role of Orpheus. The recently bombed ruins of Saint-Cyr, France's military academy, are used as background. *Orphée* retains two episodes from *Sang d'un Poète*: that of the passage through a mirror in order to reach the other world and two remarkable walking scenes which are strongly reminiscent of the corridor scene. The general conception of Cocteau's play, *Orphée*, of 1925, is carried over into the film of 1950, but all the details have been altered. Cocteau in his new film is still concerned, as always, with the meaning of the poet, his suicide, the secrecy of his code. The myth is both old and new, both esoteric and psychological.

If *Sang d'un Poète* is a manifesto, *Orphée* is a summa of the new art. In both films the poet is unpopular. The rite of death is important, although it is more gently enacted in *Orphée*. Eurydice's death, for example, is signified by a bicycle running alone toward a ditch. The poet who is Orpheus journeys to the unknown in order to renew his inspiration, and finds that his inspiration is death. In the play, Heurtebise is an angel disguised as a window repairer. In the film he is the princess's chauffeur, a student who had recently committed suicide, in the service of a satellite of death. His action in the film is the attempt to oppose by an act of free will a fate devised by the princess. Eurydice (played by Marie Déa) is a girl who used to work, before her marriage, at a woman's club, the Bacchantes, run by Aglaonice. She is a simple homebody, impermeable to mystery of any kind. Cégeste, eighteen years old, is the doomed protégé of the princess. He belongs to the avant-garde poets. He drinks too much and is insolent, but once he is in the zone he becomes himself, rather shy and naive and even quite dignified. The radio messages, sent by Cégeste, deceive Orphée. They were inspired, according to Cocteau, by the BBC radio used during the

Occupation. Automobiles which speak belong to modern mythology but we do not recognize them as such because they are too familiar. The message, *l'oiseau chante avec ses doigts,* was sent to Cocteau by Apollinaire in 1917, as an emblem at the end of a poem. In the film, thirty-four years later, it appropriately becomes the secret message of the poet.

Cocteau knew that his public would interpret the princess as Death, but he has said that she is no more Death than an air-hostess in an airplane is an angel. He says that she is Orpheus' death, because each one of us possesses his death who watches over us from birth on. Orpheus' love for the princess is the attraction of poets for what lies beyond the world. The theme of *Sang d'un Poète* was stated very delicately, with one finger playing, Cocteau said. But in *Orphée* the same theme is richly orchestrated. It is a theme announced in a celebrated line of Mallarmé:

Tel qu'en lui-même enfin l'éternité le change.

The poet has to die several times in order to be born.

The theatre's paradox is its need of living men and women to demonstrate its fictions. To re-enact crimes they never committed, to struggle against obstacles invented by the mind of a poet, to speak language that was never spoken by real people, the theatre demands of its comedians that they forget their own lives and characters in order to put on the immortal cloak of an Orestes or a Medea, or the costume of some eternal type of clown or prostitute or miser. Impossible for the theatre to exist, for a play to be experienced without the real presence of actors who have learned to be what they are not, who have learned to speak words not their own and perform actions foreign to their own instincts. Molière became Alceste by ceasing to be Molière, and Jean-Louis Barrault, in our own century, became Alceste by forcing us to see on his stage for two hours not a contemporary man but a reincarnation of the green-ribboned man raging against his fate of sincerity, with the same words which Molière had written and recited two centuries and a half ago.

The actor is the man whose vocation justifies the universal and normal habit of metamorphosing oneself, of making oneself into a character of many parts, even conflicting parts. We remain the same being, but perform multiple roles depending upon the situation (the *mise-en-scène*) and the people (the dramatis personae) surrounding us. We are different characters with our mother, our wife, our friend, our business associate, our students, our physician, our maid, our confessor, our children. Which is our true character? With whom are we most sincere? And under what conditions, prosperity or adversity, at Christmas or at a Hallowe'en party? The actor lives for the enchantment of metamorphosis. It is his ecstasy, and its realization is his secret, hidden even from himself. When he is perfectly metamorphosed, in the presence of his public, he enters upon a rite, so ancient and so sacred that he moves outside of a timed existence into one reminiscent of a sacrificial and hieratic order. This mystery of the actor equals in importance the poet's mystery. If the poet is a demiurge in his creation of a play, the actors are his priests necessarily repeating the ceremony for the dead words to take on their meaning and for the action to be performed. The artificial world of the stage is not falsehood. It is convention for the re-enactment of a mystery.

The actor strives to become the being imaginatively created by the dramatic poet who, like a god, needs human beings to incarnate his ideas. The text of a tragedy, which always centers about a play of will, has more energy, more dynamics than other literary forms. A play is composed of characters who first will to live and then will to commit an action. The poet in creating them is obsessed with the actors who will play his characters. By thinking of how a character will be performed, the poet is helped in creating the character. The great dynamism of dramatic writing comes from this imperious need of creating living characters. No set of rules, no recipes can be called upon to produce this art of the theatre. A Racinian destiny is a direct willful descent into the abyss, an implacable descending destiny which consumes its victim. A Molière comedy resembles more a ballet, pantomime and dancing, endless entrances and exits. A Shakespearean drama is a complex mirroring of all of life, a cosmic universal reproduction of multiple parts. But all of these plays need actors in order to make of the texts something that is purely human.

A trapeze act in a circus may possess the purity of a poem, and even the purity of a tragedy. But its beauty depends solely on the body of the acrobat. He will die one day and his trapeze stunt, with its particular beauty and perfection, will never again be performed. But the actor performs his role within the limitations of a text. It is true that his body is as mortal and perishable as the acrobat's, but the lines he recites are immortal and the character he incarnates will continue to live in the actors of succeeding generations. In a certain sense, an actor is as ancient and as immortal as his text.

An actor's vanity is not hard to understand and accept. A play must succeed in order to be, and this success depends largely on the actors. The work of the poet, of the director and of the stage manager is forgotten at the moment of the production which is always the triumph or the failure of the actors. Jacques Copeau, in the early days of the Vieux-Colombier, grouped around him ten or twelve actors capable of populating the universes of comedy, drama and tragedy. In each one of his actors he discovered the natural bent and temperament which he used in the roles he distributed. His fanatic love of the profession, which characterizes the actor, made possible the creation of a troupe of actors who worked as one for the success of the play.

The first play Copeau presented at the Vieux-Colombier, in October 1913, was Molière's *L'Amour Médecin*. At that production, the part of Macroton, a tall cadaverous stammering figure of a doctor, was played by an unknown actor, Louis Jouvet. Later, in another Molière comedy, *L'Avare*, Charles Dullin was to triumph by so entering into the part of the miser that Harpagon and Dullin became one. Under the extraordinary inspiration of Copeau, Jouvet as Macroton and Dullin as Harpagon learned how a play is carried by the interpretation of the actor, and never forgot this rule when they themselves became directors of their own companies.

Hamlet's taste for the theatre and his love for the actor's vocation, which is that of interpreting all kinds of human destiny, illustrate the fundamental principle

of the actor's life. He is able to enact the most profound and most cruel experiences without suffering
from them. He becomes a given character for two or
three hours, but the very poetry he recites protects
him. The lives he plays are more serious and more exciting than his own. They serve only to show how
absurd is his private destiny of a man.

No human glory is perhaps quite so perishable as
an actor's. For two hours he is permitted to be Scapin
or Macbeth. Two hours when in an absolute sense
he feigns and pretends to be someone else. He wills
to lose his own life in order to gain another life. The
play is the triumph of his body, of his physical appearance and presence. In dramatic art, appearance
is being. The formula of an Othello is extremely simple to state and comprehend. But the dramatic greatness of Othello can never be fully felt unless he is seen
in the flesh, on the stage. And yet more profound
than the understanding of the spectators is that of the
actor who plays Othello, who becomes Othello. A
blasphemous profession, perhaps, this coveting of another life, this will to lead another existence. Little
wonder that the Church has been in the past so harsh
on the actor's profession. The last rites were refused
to Molière who practically died on the stage while
interpreting his own *Malade Imaginaire*.

During the past years there has been no diminishing
of interest in Molière. He has held the boards more
persistently than any contemporary playwright. Jean-
Louis Barrault revived *Les Fourberies de Scapin*,
with a new set by Bérard, and Jouvet revived *Don
Juan* in 1948 and *Tartuffe* in 1951. The last interpretation of Jouvet was the most harshly criticized of his
career. His understanding of Tartuffe contradicted

the familiar character. Jouvet's was more ambiguous than the Paris public had seen. He was a sorrowful man, but not a traitor, a man troubled by a terrible concupiscence. The most marked trait of Jouvet's art had always been his power of portraying ambiguity, and he used this power in his production of *Tartuffe* where the public did not laugh, because the new Tartuffe appeared sincere! The decade has been marked by a continuing and strong interest in Molière. Professor Jasinski, of the Sorbonne, has presented a new study of *Le Misanthrope* which contains especially a striking interpretation of the character Philinte, and Mauriac, in an essay, has developed the now familiar thesis of Molière's sadness, *Molière le tragique*.

No single figure in the contemporary French theatre was better known or more universally loved than Christian Bérard. His legend exceeds all others. He has been described as a character from an Oscar Wilde story or a Hieronymus Bosch painting. Jouvet used to place him in the theatre during rehearsal in order to watch his reactions. He was like a piece of chemical paper who would take on colorings and change with the atmosphere and the activities of the stage. His work of a painter—his portraits especially and his fashion drawings for *Vogue*—were as delicate as the drawings of Constantin Guys. Henri Matisse once called Bérard the "Watteau of our age." His versatility was as great as Cocteau's. For Jouvet and Cocteau he was essentially the stage designer, for Lifar he was a ballet master, for Valéry he was a poet, for Milhaud a musician, for Chanel a dress designer. Bérard was not left-handed, but he used to paint with his left hand through fear of the facile skill of his right hand.

Bérard, who was familiarly called "Baby," died on February 12, 1949, at his post in the fifth row of the Marigny, after looking at the costumes and the set he had devised for Barrault's revival of *Les Fourberies de Scapin*. After his collapse, his body was carried out by Jouvet, Barrault (still in his costume of Scapin), and by the stagehands. Cocteau described this scene as "the procession of Shakespeare's heroes." He is buried in Père-Lachaise, near the grave of Raymond Radiguet.

In the course of twenty years the contemporary theatre in France was rejuvenated and renovated by such actors and producers as Pitoëff, Dullin, Jouvet, Baty. They were all men who understood that the mystery of the theatre is in the hands both of the poet and the actor, that a play is first conceived by the imagination of a poet and then incarnated in the flesh of an actor. These men have brought to the art of the theatre a very profound understanding. In their greatest realizations, the play has given a new life, in the presence of the public, to the subconscious life of man, to his most obscure dreams, to his dormant memory, to the child he once was, to the man he might have become. All this was brought about by the presence of the actor, to which everything else was subsidiary: lighting, costumes, stage set, stage directions, speech and even text.

Movement of the human body is at the origins of the theatre: a man dancing for his gods. All acting is exhibitionistic: the woman playing Phèdre, as well as boxers, gladiators, clowns. Mimicry and exhibitionism must accompany the words. Many dramatic poets have acted or directed other interpreters. Racine taught Du Parc her role of Andromaque. Voltaire played comedies at the court of Frederick and at Ferney. Shakespeare was an actor, and Molière. Cocteau today produces his plays and speaks some of the parts. But no single production of a play, even that directed and performed by the poet, is the definitive or authentic one. Each succeeding actor will bring to the same role, not an established set of traditions, but his own understanding, his own body, his own life. The theatre is a communion, a community established around the actor. The priest is the initial actor, and each of the great contemporary actors retains some priestly power in creating out of an assembly of spectators, of varied races and stations, something that resembles a communion of the faithful. The theatre was born in the church and serves still today as one of the unifying forces of civilization.

In November 1949, two new ballets were announced at the Paris Opéra, on the subjects of *Phèdre* and *Scapin*. Prior to the first performance, celebrities and noncelebrities were interviewed in Paris on the legitimacy or feasibility of interpreting in dance form such well-known characters in the French theatre. Many of the answers pointed out that certain subjects are eternal and that it is quite appropriate to continue giving to myths new aspects, new emphases. Choreographers as well as playwrights have to take their subject matter where they can find it. If Picasso can use Greek sculpture as inspiration, there is no reason why the modern ballet should not use the curse of the house of Atrides. The more a work becomes celebrated, the more it becomes mythological, and the more it lends itself to alteration and metamorphosis.

The dance-form has the tendency to divest the theatre of its pure intellectuality. But the theatre was born out of dancing, which is, according to Valéry, "the pure act of metamorphosis." A drama secretly inhabits the ballet and imposes its form, its architecture, its limitations on the movement of the dance. Even in such ballets as those of *L'Amour Médecin* and *Le Bourgeois Gentilhomme,* the form does not exist separate from the text, as a kind of concession to popular taste. It is a part of the work itself, a moment when the comedy becomes more purely formal, more purely diverting. The ballet is one of the surest means of attaining to caricature, to a world of fairy enchantment, to a comic stylization, to a poetic transcription of sentiment. Each time a group of ballet dancers come upon the stage and make their circular walk preparatory to the real beginning of the ballet, we know that we are about to witness a work of purely organized perfection from which all chance has been removed. We watch with delight the seeming frailty and delicacy of each girl, and know all the time that in reality she is a monster of strength and skill. She is inhuman in both her strength and her infinite grace. A salamander, she lives in the two worlds of fire and air. She is the extreme expression of the actor, the living creature incarnating a fictional character. The actor, at one end of the experience, makes life out of fiction, and the ballet dancer, at the other end of the same experience, creates a dream out of reality.

Styles of acting change from generation to generation, but the sacredness of the actor's profession remains. In many cases the actor outlives his roles and becomes greater than his roles, although his greatness comes from the fact of his being an actor. Mistinguett, for example, is the champion of the actor's endless career. Even several years ago we were told of her great age and of the mystery by which she continued to depict youth and vigor on the music hall stage. Each time she appeared, she was *la Miss du promenoir,* whose hoarse, rasping voice and animation held everyone in the audience. It was always a thrilling experience to love Mistinguett, with everyone loving her at the same time. In the first part of each review, she always played the role of a street urchin or a prostitute. But the review inevitably ended with the stairway scene. Mistinguett, dressed in light blue and covered with feathers, walked down the flight of stairs between two rows of chorus boys, their hair plastered with brilliantine. At the foot of the stairs they lifted her in their arms and turned her around in the air several times as if she were one of her own feathers. These two scenes marked her origins and her triumphs. She continued to play them during all the lesser and successive reigns of Josephine Baker, Lucienne Boyer, Charles Trénet, Edith Piaf.

Only Maurice Chevalier, perhaps, remains close to her longevity. His straw hat has become the symbol of French wit and seduction, as Mistinguett's feathers symbolize the female conquest. Both artists have remained very close to the people. They have carefully preserved their pure accent of the Place Pigalle. Their faces, when submitted to the full glare of the white spotlight, seem stripped of all secrets. They hold nothing back from their public. The Paris public loves them just a bit more than the two great clown actors, Raimu and Fernandel, who are more subtle and more pathetically human.

Raimu's celebrated Marseille anger, his sentimentality, his laughter made him into the leading artist of the French cinema. But with Fernandel, one has the best contemporary example of the plastic art of the mime, whose grimaces, gesticulations, agility, volubility come from the already distant genius of the *commedia dell'arte*. He is a comic virtuoso whose art, in his own country at least, goes back to the medieval juggler and acrobat, the man who doubtless played the devil in the "mysteries" and who was soon to become Arlequin (Hell-König, Hellequin?). His face is a multiple mask of all the simple recognizable emotions. He is most often the rustic clown, reminiscent of the Zane from Bologna, whose contemporary American counterpart is Li'l Abner, created by Al Capp. He summarizes many versions of the same actor: Arlechino of the *commedia dell'arte*, Watteau's *Gilles*, the lunar melancholy of the romantic hero, Don Juan, the Neapolitan Pulcinella, London's Punch, Lyon's Guignol of the eighteenth century, the Russian Petrouchka, the American Chaplin. When the personality of the actor is supreme, as in the cases of Mistinguett and Fernandel, the actor becomes his role.

Pierre Fresnay is the purer type of actor in France today, who, each time he portrays a part, becomes a different character. Jean-Louis Barrault is somewhere between the two extremes of Fernandel, eternally the same, and Fresnay, miraculously diversified. Barrault appears as a kind of archangel, as Pan at the head of a troupe of actors. His temptation is poetry, a poetic stylization of every role he plays. In his Hamlet we see the mime, and in his literal characterization of a mime (as in *Les Enfants du Paradis*) we see a man tormented by poetry and ideas. Barrault comes at the end of an illustrious line of actor-directors: Copeau, Dullin, Baty, Pitoëff, Jouvet, who have renovated and purified the art of acting on the Paris stage.

Love of the theatre easily turns into worship of the actors. What we see on the stage concerning the existence of Bérénice or Lear or Célimène is only fragmentary. A play is more of a dream than life is. But the actress playing Célimène and the actor playing Hamlet are real and more familiar to us. The modern public has become a jury judging not so much the art of the play, as the skill and the beauty of the actors. The public wants to follow not only the private life of the king depicted on the stage, but also that of the actor playing him. The poet was at one time not much more than a domestic of the wealthy. He is still that to some degree. But the actor depends even more on the whim and the buying power of a few. Only when the actor succeeds in seducing the public can he remain the actor. And in order to continue seducing the public, he needs to play the part of some enigmatical figure, such as Don Juan or Hamlet, who can be created or recreated only by the genius of a great poet. Since Racine and Molière, the greatest of the French writers have not been dramatists. With only one exception: Paul Claudel. Even such excellent dramatists as Marivaux and Musset are not in the highest category. The recent dramatic successes in France have come from writers who turned to the theatre after distinguishing themselves as novelists: Mauriac, with *Asmodée;* Camus, with *Caligula;* Mon-

therlant, with *Le Maître de Santiago;* Sartre, with
Les Mains Sales; Julien Green, with *Sud.*

The actor has to wait for such unexpected turns
of fortune as these. A renascence of the poetic theatre,
or the exceptionally literary theatre, is his present
hope which has already been realized in such successes as Claudel's *Soulier de Satin,* Eliot's *Murder in
the Cathedral,* Lorca's *Yerma,* Pichette's *Les Epiphanies,* Beckett's *En attendant Godot.*

Man is an immemorial mimic. The theatre is the
principal art where his conscience may at least be
temporarily eased by watching on the stage the depiction of his fate: his eternal restlessness in the presence of the mystery of life. The actor is the mask, the
sacred magical instrument forged very early in the
history of man to counteract the pain of living by
transcending it. The sacred dances of India, the ballets of Lulli and the dialogues of Marivaux are all related in being aspects of the same art which tries to
give some measurement of human genius. No matter
how clarified and disciplined the characters appear,
thanks to the poetry, say, of a Racine, they have always some element of the sacred intoxication of
Dionysus.

EIGHT

POETRY

I: LEGACY OF SYMBOLISM

Ever since the rich period of Symbolism, in fact, ever since the work of the two leading forerunners of Symbolism, Nerval and Baudelaire, French poetry has been obsessed with the idea of purity. To achieve poetry of a "pure state" has been the persistent ambition of a century of literary, and specifically, poetic, endeavor. This ambition is to create poetry that will live alone, by itself and for itself. In a very deep sense, it is poetry of exile, narrating both the very real exile of Rimbaud from Charleville and from Europe, and Mallarmé's more metaphysical exile within his favorite climate of absence. In this effort of poetry to be self-sufficient and to discover its end in itself, it has appropriated more and more pervasively throughout the span of one hundred years the problems of metaphysics. As early as Nerval, who actually incorporated the speculations of the eighteenth-century *illuminés,* poetry tried to be the means of intuitive

226

communication between man and the powers beyond him. Nerval was the first to point out those regions of extreme temptation and extreme peril which have filled the vision of the major poets who have come after him.

This search for "purity" in poetic expression is simply a modern term for the poet's will of all ages to break with daily concrete life, to pass beyond the real and the pressing problems of the moment. Poets have always tended to relegate what may be called "human values" to novels and tragedies or to their counterparts in earlier literary periods. Poetry is the crossroads of man's intelligence and imagination, from which he seeks an absolute beyond himself. That is why the term "angelism" has been used to designate the achievement and the failures of the modern poets, especially those of Rimbaud and Mallarmé. Baudelaire called the poet "Icarus," and Rimbaud called him "Prometheus, fire-stealer." The progressive spiritualization of modern art in all its forms is its leading characteristic. It brings with it a mission comparable to that of the angels, and also a knowledge of pride and defeat which, strikingly, are the most exact characteristics of some of the great poetic works of our day. Defeat of one kind is in Mallarmé's faun and in his *Igitur*. Claudel, in discussing *Igitur*, called it a "catastrophe." Defeat of another kind is in the long literary silence of Rimbaud, after his 20th or 21st year. And still another kind of defeat lies in most of the poetry of the Surrealists who found it impossible to apply their poetic theory rigorously to their actual poems.

The example of Mallarmé's art was never considered so fervently and piously as during the decade

1940-50. His lesson is the extraordinary penetration of his gaze at objects in the world, and the attentive precision with which he created a world of forms and pure relationships between the forms. His will to abstraction isolated the object he looked at and his will of a poet condensed the object into its essence and therefore into its greatest power of suggestiveness. The object in a Mallarmé poem is endowed with a force that is latent and explosive. The irises, for example, in *Prose pour des Esseintes*, have reached a "purity" from which every facile meaning has been eliminated. Such flowers as these come from the deepest soil of the poet's consciousness and emotions. They retain in their "purity," exempt as they are from all usual responses, the virtue of their source in great depths and dreams. Their purity is their power to provoke the multiple responses of the most exacting readers, those who insist that an image appear in its own beauty, isolated from the rest of the world and independent of all keys and obvious explanations. Whatever emotion, whatever passion was at the source of the poem, has been forgotten in the creation of the poem. Poetry makes no attempt to describe or explain passion—that is the function of the prose writer, of the novelist; rather the object or the image is charged with the burden of the literal experience. The image becomes the experience, but so changed that it is no longer recognizable.

The metaphor is an image endowed with a strange power to create more than itself. Mallarmé's celebrated sonnet on the swan caught in the ice of a lake, *Le vierge, le vivace et le bel aujourd'hui*, illustrates this power of a metaphor to establish a subtle relationship between two seemingly opposed objects in the world: a swan and a poet. The relationship is not stated in logical specific terms, but it is implied or suggested or evoked by the metaphor. The reader's attention is fixed on the swan, as it is almost never fixed on an ordinary object in the universe. This attention which the metaphor draws to itself becomes something comparable to a spiritual activity for the reader, as it had once been for the poet. His consciousness is contained within the metaphor. When the metaphor is an image of a sufficiently general or collective meaning, it becomes a myth, not merely establishing a relationship with another object, but translating some aspect of man's destiny or man's nature. It is often difficult to draw a clear distinction between a metaphor and a myth, as in the case of Mallarmé's swan, which testifies to a basic human struggle and defeat.

Today, in the middle of the century, sixty years after his death, Rimbaud's fame is higher than ever and the influence of his poetry is felt everywhere. Editions of his work multiply each year. More than five hundred books about him have been written in all languages. Perhaps never has a work of art provoked such contradictory interpretations and appreciations. One hears of his legend everywhere, and underneath the innumerable opposing beliefs, one continues to follow the legend of a genius who renounced his genius to embrace silence and conceal whatever drama tormented him. He was the adolescent extraordinarily endowed with sight and equally endowed with speech, but with the advent of manhood he deliberately desisted from the prestige of letters and a poet's career. The period of wonderment about his life and his flight from literature is just about over now. In its place, the study of the writings themselves is growing into its own, and it is obvious that their mystery far exceeds the actual language of the writings. With Mallarmé's, it forms the most difficult work to penetrate, in French poetry, and the most rewarding to explore because for both of them, poetry was the act of obedience to their most secret drama.

The work of Rimbaud is far more knowable than his life, but in his case especially, the one cannot be dissociated from the other. The example of his human existence has counted almost as much as the influence of his writings. Breton named him a Surrealist by his life, and Rivière named him the supreme type of innocent. Although it must, in all justice, be noted that Breton modified his earlier view and called Rimbaud an apostate, one who renounced his discoveries and called them "sophisms." Nerval's suicide and Lautréamont's total disappearance would please the Surrealists more than Rimbaud's final choice of another kind of life to that of poetry.

Rimbaud's example will remain that of the poet opposing his civilization, his historical moment, and yet at the same time revealing its very instability, its quaking torment. He is both against his age and of it. By writing so deeply of himself, he wrote of all men. By refusing to take time to live, he lived a century in a few years, throughout its minute phases, rushing toward the only things that mattered to him: the absolute, the certainty of truth. He came closest to finding this absolute in his poet's vision. That was "the place and the formula" he talked of and was impatient to find, the spiritual hunt that did not end with the prey seized. Rimbaud's is the drama of modern

man, as critics have often pointed out, by reason of
its particular frenzy and precipitation, but it is also
the human drama of all time, the drama of the quest
for what has been lost, the unsatisfied temporal existence burning for total satisfaction, for total certitude. Because of Rimbaud's universality, or rather
because of poetry's universality, the Charleville adolescent can seemingly appropriate and justify any title:
metaphysician, angel, *voyou*, seer, reformer, repro-
bate, materialist, mystic. The poet, as Rimbaud conceived of him, is, rightfully, all men. He is the supreme savant. The private drama of one boy, which
does fill the poignant pages of *Une Saison en Enfer*,
is always deepened into the drama of man, tormented
by the existence of the ideal which he is unable to
reach. And likewise, the pure images of *Les Illuminations*, which startle and hold us by their own intrinsic
beauty, were generated and formed by a single man
in the solitude of his own hope to know reality.

To the role of magus and prophet for the poet, so
histrionically played by Victor Hugo, was substituted
the role of magician, incarnated not solely by Rimbaud (whose *Lettre du Voyant* of 1871 seems to be
the principal manifesto), but by Nerval and Baudelaire, who preceded him, by his contemporary Mallarmé, and by his leading disciples, the Surrealists,
thirty years after his death. This concept of the poet
as magician dominates most of the poetic transforma-
tions and achievements of the last century. The poem,
in its strange relationship with witchcraft, empties itself of much of the grandiloquence and pomposity
of Romanticism. The poet, in his subtle relationship
with the mystic, rids himself of the traits of the
Hugoesque prophet and the vain ivory-tower attitude

of a Vigny. This emphasis on the poet as the sorcerer
in search of the unknown and the surreal part of his
own being has also caused him to give up the poetry
of love, or especially the facile love poetry of a
Musset. Except for the poems of Eluard (and a few
pages of Breton), there has been no love poetry in
France since Baudelaire!

The modern poet in France has become the magician, in accordance with the precepts of Mallarmé, or
a visionary, in the tradition of Rimbaud, by his willful or involuntary exploration of dreams and subconscious states. He prefers, to the coherence and the
colors of the universe which the Romantics celebrated, the incoherence and the half-tones of the hidden universe of the self. There they have learned
to come upon thoughts and images in their nascent
form, in their primitive beginnings before a conscious
control had been exercised over them. The *vert
paradis* of the child's world, first adumbrated by Baudelaire, is the world which the modern poet has tried
to rediscover. To descend into it brought about a di-
vorce between the poet and the real world around
him. The world of childhood and innocence is so
obscured in mystery and has been so outdistanced by
the gadgets of adulthood, that to return there, a system of magic, a new series of talismans, has to be invented. The richest source of the poet turned out to be
the subconscious, precisely that in himself which has
not been expressed. The pride of the Romantic poet
and the somewhat melodramatic solitude he so often
created for himself unquestionably helped him later
to discover the new regions of his spirit. The historical
period of Romanticism is seen more and more clearly
to have been the preparation for the far richer periods

of Symbolism and post-Symbolism when the poetic word is understood in terms of its potential magic and the symbol in its power of exorcism.

The critical writings of Baudelaire, Mallarmé and Valéry are as important as their poetry. They discovered, as if for the first time, some of the oldest laws of poetry. What Racine did in the seventeenth century for the ageless laws of tragedy, Baudelaire did in the nineteenth for the ageless laws of poetry. He saw the constraints of rhythm and rhyme to be, not arbitrary, but imposed by a need of the human spirit. A great line of poetry combines a sensual element with an intellectual vigor, and Valéry marveled at the delicate equilibrium which poetry established between them. This very equilibrium was defined by the modern poet as the witchcraft, or the incantation of the word, which no other kind of word possesses. Poetry is not, therefore, the art of obstacles and rules, but the art of triumph over obstacles, the art whose beauty is accomplished by the enveloping of obstacles and transcending of adventure, brutality, love, sorrow. Modern poetry will one day be described as the revindication of the profoundest principles of classicism where the most universal problems of life are transcribed in a style of language that has reached a high degree of enchantment. The most obscure mysteries of the French language, and of language in general, were explored by Rimbaud, in his seeming anarchy and disorder, and by Mallarmé, in his seeming abstractions and absences. The poetry toward which they were moving, almost without fully realizing it, and which they almost reached, was poetry which would have sung only of itself. Claudel and Valéry, in their time and in their acknowledged role of disciples, realized more acutely than Rimbaud and Mallarmé the perils of such an attainment, and they willfully diverted poetry from anarchy or verbal alchemy to a religious celebration of the universe, and from the dream of poetic purity to a celebration of the intellect.

Just at the moment when poetry might have become an abnegation or a defeat, it was redefined by Claudel as a conquest of the universe. Claudel's method, the new freedom of poetic expression developed by Léon-Paul Fargue, the new strength of poetic enumeration and breath discovered by St.-John Perse, helped to close off the danger which poetry courted in the writings of Rimbaud and Mallarmé. If with Mallarmé, poetry stopped being essentially a lofty mode of expression, it became in the subsequent poets what it had been only partially with Mallarmé, an instrument of knowledge, an art in the service of the human spirit utilized in order to reach a higher degree of domination and knowledge of self. Cubism, Surrealism, Existentialism, have been some of the successive chapters in this same quest dominated by poetic experimentation. One of the most recent episodes is Lettrism, revealed by Isidore Isou in his book, *Introduction à une nouvelle poésie et à une nouvelle musique*. This criticism of language, remarkably youthful in its violence and boldness, will in time be rightfully attached to Rimbaud's revolution. Older thinkers in France today, men like Rolland de Renéville, Thierry Maulnier, Jean Paulhan, Jules Monnerot, Roger Caillois, Maurice Blanchot, have devoted the major part of their work to inquiries into the meaning and the scope of poetry. Their investigations and elucidations are varied, but they all agree on seeing poetry as one of the extreme "experiments" of modern

times. The basis of their important works is in their
several interpretations of Symbolism, in their effort to
analyze the indifference of the Symbolist toward the
world, his narcissism, and the closeness he came to a
destruction of poetry by itself. They are the major
critics who have seen the poetry of post-Symbolism in
France, the poetry that has been published between
1900 and 1950, as the reconstruction of poetry.

Because of the extreme solitude of the poet, spoken
of by Baudelaire and poignantly epitomized in the
life story of Rimbaud, and because of the extreme detachment from the world exemplified in the art of
Mallarmé, poetry almost ceased being the full creation that it really is, that of a word which bears in
itself the very substance of man. The past fifty years
have witnessed a return of poetry to the joys and suf-
ferings of man. This has represented a revindication of
the complete freedom of poetry, after the dizzying
lessons of magic and abstractions, of Rimbaud's alchemy and Mallarmé's purity. The act of constructing
a poem has helped the poet to construct himself.
The miracle of poetry has always been the conferring
of a new life on that which already has life. By means
of the word, designating signs in the physical world,
the poet creates a world which is eternal. The lucidity
with which the modern poet has learned to do this,
would probably not have developed without the examples of Baudelaire and the two major poets who
succeeded him.

A poem is a marriage between expression and
meaning. In order to compose the poem, the poet has
to question everything all over again, because a successful poem is a new way of seeing and apprehend-
ing something which is familiar. This is Mallarmé's

profoundest lesson and it seems now to be fully incorporated in the contemporary poetic consciousness.
The poet's power of questioning the universe is essential. His capacity to be amazed at what he beholds
is his sign. Without it, his poem will never be the
revelation it should be, the revelation to himself and
to his readers of what his questioning glance has resurrected, illuminated and understood. In order to be
amazed, the poet has to practice a freedom which is
unusual, because it is related to everything: the physical world, morality, mythology, God. The practice of
this freedom insures what we may best call the poetic
response to the world and to everything in it. This is
vigilance, attentiveness, lucidity: all those disciplines
which are impossible to define but which the artist
needs in order to achieve his work.

Since 1940, French poetry has drawn its themes
more directly from the tragic quality of contemporary
events: blood, catastrophe, hope, than it did in the
periods of Baudelaire or Mallarmé. And yet this poetry is far from being a *reportage* or direct transcription. The lesson taught by Mallarmé that there is no
such thing as immediate poetry is to such a degree the
central legacy of modern poetry that the younger poets move instinctively toward the eternal myths, like
that of Orpheus, which are just beyond the event, the
first reactions and the first sentiments. The myth is
man's triumph over matter. It is his creation of a
world drawn from the world of appearances. It is the
world of poetry we are able to see and comprehend
far more easily than the real world. This process was
once called inspiration or enthusiasm by the Greeks.
The modern poets prefer to call it the alchemy or the
quintessence of the word. The part of poetry has al-

ways come from a new ordering of the real, a new arrangement of ordinary words and common phrases
created as a means to hold on to the real and con-
template it. This was the fundamental belief of Symbolism which has continued to our day and by which
the modern poet denies that poetry is an arbitrary convention. Rather it is an enterprise of the human spirit,
directed toward the living words of speech, or rather
toward that invisible world which provides words
with their life. Between the object and the symbol,
there is a distance to be covered, an experience to be
explored which is the very act of poetry: the imposi-
tion of order on words.

II: THE GENERATIONS

At the turn of the mid-century, French poetry is
still fully engaged in one of the richest periods of its
long history. Its roots are essentially in Symbolism and
in the achievements of poetry between *Les Fleurs du
Mal* of Baudelaire (1857) and the death of Mallarmé
(1898). Especially in France the creative spirit has
always been fully conscious of its heritage, of its belonging to the past, of its role destined to continue and
perfect a tradition. During the past fifty years, the
youngest and the oldest poets have been proud of the
fact that the art of poetry has enjoyed an extraordinary prestige. The wealth of modern French poetry
and its high quality have jealously preserved this prestige. More than the novel and more than drama, poetry has continued to renew itself. Only perhaps the
realm of literary criticism has been productive to a
similar degree, and the most vital books of criticism
have considered the problems of poetry and poets.

The half-century has been dominated by four major

writers, all born around 1870, none of whom is still living, and who have reached now the status of classical writers. Two of these are prose writers, Proust and Gide; and two are poets, Valéry and Claudel. Their common background was Symbolism. They were initiated into literature by the stimulation, the achievements and the manifestoes of Symbolism. Each reacted to Symbolism in his own way and according to his own purposes. In a certain sense the twentieth century did not begin until 1914. The first decade was still very much a part of the 1890's. These four writers had begun writing and publishing by the literal turn of the century, but recognition of their importance did not come until soon after the first World War, about 1920.

Mallarmé and Rimbaud are the greatest poets of the Symbolist period, although, paradoxically, neither one is purely representative of the Symbolist creed. Mallarmé was guide, director and high priest of the movement, but his poetry far transcends the doctrine and the art of the lesser poets. Rimbaud repudiated a literary career, and he had no direct influence on Symbolism, although he wrote between 1869 and 1875. To a far lesser degree, the example of Verlaine counted also in the Symbolist period. His was the poetry of the heart and pure sentiment, a tradition maintained, for example, by Francis Jammes (1868-1938) who belongs to this first generation of twentieth-century poets. Even more isolated from the central evolution of French poetry, stands Charles Péguy (1873-1914), celebrated for his deeply religious poetry on Notre Dame de Chartres and for his *Mystère de la Charité de Jeanne d'Arc* (1910).

The second generation of poets were those men

born at the end of the century. On the whole, they participated in the experience of the first World War much more directly than the generation of Valéry and Claudel. In fact, some of the most gifted writers of this generation lost their lives in the war: Apollinaire, Alain-Fournier, Psichari, and Péguy (although Péguy was slightly older and belongs more strictly to the other generation). This group of writers, particularly in the years after the war, demonstrated a changed attitude toward the role and the activity of the writer. The poet was for them a far less exalted being than he had been for Mallarmé and Rimbaud. The excessive intellectualism and aestheticism of the late Symbolist period were drastically modified and diminished. The experience of the war and the rise of the cinema were only two of the many new forces which were shaping the younger poets at that time.

The oldest figures of this second generation were Max Jacob and Léon-Paul Fargue, both born in 1876. They had begun publishing their poetry long before the war, but their influence was felt after the war. They and the younger poets following them no longer exemplified the distinct influence of either Mallarmé or Rimbaud. Such influences were combined in them. Stylistic traits, for example, of Verlaine and Laforgue, are as present in their writing as characteristics of Mallarmé and Rimbaud. They were both friends of painters and musicians, and participated actively in the avant-garde movement in France. They were both (especially Fargue) poets who wrote of Paris. Jacob died first, in the German prison of Drancy, in 1944, just before the end of the war. Fargue survived the war, and died in 1947.

By his creation of a style of poetry distinctly modern, Guillaume Apollinaire, born in 1880, occupies a more significant place in the development of French poetry than either Jacob or Fargue. His influence is apparent in the writing of Blaise Cendrars (born in 1887), who is a greater prose writer than a poet, and who illustrates the non-bellelettristic approach to writing. His autobiography of 1945, *L'Homme Foudroyé,* is written in the prose of a poet.

Surrealism was the most significant literary movement in France between Symbolism and Existentialism. It flourished especially in the decade 1925-35, and attracted many of the younger poets of that period, most of whom are still living. Reverdy, born in 1889, was as closely allied to Symbolism as to Surrealism. Tristan Tzara, born in Rumania in 1896, was the founder of the Dada movement, in collaboration with Jean Arp and Hugo Ball, in Zurich in 1916. Dadaism was the immediate forerunner of Surrealism. The leading spirit and theorist of Surrealism was André Breton (born in 1896) who even since the second World War has made attempts to revive Surrealism as an organized movement. But most of the poets who at one time or another adhered to the tenets of Surrealism are today writing poetry that is no longer strictly Surrealist. Breton himself and Benjamin Péret have remained closest to the beliefs and practices of orthodox Surrealism. Péret took part in the Civil War in Spain, and has been living in Mexico since 1942. He was perhaps the best satirist of the group, the closest spiritual descendant of Alfred Jarry, whose *Ubu-Roi,* of 1896, was a major text for the Surrealists. Some of the purest of the Surrealist writers have died: Crevel (1900-1935) committed suicide; Artaud (1895-1948) spent most of his last years in an insane asylum. Others have continued only intermittently with the writing of poetry: Soupault (b. 1897), Léiris (b. 1905), and Georges Hugnet (b. 1907), who was active in the Editions de Minuit, the publishing house of the Resistance. Aragon, born in 1897, became the best known Resistance poet, but by that time he had broken all ties with Surrealism. The greatest poet from Surrealism is Paul Eluard, actually the oldest of the entire group, since he was born in 1895. The miracle of Eluard's work is the extremes it contains, and the ease with which he moves from one extreme to the other, from the poet's solitude, from his deep and secret intimacy, to his sense of communion with everyone, to his civic hope. His solitude is his generosity. His sense of the collective comes from what is most individual in him. He is the poet of love, in one of its highest forms, love which will not allow a man to remain within himself.

To this list, which is not exhaustive, of the major French poets associated with Surrealism, should be added many other names of poets who wrote during the same decade, and who have continued to write since, but who had no formal connection with any literary school or movement. The contribution of Jules Supervielle (b. 1884) is distinguished and abundant, although his best books seem to have been written before the second World War. Jouve (b. 1887) in recent years has grown into a poet of great influence. His universe of catastrophe is described in poetry of a lofty Christian inspiration. Since 1940, St.-John Perse has lived in the United States where he wrote *Exil,* one of the profoundest poetic statements on the war. Jean Cocteau (b. 1892) has written poetry intermittently throughout his career. He remains one of the most gifted poets of his generation, even if his signal success in other genres: theatre, cinema, criticism, has somewhat detracted from his position as poet. One of the most independent modern poets, Henri Michaux (b. 1899), has enlarged the domain of poetry. He was discovered in 1941 by Gide whose fervent criticism introduced him to a wider public than he had known. Audiberti (b. 1899) is as well known in the fields of the theatre and the novel as he is in poetry. He is the most highly endowed rhetorician of the new poets. The torrential flow of his lyrics and his purely verbal virtuosity give him a distinctive place among his contemporaries. With Aragon, Prévert (b. 1900) is probably the most widely read of the French poets. More important than his poetry is his writing for the cinema. *Les Visiteurs du Soir* and *Les Enfants de Paradis* are two of his major successes.

The third and youngest generation of poets writing in France at the turn of the mid-century is more dramatically allied with action, with the war and the Resistance, than the poets of the other two generations. Sartre defined the new literature as being "engaged" (*la littérature engagée*), and this term applies to the poetry of this generation so directly concerned with the actual circumstances and events. The greatness of Jouve (who chronologically belongs to the previous generation) brilliantly illustrates this use of the immediate event in poetry. Pierre Emmanuel (b. 1916) has written generously of his admiration for Jouve and of the influence which Jouve's poetry has had on his own. One of Emmanuel's noteworthy achievements is the vigor he has given to poetry of a well-defined subject matter. He has mingled, for example, the Orpheus theme with the redemptive

power of Christ in one of his early works, *Le Tom-
beau d'Orphée,* where the mystery of man is not separated from the mystery of the exterior world.

The ambition of this youngest generation has been,
in general, to recall the poet to reality, after the long
experimentation of poetry with language, with the
symbol, with the hieratic role of the poet. The new
writer has felt a greater desire for communication,
for immediate communication, we should say, with
the reader. On the whole, he is less subjective than
the earlier poets. He appropriates the common basis
of world events and world problems for his verse. This
tendency was already visible in the poetry of Eluard,
of Supervielle and of Michaux. The earliest poetry of
Patrice de la Tour du Pin (b. 1911) was published in
1932 and seemed to prophesy the advent of a very
great poet. His six hundred page *Somme de Poésie* has
not justified these hopes, but the work illustrates the
ambition of discovering for the modern age a common
body of metaphysics.

Existentialism, as a literary movement, has not developed any poets, with the possible exception of
Francis Ponge, on whose work Sartre himself has written a long essay. Although Ponge was born in 1899,
his first important publication was in 1942, *Le Parti
Pris des Choses,* a poetic work of great rigor and objectivity, and one completely lacking in any subjective
lyricism. In describing an object: a pebble, for example, or a piece of bread, Ponge can also write as a
moralist, as a contemporary La Fontaine.

Robert Ganzo, born in 1898, and therefore a contemporary of Ponge, also attracted for the first time
serious attention in the 1940's. A skillful, meticulous
technician, his poem *Domaine* is a remarkably

achieved poem on a jellyfish as symbol of the poet's conscience reflecting all appearances. Although Raymond Queneau, born in 1903, has written principally and prolifically in the domain of the novel, he is also a poet. His central preoccupation with language, with what he considers a needed revolution in language, places him very centrally among the poets. His influence is wide, exceeded only by the more massive influence of a writer like Sartre. By advocating the reintegration of the vitality of spoken language, each book of his is a "stylistic exercise." His powers seem to be tricks with words, and in the freedom of composition he practices he is often reminiscent of Surrealism with which he was in fact at first associated. His writing mingles all the contemporary scenes: the suburbs, the "zone," the movies, autocars, but his distortions of caricature are suffused with what is an essentially poetic atmosphere.

Henri Thomas (b. 1912) is as spontaneous and youthful in his writing as Maurice Fombeure (b. 1907), who maintains in his verse elements of the refrain, the *chanson*, a certain shrewd, peasant-like quality, not absent from Apollinaire, who is still in France the leading modern poet of this style. Luc Estang (b. 1911) recalls persistently the art of the Symbolists. Jean Cayrol (b. 1911) is almost prophetic in his use of the great myths of humanity and in his preoccupation with the spiritual. By many, and especially by Breton, Aimé Césaire (b. 1913) is considered the first major colored poet in French. He lives in Martinique. Not until after the second war was his poetry discovered in France. Breton has acclaimed him as one of the legitimate heirs of Surrealism, by reason of the violence and richness of Surrealism, and by his spirit of revolt against an unjust society. Alain Borne (b. 1915), in company with Patrice de la Tour du Pin and Luc Estang, represents the Catholic tradition. The Catholicism of Loys Masson, born also in 1915, is perhaps less orthodox. A poet from l'Ile Maurice, Malcolm de Chazal, has recently been discovered by Jean Paulhan, who has for many years exercised a very powerful role as literary critic and judge in the house of Gallimard. In 1947, the lyric play, *Les Epiphanies,* by Henri Pichette (b. 1924) was a marked success for the experimental theatre and for the talent of one of the youngest poets.

These, then, are some of the most representative of the three generations of French poets writing at the mid-century. During the tragic years of the war and the German Occupation of France, the poets reached a larger audience than usual. At the grave moments of history, humanity is wont to turn to its poets in order to reconsider man's fate, to understand more profoundly the relationship of man with the universe, and to enjoy the poetic word as the expression of the ideas by which men live. The last generation is the most difficult to judge. There are signs in it of impatience and haste, but its poetry has in common with the poetry of the two preceding generations the visible influence and even domination of the same gods of modern French poetry: Rimbaud and Apollinaire, especially, and then the less visible but always present influence and examples of Baudelaire and Mallarmé.

III: ST.-JOHN PERSE

The art of St.-John Perse provides one of the loftiest contemporary lessons on the meaning of poetry and

on the role of the poet both in his own time and in
all times. His poetry is always the act of understanding, which is equivalent to the seizure of the intimate
and essential relationship existing between orders or
phenomena or objects. This seizure he narrates in such
sumptuous language, of such dazzling spectacular
beauty, that a unity is engendered surrounding and
combining all diversity, all antinomy. The consciousness of this poet is the principal instrument of his art:
it is the rapport between man's deepest instincts he
learns and sings. He wills to learn and therefore to
know and dominate whatever there is to see and feel
and hear in the universe. It is his will toward—eternity, rather than immortality, in this particular case.
Behind every manifestation of mobility and fluctua-
tion he finds a pure and constant relationship, a pure
and constant truth, a sign of the immutable. The real
world, in the poetry of Perse, becomes less approxi-
mate and less degraded. To man and to every aspiration of man he ascribes some eternal meaning. Everything precarious and ephemeral appears less so in the
condition of his poetry, which is a relentless conquest
of reality, a transcription of reality outside of time.

The present is sung of in this poetry so flagrantly
and pervasively that it becomes eternal. The oneness
of the poet is lost when he sings. What in him as a
human being is a state of becoming is miraculously
transposed into a state of being. This is like a decisive
event which explodes and marks the end of some temporary state and the beginning of an eternal one. The
sorrows and joys we associate with time lose their
temporal aspect in the poems of Perse, and find a new
meaning, a new accomplishment. The poet discovers
in them new resources and new reasons. This is per-

haps vision. At least it is consciousness by which all
color and form are modified. The universe is recognizable in these poems, but it is changed. It has es-
caped the tyranny of minutes. It is more sovereign,
more real, more powerful. And the poet, too, is more
than a mere individual. He reaches in his function of
poet a fullness of being which leaves far behind the
imperfect and limited individual he is in every other
function. What elevates him must be this new sense of
existence, this new energy which joins him with the
cosmos. His consciousness is an act of such fullness
that it recreates him so that in him the absolute is
consummated.

Alexis Léger was born in 1887, on a coral island
near Guadaloupe, Saint-Léger-les-Feuilles, which be-
longed to his father's family. His early years were
spent there and on Guadaloupe itself where his mother's family owned plantations. At the age of eleven
he went to France to complete his education. In 1914
he entered the Diplomatic Service, and was sent to
China in 1917. In 1922 he attended the Disarma-
ment Conference in Washington in his capacity as
expert on the Far East, and then accompanied back
to Paris Aristide Briand, whom he served for the next
ten years. Legend has it that while walking with the
poet beside the Potomac, Briand was struck by Léger's statement that a book is the death of a tree. (*Un
livre, c'est la mort d'un arbre.*) At Briand's death, in
1932, Léger became permanent Secretary of Foreign
Affairs. At the capitulation of France, in 1940, Léger,
rather than submit to appeasement, left for England,
and arrived in Canada on July 14th. Archibald Mac-
Leish offered Léger a post at the Library of Congress
where the French poet took up an important service

for the library and French letters. At this time he wrote *Exil*, which initiated a new series of poems. He still lives in Washington today.

Eloges was first published in 1910, in the Editions de la Nouvelle Revue Française, with the signature Saint Léger Léger. The new edition, of 1925, appeared with the signature St.-John Perse. The name may well have been chosen because of Léger's admiration for the ancient writer Persius. *Eloges* are poems evocative of childhood spent in the midst of exotic vegetation, in a harbor cluttered up with colonial merchandise. The vision of the sea dominates this childhood, with its memories of cyclones, plantations, volcanoes, tidal waves. *Anabase*, first published in Paris in 1924, preserves the memory of the five years Léger spent in China and the Gobi desert. This work, translated by T. S. Eliot in 1930, is one of the key poems of our age. It represents the poet as conqueror of the word, in the guise of a literal conqueror associated with arms and horses, with a willed exile in foreign places. As soon as the plans of the future city are drawn up, the conqueror leaves. Experiences and joys are enumerated, but there is always more to see and to hear: *Beaucoup de choses sur la terre à entendre et à voir, choses vivantes parmi nous!* But the literal conquest related is not so important as the actual conquest of language carried out by the poet in the writing of his poem. The primitive meaning of words is fought over and won. The history of the poet is the history of man seeking possession of the entire earth.

In March 1942, *Poetry* (of Chicago) published the original French text of Léger's poem *Exil*. This is much more than a poem on the war and on the exile of Perse. It is a more profound work on the same theme of *Anabase*, on the poet's exile, on the necessary "absence," which precedes every work of art: *un grand poème né de rien*. This concept, traditionally associated with Mallarmé, is explored and revitalized in *Exil*. The poet is the man who inhabits his name. His syntax is the pure language of exile. Isolated from the rest of the long poem, the final line is both the summation of the work and the announcement of the poems to come:

Et c'est l'heure, ô Poète, de décliner ton nom, ta naissance et ta race.

The sensations which come to him from the rains, the snows, the winds and the sea are each in turn to be the subject of the new poems. The form of these poems is nontraditional. Léger has perfected a broad stanza containing its own beat and pulsation. He observes the world and spells it out in his verse, as it comes to him in his meditation. His speech is breath and concrete words. He enumerates all parts of the familiar world surrounding man: animals and plants and the elements, and he does not hesitate to use precise technical terms. The poem is a ceremonial, involving all the diverse activities of man, and stating them in successive gestures. The world of his poetry has the freshness of a new creation. It is total and totally present. Whatever legendary elements remain are actualized in this poetry which is always praise, as the title of the first volume, *Eloges*, revealed.

It is impossible to separate the scansion, or the articulation, from the words of the line in Perse's poetry. One supports the other, one authorizes the other, and to such a degree that sound and meaning are dilated far beyond their usual limits. The poem seems to form and grow before one's eyes. Language creates the work of art, and the work of art grows out of the language. Almost every critic who has written on Perse has been struck by the opulence of his work, by its solemnity, by the persistent use of *grand* and *grandeur*, of *haut* and *hauteur*, of *vaste*, and other such words which provide the work with cosmic dimensions. The figure of the Prince is associated with the themes of power and exile and language. The prince in his world is the prototype of the poet in his poem. Each has to undergo a similar paradox and learn to live in accordance with two seemingly opposed regimens. The prince: in power and impoverishment, in adornment and nudity; the poet: in silence and language, in magic and mysticism.

St.-John Perse is heir to one of the richest poetic traditions. The form of his poetry, as well as the metaphysical use he puts it to, recalls the examples of Rimbaud in *Les Illuminations,* of Lautréamont in *Les Chants de Maldoror,* and of Claudel in *Cinq Grandes Odes*. He is the contemporary poet who comes perhaps closest to considering himself the instrument of superior revelation. When he speaks as a poet, something is affirmed in him and in itself. He knows that the most simple object or the most trite event is capable of giving birth to a poem. In this sense, his being is the restoration of eternity, the actualizing of eternity. This does not mean that he always knows the full significance of what he says and does. On the contrary! His poetry is the yielding to something more imperious than his own voice, something that cannot be defined with the research and the precision which are found in the actual stanzas. Yet the poetry reveals the desire to reach this inaccessible source. It is constantly striving to make present what is for all time. This will, by definition, is never without a struggle against death. The poet has to accomplish simultaneously two acts which appear contradictory. He has to represent himself outside of his normal state of becoming a mortal man, and at the same time he must abolish any part of his personality, any part of his uniqueness. To become possessed by such a will is equivalent to being its martyr. Perse is obsessed and martyred by his vision, as Mallarmé and Rimbaud were by theirs. The poet's vocation is his drama. To transcend one's existence by participating in it more profoundly is the poet's honor and suffering. Whether it be Besançon or Aden or Washington, the poet's exile is his solitude and his ethics.

St.-John Perse revindicates, reactivates the ancient belief that each event in the history of man signifies something else. In this sense, the work of the poet is comparable to the work of the psychoanalyst who explores the meanings of things and at the end of the search illuminates them. Poetry is a combination of two languages: one, the words defined in dictionaries and used by the contemporaries of the poet, the vocabularies of the uneducated and the educated; and the other, the rhythm of language, the spell created by combinations of words. This second language is in reality the poet's effort to move beyond language, to reach the ineffable. Language itself may be for man his deepest spiritual experience. Beyond language extends the void, the unmeasured spaces inhabited by the winds of which Perse speaks in his poem *Vents*. The meaning of the winds which blow over the face of the earth and disturb all perishable things is the subject matter of his poem. The opening words speak of the winds in quest, of oracles and maxims, and of the narrator who seeks the favor of a god for his poem.

St.-John Perse, as the contemporary poet, does not borrow from the traditional forms of poetry, but from the words of language itself and from the sentiment of vertigo felt by the poet on the brink of space, in the midst of limitless winds. As much as any man of any period, Alexis Léger has traveled along the high-ways of many lands and across the oceans of the world. The course of his poem is the meaning of such travels, the new style of grandeur he refers to, and the pure song about which there is no real knowl-edge. The weight of the words would seem to be the only force not dispersed by the winds. The words, riveted to the pages, are those signs, fixed forever, of things which move with the wind and die in it. "Ashes and squams of the spirit," he says, "taste of asylum and casbah."

At the opening of the poem, other words, deeply imbedded in the text, appear almost synonymous with "winds": "dreams," for example, when joined with such an adjective as "favorable"; and "intoxi-cated," whereby "wine" is associated with the inva-sions of doctrine. Such words have the same power of describing circles around the earth. The poet who is "still with us" has once again spoken the words of a living man which recreate his world with some of its multiple meanings. He is the one taught to think something else. Poetry, in such a work as *Vents*, reaffirms its power and its destiny to draw upon all forms of knowledge: psychoanalysis, history, phenomenology, autobiography. It is perhaps the one art of synthesis, able to show at moments of intense illumination the once complete form of our shattered world.

Certain poems, like the one under discussion, can only be composed because man inhabits what Perse calls "the calcinated earth of dreams." We may be certain that whatever thought occurs to us, its depth and its originality will not at first be recognizable to us. The finite brief character of a human existence echoes depths which will never be sounded. No one thought remains for long what it seems to be at first. The poet is precisely the one who torments traditionally accepted words and things until they release some of their unsuspected meanings. In order to rise up once again into the world, such meanings had to take detours and even provoke ruses and deceptions.

Claudel, in his essay on *Vents,* published first in *La Revue de Paris* of November 1949, says that the second part of the poem evokes America, both the puritan melancholy of the North and the stagnant stupor of the South. Certain words in the text clearly justify this belief: Audubon, sumac, hanging moss, Columbus. The poem unfolds in wave after wave of images, almost as if they preceded the poet, because their very profusion might have paralyzed him. Their forms do not appear in the least contestable or corroded, and yet they proclaim the primacy of the obscure, the sulphurous, the pythic. The winds, in this section of the poem, carry with them the smell of fire. They may well establish an "ascetic rule."

The poet, the man "assailed by the god," speaks equivocally. He speaks with brilliance about the negative traits of his art. He knows what his method is not: an intellectual program, a will to please, a self-complacency not always communicable. What his method is, is too vast to define, too close today to our manner of reading poetry. *Vents* of St.-John Perse, as well as *Les Illuminations* of Rimbaud, and to some extent *Les Fleurs du Mal* of Baudelaire, are among those modern works of poetry reflecting the complex degree of sensibility which man reached in the nineteenth century and continues to maintain in the twentieth. Perse has taken his place beside the four or five major poets of modern France: Baudelaire, Mallarmé, Rimbaud, Valéry, Claudel. Like theirs, his work defies any facile nomenclature of romantic or classical. A major poetic work will always appear in excess of the literary school closest to it. Adherence to classicism seems to imply an emphasis on form, on the poet as demiurge and creator. Romanticism is revealed in the poet's passivity to the exterior world, to the cosmos of matter. Perse and the other poets whose tradition he continues represent extremes in their role of demiurge and in their trait of passivity to the cosmic forces. They are extraordinary technicians drawing upon all the known resources of their art, upon the most modern beliefs in ancient poetic vision, and upon the most ancient tenets still visible in Symbolism and Surrealism. Each in his own way strives for some balance between his inner psychic tensions and his virtuosity. But the balance reached has many degrees. The art of Valéry and that of a typical Surrealist would represent extremes of this very balance.

Part three of *Vents* evokes the history of the conquerors, their long itineraries, the new lands, the setting up of new trade. The poet too belongs to the

race of discoverers: to the *conquistadores,* well-dig-
gers, astrologers. In his acquisitions he seizes with
similar boldness the goals of his search, of his humor
and of his sorrow. Into a poem he puts the originality
of his discovery as one puts the essence of flowers
into a flask.

The general effect of the entire poem, and especially of the third section, where the wanderers are
men with antennae, is one of constant movement
through fear that all movement will cease. In the
midst of the poem, it is impossible to believe that it
will ever end. The poet is no longer the prisoner of
his form; he is the prisoner of his poem which is
limitless. Each stanza, as it moves ahead, acts as a
detonator for the next. No one picture is allowed to
remain static for fear that it might settle into a symbol with an established human relationship. This is
no poem to be anthologized where it might testify
to a moment in time and to the achievement of a literary school. It testifies only to itself, to the honor of
men and their failure, to their torches held in the
wind and extinguished, to the conjunction of their
experiences. Even the form of the novel would attempt the imposing of greater limitations on such an
inexhaustible subject matter. All the characters are
phantoms in these winds, liberated, authentic phantoms whose power is never confused with any vulgar
opportunism.

The wind is the element giving us life. It is in our
lungs and in our mouth in capsules of emptiness,
necessary for us whether we move over distances
covered by a Drake or a crusader, or whether we
remain in one corner of the planet and perish through
excess of wisdom. Poems, in a destiny comparable

to the winds, bear seed and fruit. A book is a series of separations, departures, returns, of changings of speed. The fourth section of *Vents* evokes not only the plateaus of the world and the aging roads of pilgrimages. It evokes as well the dilemma of man's ceaseless questioning and the equivocal mask of art placed over all interrogations. The poem here is less a novel or an epic than it is a cosmology. A cosmological novel, perhaps.

The poet's experience which made possible such a poem as *Vents* is beyond question irreplaceable and unique. But the poem is also the history of contemporary sensibility. The paradox is constructed around the subjective uniqueness of the poem and its universality. The rigorous methods employed in the writing of history will never succeed in providing the kind of history of modern man narrated in such a poem as *Vents*. Historians are quickly dated even if their subject matter never goes out of date. Poets take generations and even centuries to come into some kind of comprehensible focus, and their poems, more intense and penetrating than written history, combine with the future in order to bring it about.

The action of a literary school, such as Symbolism or Surrealism, tends to serve as the history of a moment and a sensibility. The major poet is usually characterized by his separation from the school and from any historical approach. This was the case of Mallarmé and Rimbaud. It is the case today of Claudel, and St.-John Perse. Exile and solitude are themes in the poetry of Perse and they appear to be the conditions of the present life of Alexis Léger. The major traits of his art tend to make it into a sacred text: elegance of circumlocution, unusual words, constant reference to celebrations and rituals, ambiguities arising from the juxtaposition of the cultivated and the elemental, the baroque and the bare.

No message is visible in *Vents*, but the poem is a remarkable statement of the poet's principal paradox. The poet is both separated from human activity and deeply involved in customs, beliefs, rites, relationships. He is both contemplator of what the world holds and participant in his social group and in his national life. The seriousness with which he considers life seems to come from this combination of homogeneity and isolation. The official attitude of the Symbolists was aloofness. The official attitude of the Surrealists was aggressiveness. St.-John Perse represents a more traditional, more central attitude of the poet. The precise word is difficult to choose, because on the whole this attitude is seldom felt today, but it would be perhaps solemnity or sacredness. It would be a word powerful enough to contain and harmonize the contradictions of man's fate as it appears to us within the limits of time and space.

IV: RENÉ CHAR

René Char was born in 1906 in Vaucluse, a section of Provence. He lives today in a town near Avignon, Isle-sur-la-Sorgue. The Sorgue River starts at the fountain of Vaucluse (once immortalized by Petrarch) and flows into the Rhone. Although Char has been associated for more than twenty years with contemporary French poetry, it is only since the war that he has received the attention he deserves. Many critics believe him to be the outstanding poet of his generation, and one of the greatest ever to come from Provence. The world of his poetry is rural and Mediter-

ranean. All the familiar elements of his native prov-
vince are in it: crickets and almond trees, olives,
grapes, figs, oranges, grass, branches of mimosa. The
frequently recurring name of Heraclitus helps to
fuse the Greek spirit with the Provençal. The country he describes is sun-flooded, a kingdom of space
and dazzling light. Char's love of the land and his
solicitude for living growing things are traits of the
peasant in him. His manner of considering the objects of his landscape, of undertaking the hardest
tasks and facing the gravest risks might also be traced
to peasant background, or more simply, be explained
by the deep sense of fraternity which characterizes
Char's love of man and of the soil. Like most lovers
of the land, he has often shown hostility toward
modern mechanization and modern forms of exploitation.

About 1930 René Char joined the group of Surrealists. This marked his first formal affiliation with a
literary movement. Although he soon cut himself off
from any strict allegiance to Surrealism, he profited
from many aspects of the school. From a spirit of
revolt, first, which permeated all of Surrealism. He
learned that revolt against conformity is a natural instinct of the poet, a natural instinct of poetry. The
boldness and novelty of Surrealist imagery taught
Char that there is a kind of poetry totally opposed to ordinary discourse, to what is called in
France *éloquence*. Surrealism was a collective ex-
periment which must have deepened Char's sense of
brotherhood. The effort made by Breton, Desnos,
Eluard to create out of their poems unusual per-
spectives and paradoxes by writing at maximum speed
and adding image on image affected Char more than

the philosophical inquiry, semi-Bergsonian, semi-
Freudian, of Surrealism.

Char's initiation during the thirties into practices
and theories of Surrealist art was followed in the
early forties by his admirable participation in the
Resistance movement, in his role of captain of the
maquis in Provence. Today most of the Resistance
poetry, which was so warmly welcomed at the time
of its clandestine publication, appears outmoded and
ineffectual. Aragon's particularly has lost its freshness
and vigor. Char's partisan poems were quite different
from the others, and they form the noblest of the war
poems and the most likely to endure. The group, for
example, *Feuillets d'Hypnos*, dedicated to Albert
Camus and included in the important volume of 1948,
Fureur et Mystère, represent best the poetry written
between 1940 and 1944. The claim has been made,
with considerable justice, that they correspond to
Apollinaire's *Calligrammes*, the best poetic testimonial of 1914.

The maquis provided Char with a new poetic vision, a new contact with reality. The boldness of his
early poems became more marked in the war poems
where the images joined with the impassioned meaning of war and resistance. Some of the poems are
today as well known as when they were first distributed in secret. One, for example, often anthologized, in which he tells of the execution of a close
friend, which he permits because the village has to
be saved at all costs. Char's deep love of mankind
replaces religious experience which seems to be totally absent from his work. His war poems, those in
Seuls Demeurent and *Feuillets d'Hypnos*, were not
built solely on noble sentiments, as were so many

Resistance poems which are no longer read, but on a rhythmical movement as strong and original as the rhythms of Pascal's prose and of Rimbaud's prose poems. They were never solely war poems for Char. They were first the communications about something ineffable which all poems must be.

This definition of the ineffable as the secret source of all poems explains what has been called the obscurity of Char. His is not the more purely linguistic obscurity of a Mallarmé or a Rimbaud. It is more metaphorical, more reminiscent of Surrealist obscurity since it is language seeking essentially to transcribe the subconscious. This concern with the subconscious was the major poetic endeavor during the period of Surrealism and has continued to be that ever since the thirties. For such a poet as Char, the miraculous or the magical is the objective of his search, wherever it is carried out: in a real object, in hallucination, in the experience of love or sleep or sexuality.

Everything is made present in poetry, because poetry is presence. What is generally considered a thought does not primarily interest the poet. His concern is with the source of thought, the movement, half-sensation, half-emotion, which precedes any formulation of logical thinking. The unknown is the real subject matter of poetic knowledge. René Char's best pages illustrate the principle that the unknown provides the richness of man's mind. The initial perception counts far more for the poet than the calculated notion.

Throughout the suggestive statements comprising *Partage Formel* (in the volume *Fureur et Mystère*), Char analyzes this basic mysteriousness of all poetry.

Le poème est l'amour réalisé du désir demeuré désir.
Heraclitus also was called obscure in his will to
effect harmony between opposites. The transformation of time into eternity, associated with the philosopher, has its counterpart in the poet's will to fix in
rhythmical language an emotion destined to pass
quickly. The strength of the poet grows midway between the state of innocence and knowledge, between love and the death of love. *Entre innocence et
connaissance, amour et néant, le poète étend sa santé
chaque jour.*

These maxims on poetry stress an admirable belief in the laws of chance whereby each day for the
poet a subtle exchange can be carried on between
himself and the things of the world. Poetry is looked
upon as a dialogue between the poet and the objects
he sees. Words used in this dialogue are found to
have surprising properties. The subtlest exchange of
all is that existing between the object named and the
name which the poet gives to the object. This poetic
exchange is comparable to the one existing within
the experience of love, between exaltation and meditation, between what Char calls *fureur et mystère.* In
accordance with the most ancient tradition of all,
Char believes that poetry is inseparable from enthusiasm. The extreme poles of inspiration and labor, of
emotion and thought, are hostile only in a superficial
way. The poet's work is achieved by their fusion.

In his most recent publications, *A une sérénité
crispée* (1951) and *Lettera Amorosa* (1953), Char
continues using the form of maxim or poetic pro-
nouncement he had evolved in *Feuillets d'Hypnos.*
The oxymoron of the first title, "To a tensed serenity,"
so reminiscent of other Char titles: *Les Loyaux Ad-*

versaires, Le Poème Pulvérisé, Fureur et Mystère, is
in keeping with his master Heraclitus, who, according to Char, "emphasizes the exultant alliance of opposites." Char the moralist is never estranged from
Char the poet. His use of the natural world helps him
to formulate not only his enthusiasms, but his mode
of behavior and the reason for his love as well. A relationship exists between the enigmas of poetry and the
actions of the poet. *J'aime l'homme incertain de ses
fins comme l'est, en avril, l'arbre fruitier.* The serenity
he has reached is rightfully called "tensed," because it
involves a lucid understanding of the diabolic in human nature, of the deception man perpetrates daily,
even if it is irresponsible deception in many cases.

In a recent maxim, Char states that the bird and
the tree are joined in us. Whereas one moves back
and forth, the other grows. With the accumulation of
such formulas, it is increasingly evident that this poet
is chartering a course for poets, which, if it is not
new, appears refreshing and clarified. He would lead
us to believe that the art of the word is still in its
prehistorical period. It is still waiting to live more
fully in its own domain. Despite all the advance of
science and despite the successive volumes of modern
verse: Baudelaire, Rimbaud, Mallarmé, Lautréamont
—man is still unable to capture the full energy of the
sun and the full energy of the poetic word.

Thus conceived, the word was at one time in history the exclusive property and privilege of the priest.
Victor Hugo considered the poet the new priest and
prophet of modern times. René Char, in agreement
with a precious belief of Surrealism formulated by
Lautréamont and Rimbaud, would probably say that
the new poetic word will tomorrow become the voice

of each man, a collective voice in accord with the orchestration of the universe. A force closer to the universality of music and no longer jealously guarded by the few elect. Char, in his backward glance across the centuries to Heraclitus, has divined something about the original source of the word. *In principio erat Verbum.* But ahead of him there is a legitimate place, the first perhaps, to be won. The poet, more than other teachers today, indicates the way ahead in the direction of the beginning.

Genius is by definition inexhaustible, and poetic history is composed not so much by the appearance of poems as by periods of silence, such as Rimbaud's. The fullness of the word can only be guessed at from the multiple signs of the poems consigned to paper. The role of René Char is today what has been the role of each previous major poet, that of teaching the belief that poetry must lead somewhere. The quest of the poet remains far more lucid than the actual poems which are the confused opaque testimonials to his quest.

NINE

THE ESSAY

No literary form in this century has been so ruth-
lessly attacked as criticism. The critics in France have
been subjected to the same scornful treatment which
American and English critics have known. Sartre has
called critics "cemetery keepers." And yet the art of
criticism is indispensable to the cause of literature.
The first generation of the twentieth century was one
of the most brilliant in French literary criticism.
Péguy, Valéry, Gide and Claudel added to their major
work important contributions in their essays and critical writings. Péguy re-evaluated and reinterpreted
Corneille and Hugo (*Victor-Marie, Comte Hugo,*
1910). Valéry, on many occasions, analyzed the origins of his poems and the art of poetry. In his critical
judgments, as they appeared in essays (*Incidences,*
1924; *Interviews Imaginaires,* 1942) and in his
Journal, André Gide directed the literary taste of
two generations. Claudel's *Art Poétique* (1907) is a
significant manifesto, which is elucidated in his es-
264

says on Baudelaire and Mallarmé (*Positions et Propositions*, 1928 and 1934).

Since the second World War, the literary periodicals and weeklies have been publishing the reviews and essays of a group of excellent professional critics: Maurice Blanchot, André Rousseaux, Thierry Maulnier, Gaëtan Picon, Claude Roy, Maurice Nadeau, Robert Kanters. It is obvious from their writings that the traditional literary quarrels have disappeared. There are almost no echoes today of the famous disputes between classicists and romantics, or between romantics and symbolists. In their approach to literature, these newer critics are not concerned with discussing the ways of conceiving a work of art, but rather the ways of conceiving and directing human life. They still demonstrate interest in technical problems, but the real center of most literary criticism in France today is elsewhere, in domains fairly close to morals and sociology. Even some of the most famous modern novels, such as *La Condition Humaine* of Malraux, and *La Peste* of Albert Camus, are treatises of morality, not too deliberately disguised.

Literary criticism, as we know it today, began in France with the writings of Madame de Staël and Chateaubriand at the beginning of the nineteenth century. The art of literary criticism grew out of their method of psychological analysis, with its emphasis on the Christian training in repentance and self-examination. Their method was a means of understanding a writer and explaining him. Scholarly research in literature was initiated and university chairs were founded soon after the careers of Madame de Staël and Chateaubriand, in an effort to continue and deepen in a more scientific way their pioneer work.

Sainte-Beuve (1804-1869) is, in a more recognizable way, the real founder of modern literary criticism in France. He was not a specialist. He was a poet, a novelist, and more essentially a literary critic who set himself the goal of understanding and explaining individual writers. His method combined the science of facts with an exceptional power of interpretation. In each of his essays, Sainte-Beuve sought to explain a temperament. His judgments on books seem to us today primarily judgments on men. It was not his intention to write history, but he did make claims to writing philosophical ideas and general laws. He called his essays "a course on moral physiology." His method, as expounded in Les Lundis, is the opposite of the scientific method. His Port-Royal is essentially a psychological study of one aspect of French society of the seventeenth century.

By the end of the nineteenth century, literary criticism had evolved in one direction into the more rigorous systems of Taine and Brunetière, and in the opposite direction into the personal impressionism of such lecturers and writers as Anatole France, Jules Lemaître and Rémy de Gourmont. In opposition to these two styles, the university founded, under the leadership of Gustave Lanson (1857-1934), the science of literary history, based upon research and verifiable facts. The extreme academic disciples of Lanson, and the extreme impressionistic critics, still carry on a vehement polemics on the nature of criticism. The literary essayists of the past twenty or thirty years whose influence is preponderant belong neither to the university historians nor to the impressionistic critics, but to a far older French tradition, in which Sainte-Beuve occupies a central role. It is the tradition of moralistic critics who are interested in reaching general ideas, and who are desirous of suggesting and proving literary theory by use of paradox and analogy, by a variety of tone and dimension and subject. The works of these writers may be classified as "essays."

The development of this literary genre was aided and protected by the important periodical, *La Nouvelle Revue Française,* founded in 1909 by Gide, Jacques Copeau and Jean Schlumberger. Jacques Rivière was editor from 1910-25, and Jean Paulhan was editor from 1925-40. Publication was suspended during the two war periods. It began again in 1945, with the title, *La Nouvelle Nouvelle Revue Française* (today shortened to its original form). In the early years of its existence, it published the essays of Claudel, Gide, Valéry, Péguy, Proust. It has always maintained the highest literary standard. By itself it gradually formed a "literary chapel," although it is impossible to ascribe to it any literary school. At the beginning it was somewhat opposed to Symbolism, or those traits of Symbolism which resembled obscurantism and a passive interest in life. It created an important publishing house, known today as Gallimard's, the official publisher of the contributors to *La Nouvelle Revue Française.* The essays of Rivière himself, collected in book form under the title *Etudes* (1912), illustrate the type of essay favored by the group. During the twenties and thirties, the *N.R.F.* was fairly sympathetic to Surrealism. By that time, it had developed its own brand of academism. It played a major part in revealing to France the work of such foreign writers as Chekhov, Conrad, Joyce, Pirandello.

By insisting on some of the characteristics of the literary essay in France, it will be necessary to omit certain types of criticism not essentially literary. Writers, for example, who are philosophers or theologians: Bergson, Gabriel Marcel, Gaston Bachelard, Merleau-Ponty, Emmanuel Mounier, Jacques Maritain, Denis de Rougemont, Jean-Paul Sartre, Simone de Beauvoir, Georges Bataille, Jean Wahl. We omit also the more purely literary historians: Guy Michaud, René Jasinski, Jean Pommier, Armand Hoog.

Julien Benda (1867-1956) has waged in the history of French letters a life-long battle for the cause of rationalism. His earliest campaign in the century was directed against Bergson (*Le Bergsonisme ou une philosophie de la mobilité*, 1912). He ascribes to the influence of Bergson and to what he calls the anti-intellectualism of Bergson the insistence on the part of modern readers to be moved by literary works rather than to understand them. Benda uses in his most famous book, *La Trahison des Clercs* (1927), the word *clerc* as synonymous with "thinker" and develops the thesis that the modern *clerc* has betrayed his mission which should be that of fighting for justice and truth. In *La France Byzantine*, of 1945, Benda organizes a full-scale attack on many of the leading contemporary writers. He denounces especially Gide, Valéry, Proust and Giraudoux, who represent for him the principal enemies of traditional French logic and clarity. He looks upon them as writers who oppose twenty centuries of civilization. Modern literature, claims Benda, is empty of ideas and reason and logic. It avoids the expression of clear ideas for dreams and for thought in its extreme mobility. It is literature which places the value in expression rather than in the thing expressed. The adjectives he applies to this body of literature, and which are derogatory for Benda, are "obscure," "hermetic," "precious."

Between 1909 and 1933, Alain (Emile Chartier, 1868-1951) taught the philosophy class at the Lycée Henri IV, in Paris. His pupils, on many of whom he had a profound influence, became writers, professors, administrators, who still today acknowledge their debt to him. Alain perfected the short essay which follows a recognizable pattern. It begins with a seemingly insignificant detail and develops into a generality. This short essay he calls a *propos* which is often one page long.

From the collections of *Propos,* of separate detached essays, and from his two studies of Stendahl and Balzac, Alain's distrust for professional philosophers is visible as well as his preference for poets and novelists. His doctrine on art resembles the Parnassian theory of art for art's sake and Valéry's doctrine. He looks upon art as born from passion and feeling, but formed by thought and labor. Alain is a realist moralist who estimates the limits of the human mind. He is a sceptic in religion, a pacifist in politics, and an aesthetician in literature. In recent years, Alain has been succeeded by newer masters, by men like Malraux and Sartre. To the younger readers in France, his wisdom seems overprudent, and his optimism unjustified in a world which appears to so many thinkers on the verge of catastrophe.

Bergson called Albert Thibaudet (1874-1936) the greatest French critic since Sainte-Beuve. Thibaudet was at the beginning of his career a Bergsonian. For

twenty years he was one of the principal literary
critics of *La Nouvelle Revue Française*. He was
trained as an historian, a sociologist and geogra-
pher. His method of criticism is in the tradition of
Sainte-Beuve's, midway between pure scholarship and
the impressionistic chronicle or essay. He tends to
classify writers by provinces and by generations, and
to explain literary works by a synthetic view and by
a frequent use of analogy. His pioneer work on *La
Poésie de Stéphane Mallarmé* (1912) has not gone
out of date despite the vast number of books on the
poet since Thibaudet's. His *Gustave Flaubert* (1922)
is still one of the best studies of the novelist. In his
Réflexions sur le Roman (1938), Thibaudet develops
some of his most perceptive theories and judgments.
His posthumous work, *Histoire de la littérature
française depuis 1789* (1936), is far more stimulating
and provocative than the usual history of literature.

Charles Du Bos (1883-1939) is the type of critic
whose life was totally merged with the books he read
and the essays he wrote on his favorite authors. He
expounds no particular doctrine. Du Bos taught literature only once, briefly, at the University of Notre
Dame, in Indiana. He loved literature with an abiding
passion, and all his life read certain authors continuously until he reached a penetrating understanding of the works. By means of this exceptionally attentive kind of reading, he was able to comprehend
and expound problems of literary creation. Very
early, in 1921, Du Bos guessed the plan of Proust's
complete novel, through his reading of the first two
parts.

Seven volumes of his essays have appeared under
the modest title of *Approximations* (1932-39). In

only one case did Du Bos attack an author. He was a close friend of André Gide, but he carried on a moral debate with Gide in his *Dialogue avec André Gide* (1927). In his *Journal*, which is now in the process of publication, as well as in the volumes of *Approximations*, it is possible to follow the love and understanding which Charles Du Bos bestows on his favorites: Amiel, Constant, Baudelaire, Keats, Shelley, Tolstoi, Chekhov. In each essay he performs a self-identification with the author. Reading was a spiritual exercise for him. He saw life through the mirrors of his authors. With the help of several religiously minded friends, Jacques Rivière, Gabriel Marcel, Joseph and Jean Baruzi, Du Bos was converted to the Catholic Church in 1927.

The title of "critic of critics" has often been applied to Jean Paulhan (1884-   ) who assumed directorship of *La N.R.F.* at the death of Rivière, in 1925. He has been especially preoccupied with problems of language and poetics. Paulhan is a harsh, intractable critic whose principal attack on contemporary litterature appears in his essay of 1941, *Les Fleurs de Tarbes*. The mysterious title comes from a sign which Paulhan had noticed at the entrance of a park in Tarbes. This sign stated that it was forbidden to bring flowers into the park. This he interprets as an appropriate symbol for contemporary literature. Writers today, he claims, have become philosophers, moralists and spiritual directors rather than creators of beauty. Paulhan has played almost the part of a dictator in France where he has fought relentlessly for the autonomy of literature, freed from ethics and laws. He has persistently championed the purest of the writers. Recently he has expressed a veritable cult for the Marquis de Sade, in a brilliant introduction he wrote for *Les Infortunes de la Vertu*. His role of "critic of critics" is particularly visible in *Petite Préface à Toute Critique*, in which he takes to task the critics in their mistakes over contemporary writers. He refers to the famous nineteenth-century victims of critics: Balzac, Baudelaire, Lautréamont, Rimbaud.

The career of André Malraux (1901-   ) has undergone a curious and complicated development. Before the war his position was solidly established as one of the leading novelists, whose large social frescoes of *La Condition Humaine* and *L'Espoir* had revealed a world torn by the worst catastrophes. During the war and immediately afterward his prestige declined, more in France perhaps than in America. His political alliance with De Gaulle might explain this to some degree. But then, in 1948 appeared his two volume work, *Psychologie de l'Art* (later issued under title, *Les Voix du Silence*), which is, without much doubt, one of the important books of our time. It is far more than art criticism or art history. Malraux is the most recent man of letters in France to undertake writing on art. The lineage is a noble one: Diderot, Stendhal, Baudelaire, Taine, Alain, Valéry. The book has recaptured for Malraux a place of high esteem with the younger generation. They are reading it as a hymn of love to universal art.

Malraux believes that a struggle or battle is at the origin of artistic creation. A young artist will first imitate a master and then react against him and create an individual style. This theory of the struggle for beauty, whereby a revolt lies at the beginning of each new art, is a familiar theory; but Malraux turns the

history of art into a dramatic story that has somewhat
the character of the *Iliad* or a *chanson de geste*. He is
particularly fond of the revolutionaries: Goya, Manet,
the Christian sculptors. He has a tendency to feel
and therefore to stress the pathetic and the catastrophic in art. Malraux exalts those painters who
depicted the lowest examples of humanity. Frans
Hals, for example. He exalts those painters who efface
their subject. Malraux dilates on the theme that the
princes and the bourgeois who are painted disappear
from the face of the earth and only the painter remains. He is in total agreement with Valéry when he
writes: "A painter is not primarily a man who loves
figures and landscapes; he is primarily a man who
loves pictures." The long work on the psychology
of art, written in an opulent, almost Bossuet-like
style, is exacting and stimulating. It touches on many
problems of literature as, for example, the emotion of
the spectators watching *Oedipus*. To participate in a
work of art is comparable to plunging into a con-
flagration. There is something almost satanic in
Malraux' belief that art reveals to us a secret way of
possessing the world. He sees the artist as one who
creates another universe, who corrects or reorganizes
the work of Genesis.

Malraux gives his subject startling beauty and
seduction. His book is really on the subject of human
genius. Because of its tone and fervor, Malraux is already being considered a kind of spiritual guide in
France. In his first volume, he elaborates the theory
that art is always following one of two beliefs. The
first sees man as mastering the world, as dominating
the mystery of the world. In this art, Greek and
Renaissance, the human figure is triumphant. The sec-

ond is the belief that the mystery of the world is greater than man and crushes him. Here he would live in accordance with some terror for all that is sacred. The second volume deals with that kind of art that seems to contain both beliefs, such as medieval art. In this art, as in the smiling angel of Reims or *le beau Dieu* of Amiens, Malraux studies the relationship between man and the sacred—and particularly those forms of art which represent a harmony between them. This final book recapitulates many ideas of Malraux, such as his belief that the genius is inseparable from that out of which he is born, as fire is inseparable from what it burns.

Throughout this work on art, Malraux demonstrates an evident hostility to the real. He emphasizes the originality of technique. One thinks instinctively of his vast stylized reportings: *Les Conquérants, La Condition Humaine, L'Espoir.* In art as well as in his novels, he prefers the pathetic and the catastrophic. He dilates on the theme of the painter effacing his subject and chooses as an example Manet's painting of Clemenceau where the subject is a mere figuration and the painter is everything.

There are many remarkable details in the two volumes, passages which resemble condensed essays: the comparison of Goya's three versions of "Christ expelling the moneylenders from the temple"; the pages on Giotto; the definition of "style" which Malraux considers a refashioning of the world in terms of the values of the artist who invents it; the distinction between an artist and a craftsman (an artist like Rubens or Cézanne creates forms; a craftsman reproduces forms); the dealings between the artist and the world of things (e.g., Tintoretto painting Venetian divers as angels).

Malraux makes the psychology of art an intoxicating subject. He refers to the arts of all ages and all worlds. The prehistoric cave dwellings cohabit with Braque and Picasso. His work is really on the subject of human genius, on an extraordinary awareness of man and his destiny. He insists on convincing the reader that an artistic creation is the justification of the mystery of our life. Because of the vigor and the perceptiveness of this hymn to art, Malraux has already been chosen by many younger minds in France as a spiritual guide. His eloquence is always the most vibrant in the passages dealing with the relationship between man and the sacred. One thought above all others he never tires of reiterating, namely that art does not imitate life, but that it imitates art and reveals life. The great apology he makes for art is its immortality. If not its literal immortality, at least the breath of immortality that permeates it. Malraux is obsessed with eternity and the idea of death. "Man," he says, "is the one animal who knows he has to die." But art, in being the ever renewed creation of a world, furnishes him with faith in the power of man, with faith that man bears in himself the source of his eternity.

Maurice Blanchot (1907-   ) in the two important collections of his essays, *Faux-Pas* (1943), and *La Part du Feu* (1949), does not judge the authors he discusses, nor does he establish comparisons between authors. He makes no effort to place them in literary history. He is concerned with the foundations and the origins of literature, with the facts that there are books, and authors to write them, and readers to read them. The authors with whom he has the strongest sympathy are those who have questioned the purpose of literature: Kafka, Hölderlin, Mallarmé, Gide, Sartre; or those who, when they wrote, tried to give their writing a value which goes beyond the expression: Rimbaud and Lautréamont. Blanchot, who is one of the most profound of the newer critics, is interested in analyzing the contradictions and the paradoxes of literature. In his essay *Droit à la Mort* (*La Part du Feu*) Blanchot discusses the paradox of language itself in being both the negation of life and the affirmation of life.

From Rumania comes the essayist and aphorist E. M. Cioran (1911-   ), who in his *Précis de Décomposition* (1949) gives expression to a totally nihilistic philosophy. An implacable despair pervades his scepticism and refusal to admit any social or moral reality. In his writings Cioran places the world on trial and condemns it. He claims that man's destiny is to perish with the continents and the stars. "Decomposition presides over the laws of life," he writes. Cioran is the prophet of collective suicide and a witness to the darkest kind of pessimism our age has produced. In questioning why men continue to live, he questions the value of religion and philosophy and history. He calls creative artists cowards and victims. The language in which he expresses this despair is admirable in its purity and conciseness.

The study of Proust has been greatly facilitated by the excellent book of André Maurois, *A la recherche de Marcel Proust* (1949). For the preparation of this critical and biographical study, Maurois had access to unpublished documents which he quotes and which one day will be published in their integrity, through the generosity of Proust's heir, Mme Gérard-Mante-Proust. In the meantime, two very important works of Proust have come to light and have been published, thanks to the labors of Bernard de Fallois.

The first of these, *Jean Santeuil* (1952), is an early draft of Proust's novel. *A la recherche du temps perdu* is a far superior work, but already, in *Jean Santeuil*, Proust shows himself a genius in perspicacity and analysis, endowed with a miraculous memory, with subtlety and human sympathy. He speaks of his childhood (there is the familiar scene of the hypersensitive child who will not go to sleep without his mother's goodnight kiss), of his adolescence when he fell in love with a young girl in the Champs-Elysées, the girl destined to become Gilberte in the final version, and of his early social successes.

The second of the new Proust publications is an essay in literary criticism which both in the brilliance of its analysis and judgment and in the illumination it casts on Proust's major work, offsets the familiar annual accusation against critics in France that they do not create, that they are the parasites of the real creators. Many of the pages of Proust's novel itself [1] can be looked upon as criticism, especially those pages concerning the paintings of Elstir, the books of Bergotte and the musical compositions of Vinteuil.

The full title of the new publication is *Contre Sainte-Beuve, suivi de Nouveaux Mélanges* (1954). The title essay, *Contre Sainte-Beuve*, occupies 96

[1] The new Pléiade edition (Gallimard) of Proust's novel appeared in 1955, in three volumes. This edition, in the vast number of corrections brought to the text, takes precedence over the previous fifteen volume edition.

pages of the volume. It is a discussion of Nerval,
Baudelaire and Balzac, three authors whom Proust
considered had been misunderstood and unfairly
judged by Sainte-Beuve. In the composition of this
essay, Proust addresses his mother as he outlines his
grievances against the method of Sainte-Beuve. Principally he denies the importance of documentation
on the life of an author. This important tenet in the
method of Sainte-Beuve, he would replace by another
belief, one which he will develop extensively in his
novel. Proust believes that a book is the product of an
ego quite different from the ego an author demonstrates in his daily habits and in his social life.

Proust is unfair to Sainte-Beuve in making his attack as general as he does. Certain poets of the sixteenth, seventeenth and eighteenth centuries are
more adequately explained by Sainte-Beuve's method
than are the far more complicated Nerval and Baudelaire. Proust understood some of the mysteries of
Nerval, Baudelaire and Mallarmé, and through their
example, he stresses the need to give primacy to
instinct over intelligence. These poets were contemporaries of Sainte-Beuve. Proust profited from the passage of time and the first serious commentaries on
these poets. Such works as *Sylvie* of Nerval and *Les
Fleurs du Mal* of Baudelaire have become enriched by
criticism, and today, thanks to *Contre Sainte-Beuve*,
enriched by the criticism of Proust. This posthumous
volume is not only an addition to literary criticism,
with its generous views on Symbolism and its somewhat less generous views on Balzac toward whom
Proust was not always sympathetic, probably because
Balzac was too close to him as a novelist, but it serves

also as a companion book to *A la recherche du temps perdu.*

French letters today are just beginning to emerge from the five or six years dominated by the Resistance movement and the dire experience of the concentration camps. Soon after the Liberation, in December 1946, André Malraux, at a meeting of UNESCO in Paris, began a very serious lecture by recalling that Nietzsche at the end of the nineteenth century shocked the world by saying that God was dead. Malraux continued by saying that we today are faced with the problem of whether man is dead. Many European thinkers are wondering whether the experience of the concentration world (*l'univers concentrationnaire,* as the French call it), with its demoniacal perfection in effecting mass slaughter, has not left in Western mentality a secret traumatic upheaval which will tend to invalidate the literary arts. The type of intense physical suffering to which so many men and women were submitted is perhaps unsuitable to literary transcription. It is far different from the spiritual suffering of Pascal, or the passion of Phèdre or the paternal grief of Hugo. It is possible that the face of man has been so altered by the excess of physical pain that he is no longer a comprehensible subject for the artist. Picasso's large painting of Guernica shows the human countenance and figure deformed by the alliance of death and torture.

David Rousset's *Les Jours de notre mort* (1947) is one of the outstanding novels on the concentration camp. The modern city itself appears as a concentration camp in *La Peste* of Camus. The murderer, whether guilty or innocent, has been extraordinarily studied in modern literature. Julien Sorel, in Stendhal's *Le Rouge et le Noir*, is perhaps the ancestor of a large company today: *L'Etranger* of Camus, *Brighton Rock* of Graham Greene, *Moïra* of Julien Green, *The Trial* of Kafka.

Such subjects as the Resistance movement and the concentration world have not in any way created a literary school. In fact, twentieth-century literature, despite the significant programs of Surrealism in the thirties and Existentialism in the forties, is characterized by an absence of strongly organized and formulated literary movements. Nothing today is comparable to the Romantic or the Symbolist schools of the nineteenth century. Twentieth-century literature in France may well be as rich as that of the nineteenth century, but it is far more confused and anarchical. In its search for an order of intellectual and formal values, contemporary literature has grown into an art of critical assessment. The four masters who have dominated the half-century: Proust, Valéry, Gide and Claudel; André Breton and Surrealists in general; Sartre and Existentialists in general; Mauriac and other Catholic writers have all devoted large portions of their work to critical statement and theory, to a serious attempt at explaining and justifying the more purely creative part of their writing.

It would be difficult to point out a major literary work directly inspired by any of the collective dramas and wars of the period. Proust and Gide wrote essentially the history of their minds and their sensibilities. In the wake of Rimbaud, the heroes of Saint-Exupéry, of Mauriac, of Julien Green are solitary, and at times solitary adventurers. This is true even of

the heroes of Bernanos who would teach, more than
any single Catholic dogma, that of the communion of
saints.

The death of Antonin Artaud, in 1948, which occurred at the end of a nine-year period in an insane
asylum, called attention to his particular case of solitude and to his fervent essay on Van Gogh, whom
he calls the "suicide of society." In his interpretation
of Van Gogh's madness as that of an artist's conscience beset by the creative impulse, he provides an
important document on the modern artist as seen by
a modern artist. As introduction to his central point,
Artaud compares Van Gogh to Gauguin. The latter
believed that the duty of the artist was to search for
the significant symbol and to enlarge the parts of
existence until they form a myth. But Van Gogh believed that the reality of the most ordinary objects
of the world was superior to any story or fable or
divinity. Artaud's pages on the scandal of genius
and the reasons for Van Gogh's death provide a
vibrant indictment of the age.

Each literary work is only a stage in a development
of a plan more significant and more vast than itself.
Gide and Valéry understood this condition or this
fate of literature. They knew that an author cannot
and should not merge himself totally with his work.
When Proust uses the first person pronoun in his
novel, he is far from engaging himself in any absolute
sense in his work. Montherlant has been criticized by
Mme Magny for not making adequate distinction between his personality and his writing. Mme Magny
calls literature, in this sense, a game in which everyone cheats, but it is a game in which you cannot pick
up the coins again in order to make a second wager.

There are in France today unmistakable signs of
the beginnings of a new literature. At least a fervent
search is being carried on for a new means of departure, a new will to awaken from a Lazarus-like
sleep. Twenty years ago, Jacques Rivière spoke of
the crisis of the concept of literature. Its principal
malady has been diagnosed and defined in many contradictory ways. The malady has been called a form
of preciosity or hermeticism, as well as an absence of
art. It has been called a tendency toward exaggerated
intellectualism as well as a tendency toward irration-
ality. What does seem beyond doubt is the will of
modern literature to exceed itself, to become more
than itself. Between Romanticism and Surrealism, literature has perhaps been more concerned with this
problem than we can realize today.

Midway in this period of 100 to 150 years, Rimbaud's phrase on the "supernatural powers" of the
poetic word and his celebrated silence in Ethiopia
testify to this preoccupation. And at the end of this
long period, during the most recent years, the spiritual experience of such a writer as Simone Weil
(1909-43) reveals a quest for the absolute during
which many contradictory forces and beliefs have to
be surmounted: anarchy and patriotism, tradition and
revolution, reason and faith. In her book, L'Enracinement, this young woman who had been teacher,
factory worker, militant revolutionary, mystic and philosopher, writes about the need to welcome all opin-
ions, provided they are arranged horizontally at suit-
able levels. At the summit, Simone Weil places God
for whom she has various synonyms, such as truth,
or light, or the object of the conquest of civilization, of France and of each man.

Thanks to the editorship of Gustave Thibon, the works of Simone Weil have become widely known. Hers was a philosophical mind, in love with truth, and concerned with the problems of the world today. Her spiritual experience was of a mystical order. It drew upon Greek philosophy as well as on the Judaic-Christian tradition. Her writings, even in their fragmentary form, are a testimonial on the meaning which contemporary man is trying to give to his life. Her particular *ascesis* seems to have been her will to renounce all sentiment, to empty her soul of all desire. In her two principal works, *La Pesanteur et la Grâce* (1948) and *L'Enracinement* (1949), she analyzes not only the self (*le moi*) which is the main obstacle in her knowledge of God, but also analyzes other domains, of literature, economics, religion, history, education, politics, in order to propose ways by which man can rediscover his moral, intellectual and spiritual life.

CRITICAL BIBLIOGRAPHY
OF OTHER ESSAYISTS
(*arranged chronologically*)

ANDRÉ SUARÈS (1868-1948)

Suarès is a dogmatic writer, totally subjective and totally opposed to the historical criticism of a Lanson. He has written admirable essays or "portraits" on those writers with whom he feels close sympathy: Pascal, Dostoevsky, Tolstoi. In his *Trois Grands Vivants* (1938) he discusses Cervantes, Tolstoi, Baudelaire.

PAUL LÉAUTAUD (1872-1955)

His *Journal*, now in the process of publication, justifies Léautaud's reputation for hostility to many of the authors he knew. His writings are characterized by a lack of reticence when he speaks of himself, his cats and dogs, and by a fair degree of sarcasm in his judgments on the writers of his time. At the end of his life he became suddenly famous because of a series of radio interviews, published as *Entretiens* (1952).

JACQUES MARITAIN (1882-   )

Primarily a philosopher in the neo-Thomistic tradition, Maritain has also contributed to contemporary aesthetics and poetic theory. In *Frontières de la Poésie* (1935) and *Art et Scolastique* (1935), he revealed a surprising concurrence of his own doctrinal conclusions with the beliefs of modern artists, and especially those outside any religious persuasion, concerning their art and their place in the contemporary world. Maritain's main doctrine deals with the spirituality of art, with what might be called the transcendental or transforming principle of art. He recently published in English his definitive book on this subject, *Creative Intuition in Art and Poetry* (New York: Pantheon, 1953; reissued as a Meridian Book, in 1955).

JEAN HYTIER (1899-   )

Formerly a professor at the University of Algiers, and today a professor at Columbia, Jean Hytier published in 1938 a study of *André Gide*, which Gide himself praised very highly. A series of essays on the meaning of literature appeared in 1945, *Les Arts de Littérature*. An important contribution to Valéry criticism came out in 1953: *La Poétique de Valéry*.

HENRY DANIEL-ROPS (1901-   )

Daniel-Rops began his career of essayist with a penetrating psychological study of his age, *Notre Inquiétude,* first published in 1927, and reissued in 1953. He has published literary studies of *Péguy* (1938), *Rimbaud, le drame spirituel* (1936), and *Psichari* (1947). The major part of his work is his history of Christianity, in several volumes: *Le Peuple de la Bible* (1943), *Jésus en son temps* (1945), *Les Evangiles de la Vierge* (1948), etc. In 1956 he was elected member of the French Academy.

ALBERT BÉGUIN (1901-1957)

Béguin's principal work, *L'Ame Romantique et le Rêve* (1939), has become known since the war. It is a profound study of the mystical esoteric aspect of European Romanticism.

GEORGES POULET (1902-)

Georges Poulet, professor of French literature at Johns Hopkins, follows the tradition of those critics who organize their thought around one central issue or theme. *Etudes sur le temps humain* (1950) and *La Distance Intérieure* (1952) were awarded prizes in Paris. The purpose of these books is a study of time and of the degree to which each age is defined by the concept of time as revealed in its leading writers.

THIERRY MAULNIER (1909-)

In 1936, Maulnier's *Racine* was hailed as a new and vitally suggestive interpretation. His long essay, which introduces his *Introduction à la Poésie Française* (1939), emphasizes the greatness of French poetry in the 16th and 20th centuries, and repudiates much of 19th-century poetry, especially that of the Romantics.

ROBERT BRASILLACH (1910-1945)

Like Maulnier, Brasillach was one of those critics who attacked the 19th century and who spent much of their critical faculties in demonstrating the greatness of the 16th and 17th centuries. The masterpieces of that age are treated as products of monarchy, Catholicism and the classical conception of art. His book on *Corneille* was published in 1936. Because of his services to the Nazis, Brasillach was shot in 1945, at the age of thirty-five.

RENÉ ETIEMBLE (1910-)

Etiemble is a professor of French literature at the University of Montpellier, and a critic on the staff of *Les Temps Modernes* and *La Nouvelle Revue Française*. In addition to his novels and to his collection of essays, he has published his doctoral dissertation, *Le Mythe de Rimbaud* (1952), which is a prodigious attempt to extinguish the "myths" (lies and false interpretations) of Rimbaud.

ROGER CAILLOIS (1913-   )

Caillois has stated his position especially in two books, *Les Impostures de la Poésie*, of 1945, and *Vocabulaire Esthétique*, of 1946. He belligerently calls for a return to the classicism of Boileau.

R.-M. ALBÉRÈS (pseudonym of René Marill) (1920-   )

L'Aventure Intellectuelle du 20e Siècle, published in 1950, is a brilliant attempt to classify European writers by the problems which they felt the most deeply.

CRITICAL BIBLIOGRAPHY
OF OTHER NOVELISTS
(arranged chronologically)

COLETTE (1873-1954)

Colette is famous for her analyses of young girls, of aging courtesans, of animals, gardens, orchards. In her novel *Chéri* (1920) on the theme of a mature woman in love with a young man, she proved herself a perceptive artist in her analysis of instincts and sensations. *Le Blé en Herbe* (1923) reveals an exceptional knowledge of adolescence. *Gigi* (1945) is a document on French gallantry at the turn of the century.

ROGER MARTIN DU GARD (1881-   )

Between 1922 and 1940, du Gard composed his long novel (called by the French *un roman-fleuve*) in nine volumes, *Les Thibault*. It is the story of two families, and particularly of two sons in one family, who lived during the same historical period which Proust chose for his novel. Du Gard's work is an excellent example of the traditional 19th-century novel, well organized and clearly written. He was awarded the Nobel prize in 1937.

288

JEAN GIRAUDOUX (1882-1944)

Long before his successes in the theatre, during the thirties and forties, Giraudoux was known in France as a novelist and famous for his pages devoted to his province of Limousin and the city of Châteauroux where he had attended the lycée. In such novels as *Suzanne et le Pacifique* (1921), *Simon le Pathétique* (1926) and *Choix des Elues* (1939), Giraudoux analyzes, with a deft combination of poetry and intelligence, the characteristics of *le petit fonctionnaire,* the routine of daily existence, the unexpected and modest joys of life.

In the realm of criticism, Giraudoux wrote two books to explain the greatness of Racine and La Fontaine (*Racine* [1930] and *Les Cinq Tentations de La Fontaine* [1938]).

GEORGES DUHAMEL (1884-   )

In addition to shorter works, Duhamel wrote a *roman-fleuve* in ten volumes, *La Chronique des Pasquier* (1933-45), which is the story of his own family. In 1906-7 with Jules Romains and others, Duhamel founded the "Abbaye" group at Créteil and appropriated in his writing many of the principles of Unanimism. (Cf. Jules Romains.)

JULES ROMAINS (1885-   )

After writing first for the theatre (*Knock,* 1923, was his major success), Romains turned to the novel. His *roman-fleuve, Les Hommes de Bonne Volonté,* was published in twenty-seven volumes, between 1932 and 1947. The work deals with the period in Europe between October 6, 1908, and October 7, 1933. The conception of the work draws upon the doctrine of Unanimism, which originated under the leadership of Jules Romains at the Abbaye de Créteil. Many influences are merged in this doctrine: theories of Symbolism, the writings of Whitman and Durkheim. Unanimism was a kind of social mysticism, and Jules Romains' novel attempts to describe the collective soul of a society. Despite the fact that this long work is looked upon by most critics as a failure, it has had a popular success.

ANDRÉ MAUROIS (1885-   )

Novelist (*Les Silences du Colonel Bramble,* 1918) and biographer (*Ariel, ou la vie de Shelley,* 1923), Maurois has perhaps had more success in the United States than in France. His last two studies, in which he makes an extensive use of documentation, are his best: *A la recherche de Marcel Proust* (1949) and *George Sand* (1952).

MARCEL JOUHANDEAU (1888-   )

The novels of Jouhandeau (*Monsieur Godeau marié,* 1933; *Chroniques Maritales,* 1938) form a continuous chronicle, a kind of *roman-fleuve,* with two main characters, Monsieur Godeau and his wife Elise, who are Jouhandeau and his wife. The scenes take place in a villa in Paris and the town of Chaminadour-Guéret. Jouhandeau has remained all his life teacher of the 6th class in a small *collège.*

HENRY DE MONTHERLANT (1896-   )

Some of Montherlant's favorite themes are athletics and sports (*Les Olympiques,* 1924), bullfighting (*Les Bestiaires,* 1926) and the place of woman (*Les Jeunes Filles,* 1936; *Pitié pour les Femmes,* 1937). He has written extensively on the person and the attitude of the novelist.

LOUIS-FERDINAND CÉLINE (1894-   )

Céline's most famous book, *Voyage au bout de la nuit* (1932) is a semi-philosophical narrative, an epic story of human degradation. He has exploited this same vein in other books: *Mort à Crédit* (1936), *Bagatelles pour un massacre* (1938), *Féerie pour une autre fois* (1952).

Céline was dishonored by his anti-Semitism. He was used by the Germans during the Occupation, and exiled to Denmark after the war. He returned to France in 1949.

JEAN GIONO (1895-   )

The early novels of Giono (*Colline,* 1928; *Un de Baumugnes,* 1929; *Regain,* 1930) are unique in modern

French literature in their celebration of the rural setting of Manosque and the surrounding country and mountain district, and of joy over the natural world.

ANTOINE DE SAINT-EXUPÉRY (1900-1944)

The books of Saint-Exupéry are authentic stories of adventures he himself lived. They have become widely known outside of France. *Vol de Nuit*, of 1931, analyzes the problems of a pilot in the establishment of an airline with South America. *Terre des Hommes* (1939) is perhaps the most complex and the most lyric of his books. *Pilote de Guerre*, published in the United States in 1942, is the story of a French pilot flying over the German lines in June 1940. It is a testimonial to the cult of danger and heroism.

JULIEN GREEN (1900-   )

The son of an American family from the South, Julien Green grew up in France. He is a French writer, a product of French culture, but he has felt the influence of American puritanism. He has treated French provincial life in such novels as *Adrienne Mesurat* (1927) and *Léviathan* (1928). American life is the background of *Mont Cinère* (1926) and of one of his most recent novels, *Moïra* (1950). *Moïra* is not, as it has been called, a story of carnal passion, but one of anguish over purity. It is admirable in its study of spiritual values. Several volumes of his *Journal* have now appeared. Green has announced that the complete *Journal* will not be published during his lifetime.

ROGER PEYREFITTE (1907-   )

Les Amitiés Particulières (1945) recreates the atmosphere of a Catholic school, and explores with understanding and delicacy an aspect of adolescent sexuality. *Les Ambassades* (1952) combines fiction and reportage. *Les Clés de Saint Pierre* (1955) is a very special account, half documentation, half fiction, of Rome and the Vatican.

Jeunes Proies (1956) is claimed to be largely autobiographical.

SIMONE DE BEAUVOIR (1908-   )

The novels of Mme de Beauvoir are on the whole illustrations of her philosophical essays on Existentialism. *Le Sang des Autres* (1944) is a novel of the Resistance movement. Her recent Goncourt prize novel, *Les Mandarins* (1955) is a *roman à clef*, dealing with the principal personalities of the Existentialist movement and with many of the issues with which it was concerned.

JULIEN GRACQ (1910-   )

Some aspects of Surrealism have been carried over into the novel, largely by Julien Gracq. *Au Château d'Argol* (1937) is reminiscent of the Gothic tale. *Un Beau Ténébreux* (1945) is the story of an aging Don Juan. *Le Rivage des Syrtes* (1951) tells the story of an Italian Republic.

SELECTED BIBLIOGRAPHY
(*Gallimard editions, unless otherwise stated*)

VALÉRY
GIDE
CLAUDEL
MAURIAC
COCTEAU

NOVEL
THEATRE
POETRY
LITERARY HISTORY, CRITICISM, ESSAY

PAUL VALÉRY
Introduction à la Méthode de Léonard de Vinci, 1895
Autres rhumbes, 1934 (First edition, 1927)
Choses Tues, 1932
Degas. Danse. Dessin, 1938
Eupalinos; ou l'architecture, précédé de l'Ame et la danse,
  1938
Littérature, 1930

Moralités, 1932
Pièces sur l'Art, 1934
Poésies, 1942
Regards sur le monde actuel. Stock, 1931
Rhumbs (notes et autres). Le Divan, 1926
Mélange, 1941
Mon Faust (ébauches), 1946
Monsieur Teste, nouvelle édition augmentée de fragments inédits, 1946
Tel Quel, 1941
Variété, 1924
Variété II, 1929
Variété III, 1936
Variété IV, 1938
Variété V, 1944

Books on Valéry

Noulet, Emilie, *Paul Valéry*. Grasset, 1932
Fabureau, Hubert, *Paul Valéry*. Nouvelle Revue Critique, 1937
Lefèvre, Frédéric, *Entretiens avec Paul Valéry*. Le Livre, 1926
Rideau, Emile, *Introduction à la pensée de Paul Valéry*. Desclée de Brouwer, 1944
Paul Valéry Vivant. Cahiers du Sud, 1946
Hytier, Jean, *La Poétique de Valéry*. Colin, 1953

ANDRÉ GIDE

Les Cahiers d'André Walter. Librairie de l'Art Indépendant, 1891
Le Traité du Narcisse. Ibid., 1892
Les Poésies d'André Walter. Ibid., 1892
Paludes. Ibid., 1895
Les Nourritures Terrestres. Mercure de France, 1897 (*Fruits of the Earth*. Knopf, 1949)
Le Prométhée mal enchaîné. Ibid., 1899
Le Roi Candaule. Revue Blanche, 1901

L'Immoraliste. Mercure de France, 1902 (*The Immoralist,* Knopf, 1930)

Saül. Ibid., 1903

Le Retour de l'Enfant Prodigue. Vers et Prose, 1907

La Porte Etroite. Mercure de France, 1909 (*Strait Is the Gate,* Knopf, 1924)

Les Caves du Vatican, 1914 (*Lafcadio's Adventures,* Knopf, 1925)

La Symphonie Pastorale, 1919 (*Two Symphonies,* Knopf, 1931)

Dostoïevsky. Plon, 1923 (*Dostoevsky,* Dent, 1925)

Corydon, 1924 (*Corydon,* Farrar, Straus, 1950)

Les Faux-Monnayeurs, 1926 (*The Counterfeiters,* Knopf, 1927)

Si le grain ne meurt, 1926 (*If It Die,* Random House, 1935)

Œdipe, 1931 (*Œdipus* in *Two Legends,* Knopf, 1950)

Les Nouvelles Nourritures, 1935 (*New Fruits of the Earth,* Knopf, 1949)

Journal 1889-1939 (*The Journals of André Gide,* Knopf, 1947-51)

Pages de Journal 1939-42, 1944

Thésée, 1946

Correspondance Francis Jammes et André Gide, 1893 1938, 1948

Correspondance Paul Claudel et André Gide, 1899-1926 1949

Et nunc manet in te. Ides et Calendes, 1951

Books on Gide

Fernandez, Ramon, *André Gide,* Corrêa, 1931

Hytier, Jean, *André Gide,* Charlot, 1938

Ames, Van Meter, *André Gide,* New Directions, 1947

Guerard, Albert, *André Gide,* Harvard University Press, 1951

Hommage à André Gide. La Nouvelle Revue Française, 1951

Thomas, D. L., *André Gide: The Ethic of the Artist.*
  Secker and Warburg, 1951
Martin du Gard, Roger, *Notes sur André Gide*, 1952
Brée, Germaine, *André Gide l'insaisissable Protée*, Belles-
  Lettres, 1953
O'Brien, Justin, *Portrait of André Gide*, Knopf, 1953

PAUL CLAUDEL

Poetry

Cinq Grandes Odes, 1910
Corona Benignitatis Anni Dei, 1913
Poèmes de Guerre, 1915
Feuilles de Saints, 1925

Theatre

Théâtre Complet, 2 vols., 1949
Tête d'Or, 1889, 1894
L'Echange, 1893
La Ville, 1890, 1897
Partage de Midi, 1906
L'Otage, 1910
L'Annonce faite à Marie, 1910, 1912
Le Pain Dur, 1918
Le Père Humilié, 1920
Le Soulier de Satin, 1928-29

Writings on Holy Scripture

Introduction au Livre de Ruth, Desclée de Brouwer, 1938
Figures et Paraboles, 1936
Les Aventures de Sophie, 1938
Un poète regarde la croix, 1938
L'Epée et le Miroir, 1937
Introduction à l'Apocalypse, Egloff, 1946
Le Livre de Job, Plon, 1946

Critical Writing, Essays, Letters

Connaissance de l'Est, Mercure de France, 1895-1900
L'Art Poétique, Ibid., 1906
Correspondance Jacques Rivière et Paul Claudel, 1907-1914, Plon, 1926
Positions et Propositions, 2 vols., 1928, 1934
Conversations dans le Loir-et-Cher, 1937
Correspondance André Suarès et Paul Claudel, 1904-1938, 1951

Books on Claudel

Rivière, Jacques, *Etudes*, 1911
Madaule, Jacques, *Le Génie de Paul Claudel*, Desclée de Brouwer, 1933
Madaule, Jacques, *Le Drame de Paul Claudel*, Desclée de Brouwer, 1936
Du Bos, Charles, *Approximations*, série 6 et 7, Corrêa, 1937
Peyre, Henri, *Hommes et Oeuvres du 20e siècle*, Corrêa, 1938
Fowlie, Wallace, *Paul Claudel*, Bowes and Bowes, Cambridge, 1957
Brodin, Pierre, *Les Ecrivains Français de l'entre-deux-guerres*, Valiquette, 1942
Friche, Ernest, *Etudes Claudéliennes*, Portes de France, 1943
Jouve, Raymond, *Comment lire Paul Claudel*, Aux Etudiants de France, 1946

FRANÇOIS MAURIAC

Novels

Le Baiser au Lépreux, Grasset, 1922
Génitrix, Ibid., 1923
Destins, Ibid., 1928

Thérèse Desqueyroux, Ibid., 1927
Le Nœud de Vipères, Ibid., 1932
Les Anges Noirs, Ibid., 1936
Le Fleuve de Feu, Ibid., 1923
Le Désert de l'Amour, Ibid., 1925
Le Mystère Frontenac, Ibid., 1933
Les Chemins de la Mer, Ibid., 1939
La Fin de la Nuit, Ibid., 1935
La Pharisienne, Ibid., 1941
Préséances, Emile-Paul, 1921
Le Sagouin, Plon, 1951

Plays

Asmodée, Grasset, 1938
Les Mal-Aimés, Ibid., 1945
Passage du Malin, La Table Ronde, 1948
Le Feu sur la Terre, ou Le Pays sans chemin, Grasset,
    1951

Criticism, Essays, etc.

Le Roman, Artisan du Livre, 1928
La Vie de Jean Racine, Plon, 1928
Vie de Jésus, Flammarion, 1936
Blaise Pascal et sa soeur Jacqueline, Hachette, 1931
Souffrances et bonheur du chrétien, Grasset, 1929
Dieu et Mammon, Edition du Capitole, 1929
Commencements d'une vie, Grasset, 1932
Le Romancier et ses personnages, Corrêa, 1933
Journal 1932-39, La Table Ronde, 1947
Trois grands hommes devant Dieu, Hartmann, 1947

Books on Mauriac

Du Bos, Charles, *François Mauriac et le problème du*
    romancier catholique, Corrêa, 1933
Hourdin, Georges, *Mauriac, romancier catholique,* Editions
    du temps présent, 1945

Majault, Joseph, *Mauriac et l'art du roman*, Laffont, 1946
Robichon, Jacques, *François Mauriac*, Editions universitaires, 1953

JEAN COCTEAU

Poetry

Le Cap de Bonne-Espérance, La Sirène, 1919
Vocabulaire, Ibid., 1922
Plain-Chant, Stock, 1923
La Crucifixion, Morihien, 1946

Novels

Le Grand Ecart, Stock, 1923
Thomas l'Imposteur, 1923
Les Enfants Terribles, Grasset, 1929

Plays

Orphée, Stock, 1927
Antigone—Les Mariés de la Tour Eiffel, 1928
La Machine Infernale, Grasset, 1934
Les Chevaliers de la Table Ronde, 1937
Les Parents Terribles, 1938
L'Aigle à deux têtes, 1946
Bacchus, 1952

Criticism

Le Coq et l'Arlequin, La Sirène, 1918
Carte Blanche, Ibid., 1920
Le Secret Professionnel, Stock, 1922
Le Rappel à l'Ordre, Ibid., 1926
Lettre à Maritain, Ibid., 1926
Le Mystère Laïc, Quatre Chemins, 1928
Opium, Stock, 1930

Essai de Critique Indirecte, Grasset, 1932
La Difficulté d'Etre, Morihien, 1947
Lettre aux Américains, Grasset, 1949

THE NOVEL
Beauvoir, Simone de, *Le Sang des Autres*, 1944
Beckett, Samuel, *Molloy*, Editions de Minuit, 1951
Bernanos, Georges, *La Joie*, Plon, 1929
————, *Sous le soleil de Satan*, Plon, 1926
————, *Journal d'un curé de campagne*, Plon, 1936
————, *Monsieur Ouine*, Plon, 1946
————, Estang, Luc, *Présence de Bernanos*, Plon, 1947
————, Picon, Gaëtan, *Georges Bernanos*, Marin, 1948
Camus, Albert, *L'Etranger*, 1942
————, *La Peste*, 1947
————, *The Stranger*, Knopf, 1946
————, *The Plague*, Knopf, 1948
————, *La Chute*, 1956
————, *The Fall*, Knopf, 1957
Céline, Louis-Ferdinand, *Le Voyage au bout de la nuit*,
    Denoël, 1932
————, *Mort à crédit*, Denoël, 1936
————, *Bagatelles pour un massacre*, Denoël, 1938
————, *Death on the Installment Plan*, Little Brown, 1938
Curtis, Jean-Louis, *Gibier de Potence*, Julliard, 1949
Dabit, Eugène, *Hôtel du Nord*, Denoël, 1930
Genet, Jean, *Notre-Dame des Fleurs*, L'Arbalète, 1948
Giono, Jean, *Regain*, Grasset, 1930
————, *Le Chant du Monde*, 1934
Giraudoux, Jean, *Suzanne et le Pacifique*, Grasset, 1921
————, *Simon le Pathétique*, Grasset, 1926
Green, Julien, *Mont-Cinère*, Plon, 1926
————, *Adrienne Mesurat*, Plon, 1927
————, *Moïra*, Plon, 1950
————, *L'Autre Sommeil*, La Palantine, 1950
Guérin, Raymond, *L'Apprenti*, 1946
Guersant, Marcel, *Jean-Paul*, Editions de Minuit, 1953

Guilloux, Louis, *Le Sang Noir*, 1935
Malraux, André, *Les Conquérants*, Grasset, 1928
———, *La Condition Humaine*, 1933
———, *L'Espoir*, 1937
Picon, Gaëtan, *André Malraux*, 1946
Montherlant, Henry de, *Les Bestiaires*, Grasset, 1926
———, *Les Célibataires*, Grasset, 1934
Proust, Marcel, *Jean Santeuil*, 1952
Rousset, David, *Les Jours de notre mort*, Corrêa, 1947
Saint-Exupéry, Antoine de, *Vol de Nuit*, 1931
———, *Terre des Hommes*, 1939
———, *Pilote de Guerre*, 1942
Sartre, Jean-Paul, *La Nausée*, 1938
———, *L'Age de Raison*, 1945
———, *Le Sursis*, 1945
———, *La Mort dans l'Ame*, 1949

PLAYS (*not including Gide, Claudel, Mauriac, Cocteau*)

Anouilh, Jean, *Pièces Noires*, 1942
———, *Nouvelles Pièces Noires*, 1946
———, *Pièces Roses*, 1942
Beckett, Samuel, *En attendant Godot*, Editions de Minuit, 1952
Camus, Albert, *Caligula*, 1944
———, *Le Malentendu*, 1944
Giraudoux, Jean, *Amphitryon 38*, Grasset, 1929
———, *Judith, Ibid.*, 1932
———, *La Guerre de Troie n'aura pas lieu, Ibid.*, 1935
———, *Electre, Ibid.*, 1937
———, *Sodome et Gomorrhe, Ibid.*, 1943
———, *La Folle de Chaillot, Ibid.*, 1946
Genet, Jean, *Haute Surveillance*, 1949
Montherlant, Henry de, *Pasiphaé*, 1936
———, *La Reine Morte*, 1942
———, *Fils de Personne*, 1943

————, *Le Maître de Santiago*, 1946
————, *Malatesta*, 1946
————, *Demain il fera jour*, 1949
————, *La Ville dont le prince est un enfant*, 1951
Sartre, Jean-Paul, *Théâtre* (includes *Les Mouches*, 1943; *Huis-clos*, 1945; *Morts sans sépultures*, 1947; *La Putain Respectueuse*, 1947), 1947
————, *Les Mains Sales*, 1948
————, *Le Diable et le Bon Dieu*, 1951

BOOKS ON THE THEATRE AND CINEMA
Artaud, Antonin, *Le théâtre et son double*, 1938
Bardèche, Maurice et Brasillach, Robert, *Histoire du Cinéma*, Denoël, 1943
Barrault, Jean-Louis, *Réflexions sur le théâtre*, Vautrain, 1949
————, *Reflections on the Theatre*, Rockliff, 1951
Benoît-Lévy, Jean Albert, *Les Grandes Missions du Cinéma*, Parizeau, 1945
————, *The Art of the Motion Picture*, Coward-McCann, 1946
Cézan, Claude, *Jouis Jouvet et le théâtre d'aujourd'hui*, Emile-Paul, 1938
Gouhier, Henri, *L'Essence du Théâtre*, Plon, 1943
————, *Le Théâtre et l'existence*, Paris, 1953
Houlet, Jacques, *Le Théâtre de Jean Giraudoux*, Ardent, 1945
Jouvet, Louis, *Réflexions du comédien*, N. R. C., 1946

POETRY
Aragon, Louis, *Le Crève-Cœur*, 1941
Breton, André, *Poèmes: 1919-1948*, 1948
Char, René, *Fureur et Mystère*, 1948
Desnos, Robert, *Choix de Poèmes*, Editions de Minuit, 1946

Emmanuel, Pierre, *Babel*, Desclée de Brouwer, 1952
Eluard, Paul, *Choix de Poèmes*, new edition, 1946
Fargue, Léon-Paul, *Poèmes, suivis de Pour la Musique*, new edition, 1947
Jacob, Max, *Les Pénitents en Maillots Roses*, Kra, 1925
Jouve, Pierre Jean, *Sueur de Sang*, 1933
La Tour du Pin, Patrice de, *La Quête de Joie*, 1933
Michaux, Henri, *Plume précédé de Lointain Intérieur*, 1937
Perse, St.-John, *Anabase*, 1924
    Definitive edition, Harcourt, Brace, 1949
————, *Exile and Other Poems*, Pantheon, 1940
————, *Vents*, 1946
Pichette, Henri, *Les Epiphanies*, K éditeur, 1948
Ponge, Francis, *Le Parti Pris des Choses*, 1942
Prévert, Jacques, *Paroles*, Editions du point du jour, 1946
Supervielle, Jules, *Poèmes 1939-1945*, 1946

Bilingual Editions of poetry

Mid-Century French Poetry, edited by Wallace Fowlie, Grove Press, 1955
Char, René, *Hypnos Waking*, edited by Jackson Mathews, Random House, 1956

LITERARY CRITICISM

(See also Chapter IX and Critical Bibliography of Essayists)

Astorg, Bertrand d', *Aspects de la littérature européenne depuis 1945*, Seuil, 1952
Bachelard, Gaston, *L'Eau et les Rêves*, Corti, 1942
Bataille, Georges, *L'Expérience Intérieure*, 1943
Beauvoir, Simone de, *Pyrrhus et Cinéas*, 1944
Blanchot, Maurice, *Lautréamont et Sade*, Editions de Minuit, 1949

Boisdeffre, Pierre de, *Métamorphose de la littérature*, Editions Alsatia, 1950

Breton, André, *Arcane 17*, Brentano's, 1950

Caillois, Roger, *L'Homme et le Sacré*, Presses Universitaires, 1939

Camus, Albert, *Le Mythe de Sisyphe*, 1942

———, *L'Homme Révolté*, 1952

Girard, Marcel, *Guide illustré de la littérature française moderne* (1918-1949), Seghers, 1949

Giraudoux, Jean, *Littérature*, Grasset, 1941

Kanters, Robert, *Des écrivains et des hommes*, Julliard, 1952

Magny, Claude-Edmonde, *Les Sandales d'Empédocle*, Baconnière, 1945

———, *Histoire du romain français depuis 1918*, Seuil, 1950

Monnerot, Jules, *La Poésie Moderne et le Sacré*, 1945

Nadeau, Maurice, *Histoire du Surréalisme*, Seuil, 1945

———, *Littérature Présente*, Corrêa, 1952

Paulhan, Jean, *Clef de la Poésie*, 1944

Peyre, Henri, *Hommes et Oeuvres du 20e siècle*, Corrêa, 1938

Picon, Gaëtan, *Panorama de la nouvelle littérature française*, 1949

Raymond, Marcel, *De Baudelaire au Surréalisme*, Corti, 1947

Renéville, Rolland de, *L'Expérience Poétique*, 1938

Sartre, Jean-Paul, *Situations*, 3 vols., 1947-49

Wahl, Jean, *Petite histoire de l'existentialisme*, Club Maintenant, 1947

LITERARY CRITICISM IN ENGLISH

Brée, Germaine, *Marcel Proust and Deliverance from Time*, Rutgers University Press, 1955

Fowlie, Wallace, *Age of Surrealism*, Swallow, 1950

Frohock, Wilbur Merrill, *André Malraux and the Tragic Imagination*, Stanford University Press, 1952

Peyre, Henri, *The Contemporary French Novel*, Oxford University Press, 1955

Poulet, Georges, *Studies in Human Time*, translated by Elliott Coleman, The Johns Hopkins Press, 1956

INDEX

307

Wallace Fowlie

Wallace Fowlie was born in Brookline, Massachusetts in 1908. Educated at Harvard, he completed his doctoral dissertation on the French religious thinker Ernest Psichari. A constant visitor to France and commentator on contemporary French literature Wallace Fowlie has taught at Yale University, the University of Chicago, and presently at Bennington College. Among his many books are: *Mallarmé, Rimbaud's Illuminations, Jacob's Night, The Clown's Grail, Age of Surrealism, De Villon à Peguy,* and *Pantomime.* His *Dionysus in Paris: A Guide to Contemporary French Theater* is available in a Meridian edition (M92).

MERIDIAN BOOKS

Literature, Criticism, Drama, and Poetry

Meridian Books are published by The World Publishing Company,
Cleveland and New York. For a free Meridian catalogue write to
Dept. AM, Meridian Books, 119 West 57th Street, N.Y.

MERIDIAN BOOKS

Fiction

Meridian Books are published by The World Publishing Company, Cleveland and New York. For a free Meridian catalogue write to Dept. AM, Meridian Books, 119 West 57th Street, N.Y.

MERIDIAN BOOKS

Art, Architecture, and Music

BARZUN, JACQUES *Berlioz and His Century.* M30
BERENSON, BERNARD *The Italian Painters of the Renaissance.* M40
BIKEL, THEODORE *Folksongs and Footnotes.* MG27
FRY, ROGER *Vision and Design.* M33
GILSON, ETIENNE *Painting and Reality.* M79
HUXLEY, ALDOUS *On Art and Artists.* M99
KAUFMANN, EDGAR, AND RAEBURN, BEN (EDS.) *Frank Lloyd Wright: Writings and Buildings.* MG22
NOSS, LUTHER (ED.) *Christian Hymns.* LA38
PACK, ROBERT, AND LELASH, MARJORIE (TRS.) *Mozart's Librettos.* M80
PANOFSKY, ERWIN *Gothic Architecture and Scholasticism.* M44
PATER, WALTER *The Renaissance.* M124
PHILIPSON, MORRIS (ED.) *Aesthetics Today.* M112
READ, HERBERT *The Grass Roots of Art.* M108
READ, HERBERT *The Philosophy of Modern Art.* M7
SMITH, G. E. KIDDER *The New Architecture of Europe.* MG33
STEINBERG, SAUL *The Catalogue.* M147
TOVEY, DONALD FRANCIS *The Forms of Music.* M36
TOVEY, DONALD FRANCIS *The Main Stream of Music and Other Essays.* M74

Meridian Books are published by The World Publishing Company, Cleveland and New York. For a free Meridian catalogue write to Dept. AM, Meridian Books, 119 West 57th Street, N.Y.

MERIDIAN BOOKS

Social Sciences, Psychology, and Anthropology

MERIDIAN BOOKS

Philosophy

Meridian Books are published by The World Publishing Company, Cleveland and New York. For a free Meridian catalogue write to Dept. AM, Meridian Books, 119 West 57th Street, N.Y.

MERIDIAN BOOKS

General and Reference

BOLTIN, LEE *Jail Keys Made Here and Other Signs.* MG21
ELAM, SAMUEL MILTON *Hornbook for the Double Damned.* MG47
JEFFERY, GRANT *Science & Technology Stocks: A Guide for Investors.* MG41
KIRSCHBAUM, LEO *Clear Writing.* MG38
The Meridian Compact Atlas of the World. M126
SEYFFERT, OSCAR *Dictionary of Classical Antiquities.* MG34
SIMON, KATE *New York Places & Pleasures: Revised Edition.* MG18R
Webster's New World Dictionary of the American Language (Concise Edition). MG25